Contact:

a textbook in applied communications

C. Jeriel Howard
Bishop College

Richard Francis Tracz
Oakton Community College

Coramae Thomas

PRENTICE-HALL, INC.,
Englewood Cliffs, New Jersey 07632

3rd edition

Contact

a textbook

in

applied

communications

Library of Congress Cataloging in Publication Data

HOWARD, C. JERIEL, 1939–
    Contact, textbook in applied communications.

    1. English language—Business English. I. Tracz,
Richard Francis, joint author. II. Thomas, Coramae,
joint author. III. Title.
PE1115.H75–1979   808'.066'65174   78–24303
ISBN 0-13-169052-3

Contact:
a textbook in applied communications
third edition

C. Jeriel Howard
Richard Francis Tracz
Coramae Thomas

© 1979, 1974, 1970 by Prentice-Hall, Inc., Englewood Cliffs,
New Jersey 07632

Printed in the United States of America

10   9   8   7   6   5   4   3   2   1

Editorial/production supervision and interior design
by Charlotte Leonard
Cover design by Edsal Enterprises
Manufacturing buyer: Harry Baisley

PRENTICE-HALL INTERNATIONAL, INC., *London*
PRENTICE-HALL OF AUSTRALIA, PTY. LIMITED, *Sydney*
PRENTICE-HALL OF CANADA, LTD., *Toronto*
PRENTICE-HALL OF INDIA PRIVATE LIMITED, *New Delhi*
PRENTICE-HALL OF JAPAN, INC., *Tokyo*
PRENTICE-HALL OF SOUTHEAST ASIA PTE. LTD., *Singapore*
WHITEHALL BOOKS LIMITED, *Wellington, New Zealand*

Contents

▼

Do telephone manners affect your relationship
with your fellow workers?
How do you answer the telephone?
How do you take telephone calls for someone else?
How do you place a call for someone else?
When do you take notes of a telephone message?
How do you establish a positive telephone image?
How do you give and receive information on the
telephone?
How do you end a telephone call?
What communications etiquette do you use with your
fellow workers?
How do you start out on the right foot with your fellow
workers?
What is the key to getting along on a day-to-day
basis?
What difference do words make?
How do you learn to choose the right words?

3 Business Letters 28

How do you handle abbreviations and figures in report
  writing?
How are longer informal reports written?

8 Serving on the

Problem-Solving Committee

Why are committees appointed?
Why do you need to learn how to serve on a
  committee?
On what kinds of committees will you serve?
What are the requirements for a committee member?
What kinds of problems are solved by committees?
What is the most informal type of problem-solving
  committee?
What do you do when you are a committee member?
What do you do when you are the chairperson of a
  committee?
How is the business of a committee conducted?
What attitude toward committee work and rules is
  helpful?

9 Solving Problems Logically

What is a problem? A solution? Logic?
What is the first step in solving a problem logically?
What is the second step?
What is the third step?
What is the last step?
How do you evaluate the information you gather?
What is deductive reasoning?
What is inductive reasoning?
What is reasoning to reach a generalization?
How do you test a generalization?
What is an analogy?
How do you test an analogy?
What are the kinds of causal relations?
Are the kinds of reasoning usually found alone
  or in combination?

How do you evaluate what you hear?
How should you listen to a speech?
How should you take notes on what you hear?

13 Using the Library

Why do you need to learn how to use the library?
How is a library arranged?
How are the books arranged?
Where are the books listed?
What are some standard reference works?

14 Effective Reading and Note Taking

How do you effectively use information from a book or periodical?
How do you preview a book?
How do you read the chapter effectively?
How do you read when you want to take notes?
What kind of notes will you take?
How do you take a note that is a quotation?
How do you take notes if you want all of the material and you do not quote it?
How do you take notes if you only want a summary of the original?
What is plagiarism?
Do you need to make a note of where you got the material?
In what general form should you record the notes on what you read?
Why is it necessary to use two different kinds of cards?

English Handbook

Index

Preface

The first edition of *Contact* was developed to fulfill the need for a composition text designed primarily for the students in vocational-technical programs. At that time, ten years ago, there were very few such specialized courses and no texts.

Many changes have occurred in American education during the last decade. Thousands of students who might at one time have elected a different education program or, perhaps, no program at all are now actively involved with many different types of vocational or technical training. Hundreds of schools, institutes, and private corporations now provide training programs for these students and employees. One can rather certainly predict that this trend will continue.

And there have been changes, too, in some of the communication tasks required of today's graduates. The competitive business world requires even more precision today than it did ten years ago, and the prospective employer is even less tolerant today of careless or ineffective communication. When we wrote the first edition, we had input from dozens of professional teachers who indicated to us the skills they felt students should acquire. When we wrote this third edition, we also had imput from a large number of employers themselves—office managers, personnel directors, corporation trainers—who expressed their ideas about the tools essential for effective communication.

The need today, as ten years ago, is still for direct and functional patterns of speaking and writing. Verbosity must still give way to exactness. Knowledge that cannot be communicated is still worthless knowledge. This third edition directs itself to these needs with a special focus on the skills needed by today's students. Assignments reflect a broader base of interests but continue to insist on exactness. Explanations are presented more inductively, and there are more examples to serve as working models. Students are constantly shown the importance of effective communication in their careers.

This edition begins with an expanded overview of the communication process. Students are then taken through a series of tasks, arranged from the simple to the complex, as they practice those skills. They begin, after the first two introductory chapters, with basic techniques, for getting that first important job: application letters and interviews. They proceed through various aspects of finding facts, evaluating data, reporting orally, and, finally, reporting formally through the researched study. A brief "English Handbook" has been provided at the end of the text to serve as a helpful refresher or guide to those students needing this information.

Many teachers who have used the second edition have provided us with valuable comments and suggestions for the third. The final text is derived from a synthesis of the many suggestions that we received. We gratefully thank those teachers. We wish especially to thank Professor J. Atta Korol of Jamestown Community College for her detailed and helpful comments, and we also want to thank Daniel Blaisdell, her student, for granting us permission to reprint his formal report in Chapter 17.

As was true with the second edition, we missed the valued contributions of Coramae Thomas—and, of course, we missed Mabel.

C.J.H.
R.F.T.

Contact:

a textbook in applied communications

The Importance
of Communication

What happens during the communication process?

Communication, at least in the very broad sense, is the exchange of information between two or more parties. Communication takes place any time you transfer a thought of your own to another individual. You may perform this action thousands of times a day, even when you may not be consciously aware of it yourself.

Very sophisticated theories of communication exist, but you can understand them best if you see them all as being composed of three major parts: the sender, the message, and the receiver. The sender may be a writer, speaker, a fellow student giving an oral report, or a close friend during a general rap session. The receiver may be a reader, a member of a formal or informal audience, a member of your class, or anyone who overheard that rap session.

If the receiver understands the essential message of the sender, communication has occurred. That message may be a formal fact, an idea of general importance, or just an interesting bit of gossip. The process is as simple as that shown in Figure 1-1.

If either side in the two-way process breaks down, then true communication has not occurred. If the sender's message is inexact, excessively wordy, or phrased in words not generally familiar to the receiver, it will not be understood. If the receiver does not "tune in" to the sender, does not listen attentively, or does not try to understand what the sender is attempting to communicate, the process has failed.

organization to which you wrote the application letter and as though you were an active, progressive member of the profession which you have chosen.

Because in the future you will keep correspondence and information in a well-organized file, your instructor may help you establish such a habit by asking you to keep your assignments in individual folders. For instance, in the chapter on gathering information from live sources, your assignments are to find out the identity of a principal speaker at a meeting of your professional organization, acquire background knowledge on his or her subject, and then take notes on the speech. If you were already actively engaged in your chosen profession, you would file all of this information together. Consequently, you may be asked to prepare such a file folder now. You may want to keep this folder to go into the file of information which you will gather throughout your professional life.

All your assignments should be done as you would do them if they were part of your job. If you can type your assignments, do so. Instructors, like employers, are more favorably impressed by material they can read readily. If you don't type, use blue or black ink and write legibly. All assignments should be done on one side of standard $8^{1}/_{2} \times$ 11-inch loose-leaf notebook or typing paper.

Because most of the writing you do in your future work will be done somewhat under pressure, you may, for practice, be asked to prepare some of the assignments in class. You must learn to begin writing the letter, the memo, or the report at once without procrastinating, and to write it rapidly, clearly, and accurately without mental anguish or frequent corrections and rewritings. If the student across the aisle from you writes six pages free of error in an hour while you stare at a blank sheet of paper for thirty minutes and then haltingly grind out a page and a half in the remaining half hour, picture the two of you employed in the same office. Either he will do several times as much work as you in a day, or you will put in hours of unpaid overtime.

What can you do outside of class to improve your communication skills?

Some of the most valuable information you acquire will be gained when you least expect it, just as some of your best ideas will come when you aren't looking for them. A television documentary, a speech heard on the radio, a chance meeting in the lounge car on the train—any happening may give you a fact or opinion that you can use later. Consequently, you should have a pen and a supply of 3 × 5 file cards handy. Jot down what you have just learned as soon as possible, being careful to record the facts accurately and to document the information as to source, place, and date. Later you can drop the card into the appropriate folder in your file.

As you read your favorite magazines, your professional journals, and even the advertisements and brochures that come to your desk, clip and file the items that interest you. The busier you are, the more such a practice is necessary. When you have a secretary, you can merely mark the articles you want filed, perhaps noting the heading you want used. When an article is clipped to be filed, it should be labeled with the name of the periodical, the volume number, and the date. If you or your company binds the professional journal and keeps it on hand, you will not need to file the individual article. You can file a card with the name of the article, the author, the journal, the volume number, and the date. Such cards will, of course, be filed by subject.

Why should you begin a file now?

It is not too early for you to begin your own professional file. If you have chosen your future work, you may already be subscribing to a professional journal or two from which you should be saving articles. In your schoolwork you will do research that may be valuable to you later. File your notes and bibliography as well as your completed reports and papers. You may take field trips or attend meetings or lectures on which you will take notes that you will need later. Your college teachers are authorities in their fields whom you may be underestimating. After you begin your career, you may wish you had recorded your class lecture notes by subject so that you could file some or all of them. As you take your class notes, be certain to date them and note the speaker, place and occasion.

If you begin now to keep a file and if you develop the habit of recording or collecting any information which is related to your interests and of organizing it according to a usable system, you will enter your vocation with a sizable amount of professional information at your fingertips. Moreover, you will have formed habits which successful workers find extremely valuable. In any field the expert is the one who knows where to find quickly the information needed for the task at hand. The successful business people or technicians are the ones who are always alert for opportunities to increase their knowledge and their skill. They know a useful piece of information when they see it, and they know how to preserve it until they need it.

How can you begin a file?

Your early system of file-keeping need not be elaborate. You can file material now under large headings which can be broken down later into subheadings. The important thing is that you establish some order to your collection of information so that you can use it now and so that you will be encouraged to continue collecting information. If you cannot afford a filing cabinet now or if you do not have room for one, an inexpensive cardboard file box such as is available at office supply houses or various mail order houses will probably hold all you will accumulate before you begin your career. If you wish to file separately the notes you have taken on 3 × 5 cards, an ordinary shoe box will hold them.

ASSIGNMENTS

    I. Collect examples of ineffective communication. Clip examples from current newspapers, journals, and magazines. Also make brief notes of ineffective oral communication. Pay special attention to the following situations:
        1. Sender is not interested in receiver's attitudes.
        2. Sender uses vocabulary or terminology above receiver's level.
        3. Sender has not carefully thought through his or her own message and has not phrased it carefully.
        4. Sender is indirectly revealing an attitude of superiority.
        5. Receiver is not made aware of the need to understand the importance of the message.
   II. If possible, obtain from your library or some other source copies of older texts in business writing. Compare the style of these older texts with those favored by modern business. Look at the style of the text itself and then at the style of the models it contains.
  III. Become aware of body language and its importance to the communicative process by performing the following:
        1. Watch a student walking across campus and then describe

his or her mood. Compare your descriptive comment with that made by another student watching the same subject.

2. Observe two students sitting and talking together somewhere on campus. How do their sitting positions tell you which one feels superior to the other?

3. List ways that a favorite friend of yours shows boredom and happiness with body language.

4. Look around your classroom. What attitudes are projected by dress? By posture?

5. Tell about a time when you have attempted to influence a group simply be employing body language. Were you successful? What process did you use? Was the reaction to you in body language or was it verbal?

IV. Become aware of the importance of listening skills by performing these activities:

1. Listen to a speech (or lecture) with a friend who has agreed to take careful notes while you just listen. Afterwards, see how much you can recall.

2. Join a dormitory or student-center bull session but do not actively participate. When you have left, see if you can reconstruct the main items of discussion. Also, did anyone in the group get in the way of the group's progress because he or she never really listened?

3. Play a sentence-building game. One person begins the game with a noun; the next person adds a verb. Then subsequent persons add parts to the sentence (modifiers, clauses) to expand it. The additions must make sense, and each person must repeat the sentence as it exists when it gets to him or her. How long a sentence can your group build?

V. You may not know the various kinds of communication skills that are needed in your vocational area, but this course will be more meaningful to you if you do. Contact a person who is currently active in the job area that you have selected and visit with him or her. (Do not go to your vocational instructor for this interview.) There are many different kinds of information you might want to gather, but the interview sheet at the end of these assignments will help you in organizing your interview. You will probably not want to ask the questions exactly as they are worded here. Put the person being interviewed at ease and use your own words to get him or her to talk freely and frankly about the job.

VI. You probably already have some ideas about what parts of your work you will enjoy most and what parts will be least interesting to you. Make written lists on the following topics related to the communication skills needed in your future job:
1. List all the communication tasks connected with your job that you think you will enjoy performing.
2. List all the communication tasks connected with your job that you think you will dislike.
3. List areas in which you think you need help if you are to communicate efficiently in your occupation.

VII. Begin developing a file to keep the material which you gather from this and other courses. An accordion file would probably be the most useful right now. It is quite inexpensive, and later you can easily transfer the material to a larger filing system.

Begin sorting your material into logical sections within your file. The following divisions might give you some ideas for setting up your own system:

Business Letters
Job Openings
Job Qualifications
Job Requirements
New Trends in _____ (your area)
Professional Organizations and Meetings
Professional Records

VIII. One of the purposes of this course is to help you to get to know people actually working in the vocation that you plan to enter. You will also become familiar with the organizations and publications that are important in your chosen area. Begin to learn about these by finding answers to the following questions:
1. What is the name of a national organization that serves your vocational area?
2. What is the name of a local organization that serves your vocational area?
3. Who is president of the local organization?
4. When does the local organization meet? Would it be permissible for you to attend a meeting?
5. What is the name of a periodical that is directly related to your field of interest?
6. How often is the periodical published? Does your college library have a copy?

INTERVIEW SHEET

Student interview conducted by _____ (your name)

Person interviewed _____

Occupation of person interviewed_____

Employer _____ Years of experience _____

How important are speaking and writing skills to this particular job?

How much time each week do you spend in writing or talking to customers or other workers?

How many letters do you write each month?

How many letters do you receive each month?

How many memos and bulletins do you write each month?

How often do you use the telephone in your work?

How much time do you spend giving oral instructions or reports to other workers and supervisors?

How much time do you spend with customers?

How often do you give speeches to groups of employees or to other groups?

Do communication misunderstandings sometimes interfere with the efficiency of your department?

How important is written and oral communication as a part of good customer relations?

Do these misunderstandings sometimes affect customer relations in your work?

Communications
Etiquette: Telephone,
Personal Relationships

Why is proper etiquette important?

Every segment of society, large or small, has its set of generally accepted procedures; and if you want to be successful within a particular part, you must learn to abide by whatever those procedures might be. Although certain standards of business etiquette may change slightly from one type of job to another, there are certain general standards—all related to common courtesy—that prevail throughout the business world.

No one likes to be mistreated, and verbal mistreatment is as readily detected as physical abuse. Both the successful small company and the important major corporation have built their program upon a solid foundation of good will, and at the base of that good will is most often proper communications etiquette.

Why are telephone manners so important?

Very often the first impression an outsider has of you or your employer comes from the image created during or after a telephone conversation. You can probably recall feeling yourself cut short while talking to a representative of some local firm, and it is to be hoped that you can also remember talking to someone who made you feel as though you and your problem were the only concern he or she had for the day. The secretary who answers the telephone with a hostile tone has already shaped the direction of the conversation. The receptionist who promises to have his or her employer call you but forgets to forward the message has perhaps lost business for the company and has certainly lowered the firm's reputation in your opinion.

More and more, business executives are coming to realize that the telephone is their best and most easily accessible instrument for positive public relations. A company may spend five thousand dollars in a good-will campaign but lose all its effects if an impatient or unpleasant person is assigned telephone-answering duties.

What constitutes good telephone manners?

The key to good telephone manners is thoughtfulness for others. If you are thoughtful, you will speak loudly enough to be heard and distinctly enough to be understood. You will keep your voice friendly and your manner pleasant. You will be as helpful as you can. You will never keep the other person waiting any longer than is necessary. You will avoid any suggestion of hurry, impatience, or annoyance, regardless of how rude or annoyed the other person is. You will show the person on the other end of the line the same consideration you would show if he or she stood before you.

Do telephone manners affect your relationship with your fellow workers?

What has been said about use of the telephone in regard to the public applies as much to calls from department to department, office to office, and employee to employee. Secretaries, switchboard operators, receptionists, and clerks respond to "thank you" and "please" with even more appreciation than executive board members, administrators, and customers. The latter expect tact and courtesy when you answer the phone. Secretaries, switchboard operators, receptionists, and clerks may be so surprised by your pleasantness that their short telephone contact with you may brighten their whole day. Remember: courtesy, tact, and friendliness are catching.

How do you answer the telephone?

One of your very first tasks in beginning work for a new employer should be to determine the procedures to be followed in answering the telephone. Every company has its own practices, and a competent employee must readily adjust to new methods even though they may differ from those that were used in a previous assignment.

Your company probably has a designated phrase with which you are to answer the telephone. It may be as simple as the company's name:

Rankin's Motors

or

Plain Value Grocery

However, the phrase may include some special greeting:

Good morning, Rankin's Motors

or

Thank you for calling, Plain Value Grocery

If you answer a phone that is an extension placed in an individual office or division, always indicate the office or division:

Parts Department, may I help you?

or

Mr. Fitch's office, Ms. Grayson speaking

How do you take telephone calls for someone else?

You are faced with an additional problem in protocol when your main function is to answer the phone and screen the calls for your employer. In such a situation, the direct approach is always best. One of these phrases usually works:

May I tell Mr. _____ who is calling?

or

May I give Ms. _____ your name, please?

In getting the above information, the experienced receptionist often gets much more information about the nature of the call. The receptionist can hand the employer an important file folder that he or she may need in talking with the caller. The receptionist can also caution the employer if the caller seems angry.

It is not unusual for an executive to instruct the secretary not to interrupt him or her. If your employer wishes no interruptions, or no interruptions from certain individuals at least, you must screen calls even more carefully. The best procedure is to say something like this:

I'm sorry, Mr. Fitch is not available right now. May I take a message?

Notice, however, that this approach is not good unless you use it before you ask who is calling. If you use the phrase above and then ask who is calling, the caller will not become suspicious. If you reverse the procedure, the caller will think he or she is being avoided.

No executive, no matter how important, should regularly use the "unavailable now" approach to dodge problems. It is unfair to the caller and to the secretary for the executive to depend upon this method of escape too frequently. Avoiding problem callers often only intensifies their hostilities, and it never solves their problems. A competent executive learns how to meet problems head-on and uses the "unavailable now" approach only when sincerely busy and unable comfortably to accept incoming calls.

How do you place a call for someone else?

Sometimes you may be asked to place a call for someone else. When you do, you should say, "Mr. Alpine of the Healthkit Company is calling Ms. Harcourt."

Ms. Harcourt's secretary will then reply that he or she will ring Ms. Harcourt or that she is out or in conference and that the secretary will have her call Mr. Alpine.

If the secretary rings her and she answers, you should say, "Mr. Alpine of the Healthkit Company is calling you, Ms. Harcourt. Here he is."

Be certain that Mr. Alpine will be available to talk as soon as Ms. Harcourt is reached. If you keep her waiting, you make her feel that you don't think her time is as valuable as Mr. Alpine's. Such an implication is discourteous and will create ill will for your company.

When do you take notes of a telephone message?

Everyone has had the experience of leaving a message for someone who never returns the call, and almost everyone has had the experience of having a message erroneously delivered so that it was worthless or even disastrous. A part of telephone etiquette demands that important information be handled accurately and precisely.

It is a good practice to keep a pencil and note pad beside your telephone at all times. In this way you can jot down information as your caller is speaking without having to say, "Excuse me while I get some paper." Many successful secretaries, key sales personnel, and others for whom the telephone is important reach for their jot pad and their telephone at the same time.

If the call is for someone else, correctly note the caller's name. If you have a question about the name, remember that it is perfectly correct to ask the person to spell it. Take down any information the caller wishes to leave for the third party, including a return telephone number if it is given. A final important bit of information is the time the call was made. Jot it down at the completion of your conversation.

Many persons who are using the telephone for business of their own find taking notes during the conversation helpful. In this manner, they will have before them any important bits of information such as names, dates, prices, sizes, etc. Also, these individuals often say that taking notes during the conversation keeps them on their toes and directs their attention to the caller and his or her problem rather than to what might be going on in the office around them.

How do you establish a positive telephone image?

You may have specific ideas about certain business concerns and professional persons even though your only contact with them has been over the telephone. You now recognize that one company is terribly cold and impersonal, another is too hurried, a third keeps you waiting on HOLD too long. Your dentist has an unusually pleasant receptionist, but your physician's receptionist always sounds bored when making your appointment.

You probably have had the experience of finally meeting someone with whom you had conducted business on the telephone. Perhaps you have been shocked about how the person looked. During the weeks of telephone conversations you developed a rather concrete mental image of this person and, at least indirectly, you transferred that image to represent your image of the entire company or office represented.

Millions of dollars are spent every day by people who regularly transact business over the telephone. Dozens of major companies in every city have employees who serve only as telephone sales personnel, taking orders from telephone clients. Their image is obviously important to the success of the company. But proportionately their image is no more important than that of one secretary working in an office for one executive.

There are many different building blocks toward structuring a positive telephone image. Listed here are the most important ones:

1. *Control the level of your voice carefully.* Nothing is more offensive than loud speech, and nothing is more frustrating than dialogue so soft that you can hardly hear it. Practice. Get someone to listen to you and criticize you. Learn to modulate your voice to a pleasant level.
2. *Make your voice friendly.* Like your face, your voice can frown, smile, and laugh as you speak. Try actually to smile as you talk on the telephone; your smile will show through in your voice tones, and you will sound friendly.
3. *Be patient.* Try not to sound hurried. Convince the caller by your attitude that he or she is your only business at the moment. If the caller wishes to complain, let him or her speak. Maybe the telephone call alone will relieve the frustrations. Learn techniques of telephone business that speed the conversation but do not make you sound too abrupt.
4. *Be attentive.* Devote your entire attention to the caller. Under only the most pressing circumstances should you ever ask the caller to hold the line while you receive another call or tend to other business. This caller is your business at the moment.
5. *Transfer calls efficiently.* Maybe your function is to screen calls and then channel them. Maybe you cannot solve the problem posed by your caller. In either case, transfer the call to the proper person as quickly as possible. Know the particular channels of responsibility in your company and know to whom you should transfer various types of calls. Never transfer a call without explaining your actions to the caller. A brief explanation such as "I will connect you with Mrs. Waler who is in charge of our personnel department" will do, but tell your caller what you are doing. And never leave a call on HOLD for an unnecessary period of time.

Your concentrated practice of these five basic rules will definitely help you develop a positive telephone personality.

How do you give and receive information on the telephone?

No matter how pleasant you might be in talking on the telephone, you will not accomplish your business function unless you give and receive information correctly. Handling information over the telephone is more demanding than handling it in writing because the process occurs more quickly and neither party has time to retract something that might have been said hurriedly.

Regardless of the business you are in, from time to time you will be required both to receive and to dispense information by telephone. Here are some helpful suggestions:

1. *Get to the point.* In a business call you do not need to spend time talking around your subject or about the weather. The call is made because

someone has a request or a problem; get to the point just as quickly as you would in a business letter. Identify the problem as specifically as possible if you are the caller. When you receive such a call, be certain that you understand the exact problem. Often you might restate the problem after your caller has phrased it. This technique will help both parties know they are talking about the same thing. If you are the caller and your call is unusually complicated, you might prepare some brief notes to help you remember important points.

2. *Record information exactly.* Whether you place or receive the call, you will profit from keeping brief notes. A competent receptionist usually reaches for the telephone and a pencil at the same time. First record the name of the person to whom you are talking. Then, briefly jot down the problem, adding any details necessary for your future understanding. If you keep this material on file, you might also wish to indicate the date and time of the call, and maybe even to use a special form so that all calls will be kept in a similar format. Even if you do not keep the material, the discipline of taking notes during the call will help you keep your mind on the business at hand.

3. *Take messages accurately and pass them on promptly.* If your caller wishes to talk with someone else, transfer the call immediately if at all possible. If the other party is not in, offer to take a message. Get the caller's name, telephone number, and, if possible, the nature of the call. Then, don't forget to give this material to the person called as soon as he or she becomes available.

4. *Keep important information near the telephone.* Organize your work area so that you have important information within arm's reach of your telephone. Competent secretaries often anticipate different types of calls and keep file cards with different sets of information right on top of their desks. If you have to leave the telephone to go somewhere for information, be certain to close the key to the telephone before you leave, but tell your caller what you are doing and that you will return shortly.

How do you end a telephone call?

You should close each telephone conversation on a friendly note. Using the other person's name in your closing sentence will leave the impression that you are alert and interested in the other person's problems. You might close the conversation with a sentence such as one of the following:

> *I shall be happy to tell him that you called, Mrs. Perkins.*
> *I'll call you as soon as I have the information, Ms. Ford.*
> *Thank you for calling, Mr. Lott.*

Wait for the caller to say "goodbye." You don't want him or her to think you are impatient and wish to move along to other business.

What communications etiquette do you use with your fellow workers?

Getting along with the customers is not the only accomplishment an employee must master. If you are really going to be happy in your work and if you are going to be considered a success by your associates and supervisors, then you must consciously work to get along with them. The era of the one-person office is passing; more than 96 percent of all workers today are in situations involving from 10 to 75 or more persons with whom they must communicate.

How do you start out on the right foot with your fellow workers?

Ancient Greek warriors wore only one sandal, the left one. The right foot went bare because it was the friendly foot. The left foot, the hostile, shod foot, was used in close foot-to-foot combat. If the Greek warrior extended his left foot, the man in front of him braced himself for a swift kick to the groin. If the warrior extended his right foot, the man knew he came in peace even if there was no white flag tied on his right foot. A greek warrior always took care to cross the threshold of a house with his right foot, since entering a house on the left foot was, like drawing first in the Old West, a signal to return fire. Two results of this ancient custom remain in the modern world: soldiers begin their march to war on the left foot, and we speak of making a good impression as "putting the best foot forward" and of beginning a friendship, relationship, or job correctly as "starting out on the right foot."

Fortunately, starting off your relationship with your fellow workers will not involve having to remember which foot to stand on. It will, however, involve putting the right hand forward. When you report for work, you will be introduced to the people with whom you will work. Naturally, you will want these people to like you. They probably will if you are a reasonably likable person. Your new colleagues realize, as you do, that much of the success and personal satisfaction found in a job comes from pleasant relationships with other workers. They want to like you if they can, but they are in no hurry to do so. They have seen their share of climbers, gunning for immediate promotion to their jobs; grumblers, who, finding fault with everything from the location of the pencil sharpener to the color of the carbon paper, would rather gripe than type; plotters, who spend all their working hours playing company politics; socializers, who think the office is the happy hunting ground; and procrastinators, who never do anything today they can manage to put off until tomorrow. Your new colleagues are therefore willing to withhold their friendship until they are sure you do not belong to any of these unpleasant breeds. They will begin to make that decision when they are introduced to you, so you will want to know how proper introductions are made.

What is the key to getting along on a day-to-day basis?

You will have made an impression with your fellow employees during the brief period of introductions, and perhaps that impression will last for some time. However, you must continue to practice interpersonal communications etiquette daily if you are to maintain a stable and happy relationship with your peers.

Nothing is more important to such a relationship than *sincerity.* The individual who appears to like everybody and to be concerned about everyone's welfare but is actually self-centered is readily detected and categorized in any working group. The most important word in the English language is *you,* and the most helpful communications attitude is sincere interest in other people and their problems and ideas.

Learn to listen as well as to talk. Be as concerned about the problems of others as you are about your own. Make a point to learn about Harold's plans for his future; know Barbara's favorite hobby; recall Eugene's children and where they are going to college. When you talk with these persons, reflect your interest in them and their plans. Look at them directly as they speak. Pay attention to what they are saying and do not let your mind and your eyes roam around the room or office.

Above all, don't be a grump. Almost every business office has its chronic grouch—the individual who never enjoys anything and enjoys telling everyone how miserable he or she and the entire world are. Avoid this individual because the venom is poisonous. Your work world probably occupies from one-third to one-half of your day, and that time is too valuable to spend it in chronic complaint.

What difference do words make?

Getting along with your colleagues and the public frequently depends upon saying the right word at the right time to the right person. Although two words may be defined the same way in the dictionary, they may produce entirely different responses when they are used. You will please your colleague when you praise his or her determination; refer to stubbornness or bullheadedness, and you may turn the colleague into an enemy. "It's not what you say but how you say it that matters" is good advice, but the "how" involves choice of words as well as tone of voice. Only the right words will get the right response.

How do you learn to choose the right words?

In situations that occur frequently, you may have time to experiment, to try several ways of phrasing a certain request, question, or response. If you are observant, you will discover that a certain word choice or placement of words will produce one reaction and that other words or word arrangements will produce another reaction.

Lois learned to make such experiments in her work as a receptionist in a girl's college dormitory. She had some difficulty in handling some of the telephone calls that came to the residence from the boyfriends of the girls. The girls wanted to know who had called while they were out, and the boys were reluctant to leave their names. "Who is this?" sounded abrupt and rude. "Do you care to leave a message?" and "Is there any message?" were too easily answered with a crisp "No," and the caller's name was not really the answer to either question. "May I tell her you called?" had the right tone, and it usually brought an affirmative answer. In fact, this question would no doubt have been the best one except for one thing: some callers answered, "Yes," and hung up without giving their names. Finally she fixed upon the phrase, "Who may I tell her called?" Because the phrase could not be answered with a simple "No," and because it suggested that leaving a name was customary among callers, it usually brought the desired result.

Agnes, who was a salesperson at a fashionable dress shop that catered to wealthy but frequently overweight women, had a similar problem. The good will of her customer was more important to her than an immediate sale because she wanted the customer to return and to ask for Agnes to wait on her. If the customer made a purchase, Agnes wanted her to be satisfied with its fit; if not, she wanted her to leave neither unhappy with the clerk nor dissatisfied with the line of merchandise carried by the store. Many times the dress the customer chose to try on was too small. Agnes experimented to find a way to give that information tactfully. "That dress is too small for you," implied criticism of the dress, the customer's choice of it, or the customer's figure. "It seems a bit tight," had similar implications. "I noticed yesterday that this model seems to run a little small. Let me get one that will be nearer to your usual size," was the phrase she finally worked out. It suggested no criticism of the dress, the customer's choice of it, nor of the customer's figure. It implied that some other woman had experienced the same difficulty; it removed any uncomfortable suggestion that the customer might have gained a little weight, and it carried the assurance that a dress that fit could be found.

Frank was a supervisor in a machine shop. About once a month it was necessary for him to ask some of the men in the shop to work overtime. Since such requests usually had to be made without warning, he could not expect the men to respond very eagerly. He found they would work more willingly if he used the right words for his request, however. "The boss says we gotta work tonight," was a poor choice for two reasons. It shifted the responsibility for the request to the boss, suggesting that Frank did not think it was necessary, and it carried a suggestion of compulsion, which never evokes cooperation. "Can you work tonight?" was too easily answered with a "No" and implied more choice than Frank could afford to offer. "I need you to work tonight" was better, but it failed to arouse a spirit of cooperation. Frank found he got the best results by explaining briefly why overtime was necessary and then asking the question, "Can I count on you to help?"

The situation which requires your attention will not always be such a matter of routine, but it will require careful handling just the same. When such is the case, put yourself in the place of the other person. Try to imagine how that person feels and the effect your choice of words will have upon him or her. Learn to observe yourself and your reaction to the words other people use in speaking to you. Be honest with yourself until you find why one phrase annoys you and another makes you want to cooperate, why one angers you and another soothes you. Read advertisements and observe the expert at work. See if you can see why one advertisement is successful and why another fails. See if you can tell what kind of people will respond.

Once you become observant in this way, you will notice that some words and phrases can be depended upon to raise the blood pressure. Avoid words that imply that the other person is in error and soft-pedal your own infallibility. When expressing an opinion, admit that it is only an opinion and that it might possibly be wrong. "I may be wrong, but it seems to me that . . . " suggests that you recognize that there may be more than one way of seeing the matter, gives the other person the opportunity to admit that he or she too is expressing an opinion which may be wrong, and gives you an opportunity to save face if by some strange quirk of circumstances you are wrong.

Another touchy situation is your trying to explain something to a person who is not quick to understand. Don't, whatever you do, let the other person feel that you think any of the blame for the difficulty in communication lies with him or her. If you watch your listener carefully, you should be able to tell if he or she understands. If you must refer to the communication problem, assume that you are rather poor at explaining. Say, "Let me see if I can explain that a better way," or "Did I explain that clearly?"

Although the ability to choose your words from the standpoint of the reaction of the other person will be particularly helpful in your work, it will also be valuable in all your personal relationships. Awareness of the value of tactful word choice whenever you speak, write, listen, or read is an ingredient for success in all that you do.

ASSIGNMENTS

  I. Using a stage telephone or pretending to, demonstrate the correct way to answer in each of the following situations:
1. Your telephone at home.
2. Telephone in the school library where you work as an assistant.
3. Telephone in your room at home; your mother answered the ring downstairs and told you it was from Bill.
4. Telephone to you at school; the call from your father has been relayed through the dean's office.
5. Telephone at TeTox Services, Inc., a business which you operate.
6. Telephone for Mr. Carter at TeTox Services, Inc.; you are his personal secretary.

 II. Use the following assignments to further develop your concepts of proper telephone techniques:
1. Work with your fellow class members to create imaginary telephone situations. Assign each other roles and develop dialogue and techniques that will demonstrate both positive and negative telephone manner.
2. Let one student go to the side of the room or behind a curtain. Simulate telephone calls and let the student try to project different moods just by the tone of voice. How can you tell when he or she is pleased, angry, impatient, bored, happy, etc?
3. With the assistance of your instructor (and taking all necessary legal precautions), record telephone calls to numerous business concerns in your city. You might call asking for

specific information about their products or services, for example. Vary the nature of your calls to fit the particular business called. After you have recorded several calls, listen to the recordings in class. Discuss what you can tell about the person on the other end of the line just by the tone of voice.

III. Each of the following situations demands a brief response. Even though some of these situations might ordinarily demand oral communication, write out and bring to class a written response to each. Remember that you are dealing with business people; make your response to each problem direct. Approach each subject with an awareness of how the other party will feel and attempt to phrase your comment in a way that will receive a positive response. You may want to work with another student to produce a dramatization of one of these assignments. Plan carefully. Try to project the real feelings of the persons involved.

1. You are a legal secretary whose boss has forgotten an important appointment. Remind your boss as gently as possible that he or she has to meet a client on the other side of town in thirty minutes.

2. You are assistant manager of a clothing store. You have been asked by one of the clerks to explain to a customer that you cannot exchange a bathing suit, which the customer says is too small, because it has obviously been worn.

3. You are an insurance claims adjuster who must explain to a client that his or her fire-damaged car was really worth only $350 before the fire and not the alleged $750.

4. You are a police officer in charge of school safety. You must explain to the city council that a stop sign is essential at the intersection of Elm and Piedmont. You want to hint that three recent accidents there have been the result of the council's failure to install the sign.

5. You are a medical secretary whose employer has poor penmanship. You must ask your employer to clarify for you a certain illegible statement on one of the charts.

6. You are manager of a hardware store and it is your responsibility to call and remind a customer that payment on a thirty-day account is two weeks past due.

7. You are fire marshal of a small city. In making annual inspections you discover that the mayor's secretary has a storage closet that is a great fire hazard. You must explain to the secretary that the closet must be cleaned immediately.

8. You are personnel manager of a company that has recently begun using a time clock. You must write a one-paragraph

memo explaining to all employees that they will be fired if they are caught checking in or out on the time clock for anyone else.

9. You operate data processing equipment for an employer who is noted for being very money-conscious. You must explain to your employer that it is important for you to attend an annual convention of data processors so that you might keep informed about current ideas and equipment.

10. You are an executive secretary for a very busy employer, who is trying to stall a representative from a certain company, awaiting further data on the company's reputation. The representative is now in the office, and you must persuade him or her to wait until later to see your employer.

3

Business Letters

Who sends and receives business letters?

It is difficult to imagine that there is any adult in today's society who has not received a business letter. You have probably received literally dozens of letters wanting to sell you something or letters wanting you to join some group. You may have received a letter confirming a job appointment or a letter from the college dean about your scholarship. Obviously, there are many, many types of business letters, and in the course of your life you will receive hundreds more.

Just as it is difficult to imagine anyone who has never received a business letter, it is also a bit difficult to imagine people who have never sent one. In today's society the business letter is a tool for effective communication, and almost everyone uses it. You may already have written a letter applying for a job, a letter asking about a college scholarship, or a letter to a company complaining about an error in your bill. As you complete your schooling and participate more fully in society, you will have many more occasions that require you to write letters.

Why is the business letter so important?

In spite of the large number of forms designed for simple reporting tasks and in spite of the ever-increasing use of the telephone for business communications, a large number of instances still require the formal business letter. This type of communication is still an effective means for exchanging information between two parties. Furthermore, the business letter provides a written document that may be referred to in the future and that, in certain instances, may even be used as legal evidence. Companies are often interested in the letters written by their various employees because those letters provide a collective profile of the employees' attitudes and job effectiveness.

Think for a moment about some of the business letters you have already received. Some made you feel good; some made you angry. Some were clever; some were boring. Some accomplished exactly what the sender intended; some severely missed their goals. Learning to write a business letter that works—one that accomplishes its purpose—is a first step toward developing mature job-related communications skills.

Why should you plan a business letter?

A business letter is by its very nature more formal than a personal letter; thus it is worth more time and effort to produce. Although figures vary, and they certainly continue to spiral upward, current estimates are that it costs a typical company nearly five dollars to send one business letter (stationery, typewriter cost, secretarial time, office space, postage, etc.). If a letter costs that much to produce and mail, it definitely is worth some planning.

Your best letters in the past have probably been written in your head. You get a letter from Ed, and you compose a long mental letter in reply eight or ten pages long, telling him all about your new job, your new car, and your old problems. Of course, the letter is all in your head, and you can't mail brain waves. But you have thought through what you wanted to tell Ed, and that thinking process will have helped you organize your thoughts for when you do sit down and write the actual letter.

Well, in the future you will write your best business letters in your head also. You will plan them mentally first, then you will go one step further. You will write or dictate the letter you have planned. Letters which receive such a head start will be written more rapidly, more clearly, and more completely than one that is not planned.

If the letter you are planning is to be a short one, you can make a brief mental outline of the points you wish to make. If your letter is longer or more involved, perhaps you should write out a word outline. After you have jotted down the points you wish to make, you will probably need to rearrange them. Place the most important things first.

After you have given some ideas a second thought, you may decide they are not really essential. Scratch them out. Cluttering up your letter with minor, nonessential points distracts the reader from what is really important.

Some letters will be so long, so involved, or so important that you may want to write or dictate a rough draft first. Then you can revise your letter, cutting out less important words and ideas, marking out words and phrases that do not say anything, making substitutions for hackneyed expressions, and re-forming sentences in the most forceful way.

Planning your letters in this way will save you time, both now and later. It will save you time now because the actual writing will take less time if you have already listed the points you want to make. It will save you time later because lack of planning may cause you to forget a point that you wish to make, and such an omission will probably require you to write another letter later.

With this type of preplanning, not only will you be able to handle your points in the best order, but you will also be able to handle them more completely and to express yourself more effectively. Do not have to worry about forgetting something you want to say. You can concentrate on one thing at a time. When you have covered one point completely, you can move on to the next point, confident that you will not suddenly insert something you should have said earlier and thus destroy the unity of your writing. When you have finished your letter, you will know that you have covered each point clearly and completely.

At first it may seem to you that such preliminary work is a waste of time. But in the end it will save you time. It will save your typist time. And because it will enable you to write a clearer, more complete letter, it will save your reader time.

How do you write a letter from an outline?

A typical word outline might be something like this:

Thanks
Reason request can't be filled
Suggestion where he can find it
Promise to help later

From this outline you might write the following letter:

Thanks   Thank you for turning to us when you needed information on how to train your dog. We are always pleased when our customers think of us for their pet supplies and needs.

Reason request can't be filled   We are very sorry that we cannot send you the booklet *How to Make Your Dog an Obedient Pal.* The booklet has been very popular, and we have exhausted our first supply.

Suggestion where he or she can find it   The local pet stores that carry Happy Puppy Dog Biscuits were all furnished large supplies of the booklet. You can probably pick up a copy at Peppers Pup Package store in Dalpark.

Promise to help later   We will place you on our mailing list for a copy, which we will mail when we receive the second printing.

When is the best time to write letters?

When you receive a letter that requires an answer, whether you plan to answer immediately or not, you mentally form some kind of answer. If your next move is to transfer that planning to paper and then to write your answer, you will save yourself much time. If you put off answering the morning's mail, you will have to read it twice: once when you receive it and once when you answer it. You will also plan your answer twice. If you can answer the letter without additional information, do so at once. If additional information is needed, underscore the main points in the letter as you read it. Make a note of the information you need. Get the facts as soon as possible, while the matter is still fresh in your mind. Be sure to have all the facts before you answer the letter.

You will also save time if you concentrate on your correspondence at one time, rather than scattering it throughout the day. You have probably noticed that once you start writing letters, you can just as easily write several before you stop. Your letters are also more effective because you are handling similar situations at the same time. Letter writing is one chore that invites procrastination. You can reduce the temptation to put off the task if you have a definite time when you handle most of your correspondence.

What are the parts
of a business letter?

Over the years the various conventions of usage have described what information needs to be given in the formal parts of a business letter and have suggested where these parts should be placed so they will be most helpful. Various forms for punctuation and indentation are used, and you will need to use the form preferred by your office. However, the changes are not major ones and can easily be accommodated once you have learned the form given below, which is the most commonly used of all business letter forms.

Based on the outline that you have just developed, a finished business letter to Ms. Dorian would look like Figure 3-1 and would contain the parts noted in the left margin.

If you were writing to Ms. Dorain from a company that did not have its own letterhead, you would use a different form to indicate your return address. The top part of your letter would look like Figure 3-2.

In both Figure 3-1 and Figure 3-2 the name of the state is spelled completely, but companies more and more are beginning to use the two-letter abbreviations that are approved by the United States Postal Service. The complete list of those abbreviations is on page 186 in the Handbook section of this text. When you use the abbreviation, both letters are capitalized.

How do you write the salutation
of a business letter?

You will be expected to greet your correspondent with one of several conventional phrases. The approved salutations are given below in order of decreasing formality:

For Men	For Women
Sir:	Madam:
My dear Sir:	My dear Madam:
Dear Sir:	Dear Madam:
My dear Mr. Sloan:	My dear Ms. Thompson: (or Mrs. or Miss)
Dear Mr. Sloan:	Dear Ms. Thompson: (or Mrs. or Miss)
Dear Joe:	Dear Fay:

Dear Sir and *Dear Madam* are always singular. *Gentlemen* is used

figure 3-1

Return Address	**HAPPY PUPPY BISCUITS, INC.** **8736 Prudence, Dallas, Texas 75222** **745-4447**
Date	March 14, 1979
Inside address	Mrs. Gilbert Dorian P.O. Box 516 Dalpark, Texas 76111
Salutation	Dear Mrs. Dorian:

Body of letter	Thank you for turning to us when you needed information on how to train your dog. We are always pleased when our customers think of us for their pet supplies and needs.
	
	      We are very sorry that we cannot send you the booklet How to Make Your Dog an Obedient Pal. This booklet has been very popular, and we have exhausted our first supply.
	
	      The local pet stores that carry Happy Puppy Biscuits were all furnished large supplies of the booklet. You can probably pick up a copy at Peppers Pup Package Store in Dalpark.
	
	      We will place you on our mailing list for a copy, which we will mail when we receive the second printing.

Complimentary close	Sincerely yours,
Signature	*John B. Griffith* John B. Griffith Customer Relations Manager

figure 3-2

```
                                         8736 Prudence
                                         Dallas, Texas 75222
                                         March 14, 1979


Mrs. Gilbert Dorian
P.O. Box 516
Dalpark, Texas 75111

Dear Mrs. Dorian:
```

for addressing a company, a committee, a numbered post office box, and an organization made up of men or of men and women. *Dear Sir and Madam* is used in writing to a firm consisting of a man and a woman. *Ladies and Gentlemen* is used in writing to a social group made up of men and women. *Mesdames* is the standard plural for *Madam* and is used for addressing a company, committee, or other group made up entirely of women. *Ladies* is becoming popular as an alternative salutation.

You can decide which salutation you should use by asking yourself how well you know your correspondent. If you have never met the person, you may use *Sir* or *Madam;* but these forms are going out of style. Modern communication leans toward directness. *Dear Mr. Sloan* is probably used a hundred times more often than any of the other more formal forms of address.

Did you notice how the salutations were capitalized and punctuated? The first word of the salutation is always capitalized. *Dear* is not capitalized unless it is the first word. The following are always capitalized in the salutation:

Sir   Madam   Mr.   Ms.   Mrs.   Miss   all titles   all names

Although a comma is used after the salutation in personal correspondence, only the colon (:) is acceptable after a business salutation:

Dear Mr. Colon:

In your salutation you will, of course, use any title which applies to your correspondent. Only a few titles should be abbreviated: Mr., Mrs., and Dr. The plurals for these words are abbreviated: Messrs., Mmes., and Drs. Miss is not an abbreviation and should have no period after it. Some other titles, such as Prof. (Professor), Capt. (Captain), Sgt. (Sergeant), may be abbreviated in the inside address when they appear with the correspondent's full name or surname and initials. However, in the salutation and body of the letter, when they are written with only the last name, they should be written in full:

Prof. Jane Peterson   Capt. Alfred Strate
Professor Peterson: *Captain Strate:*

Addressing governmental and other prominent officials and church dignitaries presents certain definite problems. Suitable titles and salutations are frequently unfamiliar because they are not used very often. It is important, however, that you address such people properly. In the back of any good desk dictionary are some of the most frequently used forms of address. *Merriam-Webster's Eighth New Collegiate Dictionary* contains a fairly complete listing of titles and salutations.

How do you close your business letter?

The most commonly used closes for business letters are arranged below in the order of decreasing formality:

Severely formal	Respectfully yours, Yours respectfully,
Formal but widely used	Very truly yours, Yours very truly,
Semiformal	Very sincerely yours, Yours very sincerely,
Ordinary business letters	Sincerely,
Daily business contacts	Cordially yours,
Close business friendships	Yours cordially,
Informal business relations	Cordially,
Close personal friendship with or without business	Faithfully yours,

Cordially yours and *Sincerely yours* express a warmth that is pleasing but which should also be consistent with the general tone of the letter. If the letter is reserved, the person addressed of great importance, or any doubt exists as to how much formality is required, choose the more conservative *Yours very truly* or *Very truly yours.*

The important thing to remember is that the complimentary close should match the salutation in degree of formality. If you begin *Dear Ms. Roberts,* you should not close with *Faithfully yours.* If the salutation is formal, the close should be formal; if the salutation is informal, the close should be informal.

How do you sign your business letter?

If you are writing or dictating the letter, it should be signed simply without title, and your name should be typed beneath your signature. If you are a man, your signature will present no problems. You decide early in your career that you prefer to sign your name J. J. Astor, Jacob

J. Astor, or Jacob John Astor, and you do so for the remainder of your professional life. You never attach a title of any kind to your signature. If you have a string of degrees or a title that your correspondent may need to know to be able to address an answer properly or to evaluate you as an authority, you still sign your name John Anderson. Then you or your secretary can type beneath your signature:

John Anderson, M.D.

or

Arthur McMurray
Sales Manager

The matter of a woman's signature is a bit more complicated. If you are unmarried, your proper signature is obviously your maiden name. If you wish, you may indicate *Miss* or *Ms.* by placing it in parentheses before the typed signature. Any form below is correct:

Sincerely yours,   Sincerely yours,

Agnes Head   Agnes Head

Agnes Head   (Ms.) Agnes Head

Sincerely yours,

Agnes Head

(Miss) Agnes Head

A married woman should use her given name in her signature, and, if she is known professionally by that name, in her typed signature. If she wishes to use the *Mrs.* or the *Ms.* title, she should place it in parentheses before the typed signature.

Sincerely yours,   Sincerely yours,

Agnes Head   Agnes Head

(Mrs.) Agnes Head   (Ms.) Agnes Head

In some business and social situations the woman may wish to sign her given name but to use her husband's name in the typed signature. If this is done, notice that the entire typed signature is placed in parentheses:

Sincerely yours,

Agnes Head

(Mrs. Frederick Head)

How can you make the tone of your letter positive?

The best way to make your letter positive is to keep it reader-centered. The most important person in your world is you. The most important problems in your world are your problems. You are interested in other people, for the most part, only as they fit into your world and relate to you and your problems. Many people touch your life only as they are able to help you solve some problem. You aren't deeply concerned with how much time or effort they must spend to help you solve your problem so long as they do it successfully. And if they are paid to solve your problems, the problems which arise for them in the course of doing so are even less important to you.

If these facts are true for you—and you're very unusual if they are not—they are equally true for the customers and clients of the company that will employ you. Your readers will respond to you as you make them feel that they and their problems are important to you.

In face-to-face contact, you convey your friendly interest in people with the warm smile and the firm handclasp with which you greet them, with the alert expression with which you listen to them, and with the pleasant tone with which you answer them. When you write a letter, your reader can't, of course, see your smile or alert expression, feel your handshake, or hear your voice. Your words must convey all the warmth, friendliness, and eagerness to help that can be put into a smile, a handshake, and a pleasant voice.

How can you begin a letter in a positive way?

Nowhere is warmth and friendliness more important than in the first sentence of your letter. Here you catch the readers' attention, express your interest in them, and show them that their problems are important to you. The opening sentence of your letter should be reader-centered and should establish a friendly relationship between you and the reader.

A letter that begins with the following sentence is neither reader-centered nor friendly:

> This will acknowledge receipt of your letter of June 11 in regard to Order No. 892068, in which you asked about instructions for the installation of the hydrometer. In reply, I wish to say . . .

There is no warmth in this sentence. Nothing in the sentence highlights either the reader or the reader's problem. Besides, it's wordy. Why not say, "The instruction sheet for the installation of the hydrometer which you asked about is being rushed to you today"? Now the reader knows what he or she wants to know, and knows you're eager to help.

The subject position of the sentence is one of the most important points in the sentence. Don't waste this important spot on an indefinite *this:* "This will acknowledge. . . ." Don't waste it on an inconsequential date: "Your letter of October 29 reached us and. . . ." The correspondent doesn't care when he or she wrote that letter. Checking the files can give that information if it is needed. The reader wants to know when he or she will get whatever satisfaction is being sought. If possible, make the subject of your sentence the reader and his or her needs:

> The order you sent on June 23 is being filled at once.
> The data on the enclosed sheet will cover the question you asked in your letter of August 17.
> Here is the catalog on our special fall sale which you. . . .

That first sentence of your letter is the most important, because if it is not the right sentence, your reader may not read the other sentences. Some letter writers aren't aware of this fact or they wouldn't waste those first precious words on empty participal phrases rather than plunging right into the really important matter at hand.

Participal Opening	Reader-centered Opening
Acknowledging receipt of and thanking you for your fine order, . . .	Thank you for your fine order.
Complying with your request of April 9 for a catalog, . . .	Here is the catalog you asked for.
Replying to your letter of January 18 in which you referred to information . . .	The information referred to in your letter . . .

Opening sentences should be interesting, gracious, and positive. They may do one of the following:

Tell What You Have Done for Your Reader

You should receive the data you requested by Friday.
Here is the report you asked about.
Your order for eight typewriter tables was shipped today.

Ask Your Reader a Question

Did you receive our latest specification on . . . ?
Have you investigated the success experienced by the Wharton Company since they have installed . . . ?
Is there a way we could make our service more readily available to you?

Make a Request

Could you let me know the results of your trial of . . . ?
Would you give me further information about . . . ?
Please give me the date and order number on . . .
Can you place my name on your mailing list for . . . ?

State Something Interesting

You will be glad to know the results of your trial of . . .
You are certainly right, Mr. Harcourt, when you say that . . .
The question you raised in your letter of September 3 is a good one and . . .

How do you keep your sentences reader-centered throughout the letter?

Throughout your letter, keep your sentences reader-centered by keeping in mind your reader, your reader's needs, and your reader's interests. The reader isn't interested in placing an order by June 15 so your company can clear certain items from its stocks, but he or she may want to place the order by that date if doing so will save some money. A customer isn't interested in sending in a duplicate copy of an invoice to help you keep your records straight, but might be persuaded to do so to insure prompt credit for his or her own account. Notice the difference of emphasis in the following pairs of phrases:

Writer-centered   *We* wish to announce . . .
Reader-centered   *You* will be glad to hear . . .

Writer-centered	*We* are enclosing our . . .
Reader-centered	*You* will find your check enclosed.
Writer-centered	*We* wish to point out . . .
Reader-centered	*You* will be interested to know . . .

It is not enough, however, to sprinkle a few *you*'s through your letter. More important is the friendly spirit you express toward the "you," your concern with his or her problems, and your positive affirmation that he or she is an important, worthwhile person. Your sentences must center on the interests of the reader as well as on the word *you*. Notice the difference in the following sentences:

Writer-centered	*We* have received your order of July 18 which *we* have passed on to *our* special dealer in charge of *our* company in that area.
Reader-centered	*Your* check for $25 was received to-day. We are happy to credit it to *your* account.

How do you end your letter in a positive way?

If the first sentence of your letter creates the important first impression that makes the reader want to finish the letter in good will, the last sentence leaves the last impression which determines how the reader will feel about you and your letter in the future. Do not waste this valuable spot on insipid participial endings that say nothing. You can write the following phrases on slips of paper and place them in a hat to be drawn out when you need to close a letter. You can, but if you do so you will not be an effective letter writer.

Hoping this has not inconvenienced you . . .
Trusting this meets with your satisfaction . . .
Thanking you in advance . . .
Awaiting receipt of your reply . . .

How much firmer and friendlier is the good-bye in these sentences:

We are always glad to serve you.
We are very glad to have this new business.
When we can help you, let us know.
Thanks.

Sometimes you may want the reader to take some action. If you do, say so in plain English. Since the closing sentence of your letter is the one that makes the most lasting impression, it should be the one that tells your reader what to do. If what you want requires a lengthy explanation, tell your reader earlier but repeat the main instruction in your last sentences. He or she will remember that instruction better if you keep it short.

> Send us your check today, and your order will be shipped Monday.
> Fill out the application and return it to us today, and your policy will be in force the first of the month.
> Just put your okay on the bottom of this letter and mail it to me today.
> By initialing and returning the enclosed order blank before the fifteenth, you will enable us to send you your stock in time for your January sales.

Notice that these requests are not vague. The reader knows exactly what the writer wants done. Moreover, the reader knows when the writer wants it done. The words *today* or *at once* urge the reader to reach for a pen now, not after the letter has lain on the desk for a week. The reader will also act more promptly if you have simplified the action you ask. If questionnaires and other forms are involved, they should be self-explanatory and easy to fill out. The use of questionnaires or forms can save your reader the time and effort of writing or dictating a letter, and save you time in waiting for a reply. If he or she can check a *yes* or *no* at the bottom of your letter or attach a signature or okay to a sentence you have prepared, the answer may leave in the evening mail. And if the reader can slip that letter into a stamped, self-addressed envelope which you have enclosed with your letter, the answer may go out the same day.

Sometimes you do not want your reader to do anything except finish your letter feeling friendly toward you. You might close with a sentence like one of these:

> For your sake and ours, we hope you will continue to have the kind of prosperity that prompted this fine order.
> If you are in Chicago for the trades convention, be sure to drop by our display room to say hello.

During the holiday season, you can add a friendly note by closing with such remarks as "Season's greetings and our best wishes to you" or "Best wishes at this happy season."

But however you end your letter, keep your closing sentence short, like the parting words of a visit with a friend. Do not stand at the door with your hat in your hand. When you are through, stop.

How do you proofread a letter?

After you have written your letter, you are not through. The following steps will keep you from making many errors:

- Check the spelling of the reader's name.
- Check figures, facts, and enclosures.
- Check the spelling, grammar, and punctuation.
- Reread the letter you are answering to be sure you have answered it completely.
- Read carefully every letter you sign.

The letter in Figure 3-3 is filled with errors in form and content. Read the letter carefully and then study the comments which follow it.

Disregard for a moment the awkward sentences in this letter and look only at the content and form. Notice that Mr. Rockton is writing about his account but that his paragraphs do not move in an organized manner. Both of his references to the ten-dollar payment, for example, should have been made in the third paragraph, rather than in two separate paragraphs. Specifically, notice the following errors:

line 2	*Tex* is not the abbreviation for Texas; also no comma should separate the state from the zip code.
line 3	Only a lazy person uses this form for citing a date. Write the date out in full and do not skip a line between the date and the return address.
lines 4,9	The preferred form for addressing a woman is *Ms.* unless correspondence from her has indicated that she prefers either *Miss* or *Mrs.*
lines 7-8	Keep the city and the state on the same line of the inside address. Do not separate state and zip code by a comma.
line 9	If you know the person's name, do not address her by general reference in the salutation. Follow the salutation with a colon, not a comma.
line 10	This is a wordy beginning to the letter. Actually you could strike this entire first paragraph and lose none of the meaning.
line 14	The letter should have begun here if this is what Mr. Rockton *really* is writing about.
lines 14-17	This is a very awkward sentence. It tries to do too much.

figure 3-3

```
                                   8753 Gation Drive              1
                                   Houston, Tex., 77211           2

                                   4/17/79                        3

Miss Roberta Pease, Credit Manager                                4
Sav—a—Lot Department Stores                                       5
4010 Alfred Road                                                  6
Houston,                                                          7
Texas, 77001                                                      8

Dear Miss,                                                        9

        I am writing to let you know that you have my credit      10
account all fouled up.  I don't know what has happened because    11
until this time I have always had good dealing with your company  12
and have never had to write to anyone about anything before.      13

        I am really writing about my last statement.  You say there 14
that I owe you $45.78 and that I have not made a payment in two    15
months and that you are going to close my credit account and      16
report me to the credit association.  I don't see how you can     17
say these things.                                                 18

        My wife sent you a check in February, about the 15th I     19
think, for $10.  We did not pay you in March because my little    20
boy had to go to the hospital and be operated on.  This all       21
cost me $320, and I don't make but $435 in a month.  You can see  22
I didn't have much left.                                          23

        Anyway, you should know that I will pay you when I can and 24
I hope that I will get paid this weekend and mail you a check.     25
My credit has been good with you for five years.                  26

        Besides, I don't know why we did not get credit for the $10 27
my wife sent you in February.  Please let me know.                28

                                   Yours,                         29

                                   Bill Rockton

                                   Bill Rockton                   30
```

	Probably Ms. Pease does not need to be reminded of all that Mr. Rockton was told on the last statement.
line 19	Be exact. When was the check sent?
line 20	Mr. Rockton needs only to say that he had unusual medical expenses. Ms. Pease is a busy woman and is not interested in the details of the boy's operation.
line 25	Be specific. When will a check be mailed?

lines 25-26   This sentence does not belong in this paragraph. It is intended
                to show that Mr. Rockton wishes to keep his credit rating secure,
                but it does not really say that.

line 27   This entire paragraph is badly stated and is misplaced.

line 29   *Yours* is far too casual a complimentary close. *Sincerely yours*
                would be much better.

Bill Rockton's letter could be rewritten to look something like Figure
3-4:

figure 3-4

```
                                 8753 Gation Drive
                                 Houston, TX 77211
                                 April 17, 1979

Ms. Roberta Pease, Credit Manager
Sav-a-Lot Department Stores
4010 Alfred Road
Houston, TX 77001

Dear Ms. Pease:

        I am writing about the last statement I received from your
company.  It showed a balance of $45.78 and indicated that I was two
months behind in my payments.

        My wife sent you a check (our check No. 355 Houston National
Bank) dated February 16 for $10.  I do not think that we have been
credited with this payment even though we have received the cancelled
check from our bank.  If you wish, I can mail you a copy of the check
so you can examine it against your own records.

        I admit that I did not send my payment in March, and I realize I
should have written to you then explaining why.  I had such heavy med-
ical expenses that month that I had to postpone several of my regular
payments.  But I do plan to make a double payment this month.  I
will be paid April 20 and will mail you a check for the last two
months that same day.

        I have had an excellent credit rating with your company for
five years, and I would certainly not want to lose it now.

                                 Sincerely yours,

                                 Bill Rockton

                                 Bill Rockton
```

ASSIGNMENTS

I. Letters 3-A and 3-B contain numerous errors in form and content. Using the line-by-line analysis which was used with Figure 3-3, list the errors that you find. Rewrite each letter so that it is acceptable. Remember that you might need to rephrase the entire letter to make it suitable.

II. Write letters for each of the following situations. Remember that you must include *your* return address and that you must sign the finished letter.

    1. Write to the publishers of Zme magazine inquiring why you have not received the last two issues of the publication. Your annual subscription still has five months to go, and you have the receipt from your last payment.

letter 3-a

```
                                    1113 Pert Avenue
                                    San Francisco Calif.
                                    Sept. 11, 1978


Mr. Fred Simpson
Manager
Oakwood Automobile Company
4414 Lamair
San Francisco, Calif. 94133

Dear Mr. Simpson

        You don't know me, but I bought a car from your company about
three weeks ago.  It was a brand new model.  I traded in my 1964 work
car for a down payment.

        The problem is that this new car is not running right.  It gets
too hot when my wife drives it around town.  She said she had to keep
the motor racing all the time to keep it cool.

        Also the front door on my side does not close good.  It rattles
a lot.

        I called the shop and they said they could not fix the car until
next week.  I just want you to know that I am not happy with it and that
I am going to write the regional sales office to tell them that you are
not giving me good service.
                            Yours truly,

                            Dan Paderson
                            Dan Paderson
```

letter 3-b

<table>
<tr><td>3857 Avenue M</td><td>1</td></tr>
<tr><td>Boston, Mass.</td><td>2</td></tr>
</table>

Ms. Mildred McWhorter   3
Boston, Mass.   4

Dear Ms. McWhorter   5

    I just want to write you a short letter and tell you how much I   6
appreciate the courtesy of your delivery man. I have done business   7
with five different cleaners in the last two years, and I have not   8
found anyone who is as good as your man.   9

    He always is dressed neat and clean. He is polite and courte-   10
ous. He is ready to give me the right change when I pay him. He is   11
real business like in everything.   12

    I also like the way he handles my clothes. He doesn't wad them   13
up in a tight little bundle like some delivery men he keeps them on   14
the hangers and treats them gently. When he brings them back home he   15
always puts them in the front closet while I get the money for him.   16

    I just wanted you to know that he is a good man and you should   17
be proud of him.   18

            Your customer,   19

            Louise McLoy

            Louise McLoy   20

2. Submit a letter to Plain-Clothes Dry Goods explaining that you cannot meet your monthly charge payment because of illness in your family. Indicate that you plan to make a double payment next month.

3. Write to the Credit Manager of Xert, Inc., inquiring why your charge account has not been approved. You submitted a credit application to them three months ago and have heard nothing. You have an excellent credit rating. (Include two or three good credit references in your letter.)

4. Prepare a brief letter to your mayor (or any other important official) expressing appreciation of some recent action for which the mayor has been responsible. Remember that he or she is busy and that you want only to register your positive response.

5. Write a letter to the same official, this time briefly expressing

disapproval of some action. Again remember that your purpose is to register your feelings and not to itemize details.

6. Write a letter to Improved Gasket Company asking if they have a replacement gasket to fit the manifold head of your 1949 Ford. You have been unable to find the gasket at a local supply house and have heard that they stock them. Order one of the gaskets sent C.O.D. if it is available.

III. In the previous question you wrote several letters to various persons. Assume now that you are on the receiving end of those letters and must respond to them. Write responses to at least three of the letters which you wrote for question II.

IV. Each of the following letters is writer-centered. Rewrite each to make it reader-centered. You are given only the body of each letter, but your revision of it should include all the necessary parts of a business letter.

Letter A

Replying to your recent letter, I am sorry that I am not able to send you information that you request regarding our new tomato plants.

Our supply of free brochures has run out, and we do not know when we will get any more from the printer.

Letter B

We would like for you to help us make a brief survey of working mothers. Our records show that you are one of the several thousand mothers in our city who hold a full-time job.

We are trying to determine several different things about the unique problems and/or opportunities that may face you and your job. If you complete the enclosed questionnaire for us, you will help to make our study more complete.

Letter C

We have been going through our customer records and have discovered that you have not made a purchase at our store in over a year.

We want to remind you that your credit is still good with us. We hope that you will come in soon and browse among the many new items that have been added to our inventory.

Our customers are important people to us. We want you to come see us again.

Letters of Adjustment, Refusal, and Collection

Why are letters of adjustment important?

Frequently, errors—yours or other people's—will require that you write letters requesting adjustments of those errors or agreeing to make the adjustments that other people have asked of you. The kinds of mistakes that must be adjusted are multiple. Merchandise may arrive damaged. Errors may be made in filling orders. The terms of the sale may be misunderstood. The buyer may feel that the goods received do not measure up to the description. A mistake may be made in billing. In such cases and in hundreds of others, the buyer should ask for an adjustment. If you are the seller, you would appreciate the dissatisfied buyer's giving you an opportunity to straighten out the matter and win back the buyer's good will. If you're the buyer, you are entitled to satisfaction, and the seller will want to give it to you.

Letters asking for adjustment are frequently referred to as "claim letters." In writing, however, don't use the word "claim"; in fact, you should avoid claiming anything. Instead, give the facts and ask for what you believe is the proper adjustment.

How do you write a letter asking for an adjustment?

Whether or not you receive the adjustment you ask for may be determined more than you realize by the way you ask for it. The person who has made the mistake often reacts defensively. This reaction is most frequently found in the less important, less experienced worker.

The Vice-President-in-Charge-of-Red-Tape can always find some underling to blame, but the third assistant to the stock clerk has no office cat to kick. If you are kind, that person may be amazed and grateful enough to put forth extra effort to see that your merchandise is properly packed and routed or that your statement is carefully checked.

You will be able to write more courteously if you are very sure that you yourself have made no error. So, first, you should do all you can to make sure that a mistake has actually been made by the seller and that you have all the facts. Then write your letter clearly, directly, and courteously. Show how you have been inconvenienced by the error and appeal to the self-interest and sense of fair play of the seller.

You will gain nothing by being irritable or quarrelsome. You may take some secret delight in displaying your wit through some sarcastic remark, but you may be embarrassed later when you discover that the error is really yours. And your sense of fair play should require that you give the seller the benefit of the doubt and assume he or she is honest, conscientious, and only slightly more subject to error than you. If you really are angry and must expel the venom that fills your soul, write an angry letter, then throw it away and write one that will get the kind of prompt, well-intentioned response you want.

There will be two parts to your letter. One part will give the information that the seller needs in order to make the adjustment. It will contain the date of the order or shipment, the order number, the stock number of the article if there is one, the exact nature of the complaint, and a description of the way in which you have been inconvenienced by the problem. The other part suggests to the seller the adjustment which you want made. You may make such a suggestion at the beginning of your letter in order to emphasize or clarify it, or you can give all the facts first. The order of the letter will depend somewhat upon the situation.

How can you show courtesy in replying to a letter asking for an adjustment?

When you receive a letter from a dissatisfied customer, you can be sure that somebody has made a mistake. No matter who that somebody is, use this opportunity to build good business relations. Right or wrong, do your best to see that the customer is satisfied with the experience.

The adjustment letter, more than any other business letter, should be reader-centered. Realize first that the customer is unhappy for two reasons: first, he or she has been inconvenienced by some discrepancy, mistake, or product failure that involves your company; second, the person has had to take the time to write to ask you to solve the problem, and has had to be placed in the uncomfortable position of complainer or asker of favors.

You hope, of course, that all the letters that you receive asking for adjustment are as clear, accurate, and courteous as those you will write. Whether they are or not, you should answer them as though they were. Even if you wonder why the words of the letter you have received did not set the paper on fire, calm yourself and assume that the person who wrote it is intelligent and careful, honest and conscientious, and that your company wants his or her business. Such assumptions will make a customer write more intelligently, carefully, and conscientiously next time; and such generosity will build good will and good business.

Avoid words or expressions suggesting that the person asking for an adjustment is careless:

You neglected to specify . . .
You failed to include . . .
You overlooked enclosing . . .

Do not use words that imply the person is lying:

You claim that . . .
You say that . . .
You state that . . .

Be careful not to write sentences that belittle the customer or make the customer feel that you think he or she is ignorant:

We cannot see how you . . .
We fail to understand . . .
We are at a loss to know . . .

Avoid demanding phrases that arouse the reader's rebellion:

You should . . .
You ought to . . .
You must . . .
We must ask you to . . .
We must insist . . .

Some phrases that seem friendly or polite to you may be read as sarcastic or condescending by your reader:

No doubt . . .
We will thank you to . . .
You understand, of course . . .
Please respond soon . . .

Read these phrases aloud as though you were angry. Do you see that a sneer seems to be applied? Put your own letter to the same test.

No matter what action you may feel is proper in the case, there is one important task you can perform to help customer relations. You can respond promptly. Even if you can't act more definitely without further examination of the facts, you can write the customer at once to say that you are looking into the complaint. Promptness is the key here. The customer has already been inconvenienced by an error or misunderstanding in connection with your company; do not cause further annoyance by your delay. The longer the customer has to wait, the greater he or she is inconvenienced. Moreover, you can damage the reputation of your company by suggesting that it is insensitive to the requests of its customers. Whether you can or cannot make the adjustment the customer seeks, you should show that you understand the dissatisfaction and that you are sorry for any misunderstanding.

How should you handle the error that is responsible for the letter asking for an adjustment?

Every adjustment requested involves a mistake somewhere. One of three parties may be at fault: the seller, the buyer, or a third party such as the shipping company or the post office.

If the buyer is at fault, you will have to tell him or her so, but you should do so in a way that will not cause embarrassment or displeasure. Remember, pointing out a person's mistakes often puts the person on the defensive. The buyer, even after being convinced that you are right, will not like you and your company the better for making him or her feel incompetent or stupid.

If a third party is responsible for the error, be careful not to judge too harshly nor shift completely the task of settling the matter to the carrying agent or other intermediary. And even if you feel that the third party should take care of the matter, you should still check later to see that the customer is satisfied.

Finally, if the mistake was made by your company, assume the blame courteously and firmly and quickly make a fair adjustment.

How do you handle the requested adjustment?

A fair adjustment is one that is reasonable and impartial. When you write an adjustment letter, you are judge, jury, and attorney for both parties. You will want to view the matter impartially for two very good reasons. First, your company is ethical and fair in its dealings. You wouldn't be associated with it if it were not, and it won't be there for you to be associated with very long if it is not. Second, no matter how tactfully and courteously you handle your letter, you will not make your adjustment appear fair if it is not.

You may be able to be unfair in the customer's favor, and you should probably investigate to see if you can afford to do so. Securing new customers costs money. It may be cheaper to make some concessions to hold an old customer than to court a new one. If at all possible, you should grant at least part of the request made by the seller.

Granting part of what the claimant asks is making a compromise and may require some negotiating. In such a case, explain why you can't make a full concession and what you are prepared to offer. You should usually offer only one plan of adjustment. Two or three plans are confusing to many people. However, always offer the compromise to the claimant as an arrangement that is subject to his or her approval. At the same time, take the positive, cheerful approach that you expect the customer to accept your suggested adjustment.

If you can grant all or part of the adjustment, do so cheerfully, even enthusiastically. If you act begrudging even in giving a fair adjustment, the claimant probably won't feel really satisfied. When you give in, give in all the way. You are wasting a valuable opportunity if you don't use a favorable adjustment to get every ounce of good will that you can. Phrases like the following help to show that your company is in business to serve this customer:

We are pleased to return the amount enclosed.
We are grateful you gave us the opportunity to correct our mistake.
Thank you for calling this matter to our attention.
We are glad to credit your account.
We appreciate your frank letter.

How do you say "no" to a requested adjustment?

Saying *no* is more difficult. But if you are clever and tactful, you may be able to make your *no* sound almost like *yes.* If you must say *no,* try to surround it with *yesses.* Agree with the customer as much as you can:

I would feel the same way if . . .
You are quite right when you say . . .
I don't blame you for . . .
I agree that you should be able to expect . . .
You certainly should receive . . .

No doubt you have an excellent reason for saying *no.* Your customer is entitled to know what that reason is. Don't dodge behind "Our policy will not allow. . . ." Give the facts as briefly as you can. Assume that he or she is intelligent enough to understand and reasonable enough to see your side. Appeal to fairmindedness, but don't argue.

How do you say "no" to customer requests?

It is easy to answer an order letter or letter of request when your answer is *yes.* In fact, usually no letter is required. The customer wants a part for a tractor, twenty-five dozen Christmas tree balls in time for a pre-Halloween display, or a selection of office supplies, not correspondence from you. But if you have to say *no*—if the tractor part is out of stock, a transportation strike delays your shipment, or the customer didn't include enough information with the order—then your answer will require tactful handling. Try to find some good news to include with your bad news. Perhaps the bad news won't seem so bad if you can find a positive way to state it. If you have good news, *don't bury it* among your *regrets* and *sorrys.* Bury the bad news. Tell the reader what you can do and perhaps he or she will shed few tears over what you can't do.

Good News	Bad News
We are sending you our latest model of the part you requested. We are proud of the many improvements we have been able to make over the older model.	I am sorry that the part you ordered is out of stock. Instead we are sending . . .

In spite of the transportation strike, you will be glad to know that we will be able to ship your order by October 8.

Because of the transportation strike, we will not be able to ship your order before October 8.

You will be happy to know that your shipment went out this morning. We filled your order as soon as we received your second letter containing the necessary information.

We are sorry that we did not have enough information to fill your order as promptly as you wanted it. Now that we have all the information, we can . . .

End your letter on a constructive note. Try to do something else for the customer. Suggest an alternative:

The freshman text which you ordered is out of print, but we are sending you examination copies of two similar texts which might meet your needs.

The winter catalogue and price list that you requested are being replaced by the new spring catalogue and price list which are now at the printer's. We shall send you the new ones as soon as they are available, possibly by the end of next week. In the meantime, we are sending you our latest sale catalogue. You may be able to find what you need there at a reduced price.

Show your appreciation of your reader:

We appreciate the time and effort you and your associates spent in preparing your bid. We hope the fact that we cannot accept it will not keep you from bidding on our next job. We have enjoyed working with you in the past and hope that we can do so again.

Your past patronage of our shop indicates that you had confidence in us. We appreciate that confidence and hope that this episode will not dusturb that confidence in the future.

Offer future assistance:

The next time you need help with such a problem, we hope you will call on us.

We hope that we can look forward to working with you on a future project.

We certainly regret that this delay caused you inconvenience and hope that you will give us the opportunity to show you that we can do better.

Hold the door open for a *yes* in the future:

Perhaps when we are able to expand our budget we shall . . .

We are keeping your application on file . . .

Possibly after the first of the year . . .

Figure 4-1 illustrates the type of adjustment letter you might write when you are able to grant exactly what the claimant wants.

If Ms. Galoway had been unable to make a full adjustment on the merchandise, she might have offered Mr. Turner a compromise. Figure 4-2 illustrates how she might have written such a letter.

figure 4-1

Size-Rite Clothing

1777 Main St.
Kansas City, MO 64105

April 18, 1979

Mr. Fred Turner
P. O. Box 87
Kansas City, KS 66102

Dear Mr. Turner:

     We appreciate your frank letter stating that the suit which you purchased in our store during our March Clearance Sale was defective.

     Ordinarily we do not exchange merchandise bought during a sale, but we certainly do not want our customers to be unhappy with a product that is defective. Please return the suit at your earliest convenience, and it will be exchanged for any suit that is presently selling for the same price.

     You will realize, I hope, that we handle hundreds of suits a month and cannot always spot defective material until too late. We do want you to be happy with the service that you receive from us and to know that we will always do our best to serve you. As a token of appreciation to you and to repay you, at least in part, for your inconvenience, we want you to select a complimentary tie to go with your new suit.

     If you will contact Mr. Ralph Walker, Manager of Men's Wear, he will assist you in your selection of a suit and matching tie.

Sincerely yours,

Susan Galoway

Susan Galoway, Manager
Customer Relations

figure 4-2

SIZE-RITE CLOTHING

1777 MAIN ST.
KANSAS CITY, MO 64105

April 18, 1979

Mr. Fred Turner
P. O. Box 87
Kansas City, KS 66102

Dear Mr. Turner:

You are right when you state that no one likes to spend money
for inferior merchandise. No one would like to buy a suit and discover that it had a stain on one pants leg.

In part, though, the excitement of shopping at a sale lies in
the possibility of finding something for a price below what you would
normally pay. We could not have sold a first quality suit for such
a low price. If you recall, the sign advertising the suit you purchased stated that those suits were seconds.

Ordinarily we do not exchange items bought during a sale, but
we want you to be pleased with the merchandise that you get from our
store. We realize, too, that perhaps you did not see the "seconds"
sign when you bought your suit. Let me offer you a suggestion. You
bought your suit on sale for $79.35. A first-line suit by that same
manufacturer sells for $124.25. If you will return the defective suit,
I will arrange with Mr. Ralph Walker, Manager of Men's Wear, for you
to purchase the first-line suit for only $99.50. You can readily see
that this is still quite a bargain.

Please call Mr. Walker within the next two weeks and make an
appointment to be fitted for your new suit. We hope that you will be
happy with your new purchase.

Sincerely yours,

Susan Galoway

Susan Galoway, Manager
Customer Relations

58

If Ms. Galoway had been unable to make any kind of adjustment, she might have written a letter much like Figure 4-3.

figure 4-3

SIZE-RITE CLOTHING

1777 MAIN ST.
KANSAS CITY, MO 64105

April 18, 1979

Mr. Fred Turner
P. O. Box 87
Kansas City, KS 66102

Dear Mr. Turner:

You have always had confidence in our Men's Shop and have been one of our most consistent customers. We are, therefore, more than upset when you are upset.

The suit which you purchased during our March Clearance Sale was one of 500 which we received on a special factory order. Some were only slightly irregular; others were critically inferior. The prices were set according to the defects. Apparently you got one of the very bad ones, and we are sorry.

Unfortunately we cannot exchange items purchased during a sale. The suits were marked low because of the special purchase order. We cannot buy first-line suits for that price ourselves.

You have been a customer at our store for the last five years, and we hope that you will not permit this one experience to disturb your confidence in us. We are now receiving our Fall merchandise, including a new line of suits that is slightly less expensive than those we now stock. You will enjoy browsing among the new ones in the latest fall colors. These first-line suits sell for only $92.50.

Come to visit our Men's Shop again. We will do all that we can to make you happy.

Sincerely yours,

Susan Galoway

Susan Galoway, Manager
Customer Relations

What attitude will help you write effective collection letters?

Letters that say *no* aren't the only letters that require you to exert tact, imagination, and the ability to put yourself in the reader's place. The letter that says *please* can be even trickier to handle, but *please* you must say if you are to keep accounts receivable receiving and not liquidated. When somebody owes you or your company money and you have the unpleasant task of asking for payment, you may be tempted to take one of two approaches. You may, feeling embarrassed and apologetic, hold out a trembling hand like a beggar. You may, feeling angry and abused, bang your fist on the desk and rave at the thief. Neither action will get the results you want.

In the first place, you have nothing to apologize for. If someone owes you money, that person has an obligation to pay and you have a right to that payment. It is important that you not seem hesitant about it. Speak up. Point out firmly and clearly that the payment is past due and that you expect it immediately.

On the other hand, you will lose more than you gain if you write angry or offensive collection letters. The reader does not think that he or she is thoughtless, inconsiderate, or dishonest, and your bullish, insinuating letter will not convince that person otherwise. And as a matter of fact, you don't want to do that anyway. You want to convince that person that he or she is a careful customer who wants to keep records accurate, accounts straight, credit clear, and most important, that he or she is a person who intends to write you a check for the amount due immediately after reading your letter.

What approach should you take in your first collection letter?

When you write your letter to remind a delinquent customer that a bill has not been paid, take it for granted that you are writing to an honest person who has shown a normal amount of forgetfulness. Allow him or her to save face and you will save the customer. Imply that the matter has merely been overlooked:

> Probably everybody misfiles or overlooks a statement at one time or another, and I wonder if that is what you did to our statement for June 1.
>
> Maybe you misplaced our letter of April 27. Even the most careful business person can do that sometimes.

A person as busy as I know you are might overlook a letter, and maybe you missed our letter of November 25 that way.

Keep your reminder friendly:

Just a reminder that your account for $93.95 was due on the first of the month.

We have been watching the mails for your check, but we have been disappointed.

Your check for $123.46 is not here. Where is it? In the mail? On your desk waiting for your signature? On my agenda is a letter to you saying, "Thank you for your check." Please help me get it in the mail and on your desk at once.

I am sending this friendly reminder because we have not received your check for $81.90 that was due on May 15.

The response to your letter will be made more quickly and cheerfully if you can point out the advantages of prompt action:

Just staple your check for $15.68 to this letter and mail it in the enclosed envelope to bring your account up to date and keep your rating clear.

Your check will be appreciated because it will maintain your superior credit record at Bailey's.

As soon as I receive your check, I will mail you the new catalogue for the spring clearance sale which I am sure will enable you to make big savings on several of the items which you usually buy.

What kind of follow-up letters are used?

Customers who have merely neglected to pay the bill will probably pay when they have received your reminder. A few will need to be urged a bit more strongly. You should send a second follow-up letter within the next fifteen days. Make this letter firmer and more insistent than the first, but still keep it friendly and courteous:

You will note from the attached statement that our January bill has apparently been overlooked. We are sure that we can rely upon you to take care of this matter at once.

We sent you a statement for $112.35 on June 26. This letter is dated July 18. We hate to annoy you with such reminders, but we would appreciate your check at once.

We do not understand it. We still have not received the $59.70 that you owe us.

According to the terms upon which you received your credit card, you agreed to pay upon receipt of your statement. The net amount, $89.70, was due on August 10. We did not hear from you. A second statement was sent to you on September 12, asking if there was some error. We have received no answer. Please be fair to us and yourself and mail your check at once.

Even now, when you want to be firm, and later, when you want to be firmer, you don't want to insult or anger the customer. Put yourself in the customer's place as you word your letter, and avoid any expression that could arouse hostility.

Most people ordinarily pay promptly, and delay only when they are in some sort of financial difficulty. They would like to pay now, but they think that nothing can be done to help them. If you write offering some solution to their problem, they may be able to meet their obligation and they will be grateful and loyal customers in the future. After two follow-up letters have failed to bring a response from a customer who has usually paid promptly, you might write a firm letter which closes with a paragraph such as one of the following:

If you cannot handle this matter now, please write us a note telling us when we can expect payment.

We know a good customer like you must have some reason for letting an account go unpaid for four months. If you cannot pay all or even part of the amount, please use the enclosed envelope to send us a note of explanation.

If your circumstances are such that you cannot take care of the entire account at once, then please send us part of it and make some suggested schedule for payment of the balance.

We are sure that something must have happened to you or you would have handled this matter as promptly as you have always handled your obligations. Please come by to see me, and let's talk this thing over. I'm sure we can make some arrangement that will allow you to keep your credit record clean.

When three or four follow-up letters have been sent out and two or three months have elapsed since the account was due, you will need to apply more pressure. State firmly and definitely what you want done and what you are prepared to do if it is not. Create a sense of urgency. Set a date by which the person must act. You need not become insulting or angry, however. Your purpose is still to save the customer as well as to collect the money owed you. Note the firm but pleasant tone in the following:

We find it difficult to believe that you intend to evade completely your obligations in this matter. Yet the way you have continued to ignore this account forces us to ask you to mail us a check immediately. Although we dislike to resort to legal measures, we find a further extension of time impossible.

Unless we receive your check for $243.67 within ten days, we shall be forced to turn your account over to our attorney for collection. This action is one we would like to avoid. Naturally, we want our money, but we do not want to embarrass you. Nor do we want to add legal fees to what you now owe us. All we want is your check for $243.67. Please help us avoid this action and save yourself embarrassment and added expense.

figure 4-4

Easy Way Paper Manufacturing Company
9305 Sunset Avenue
Ostego, IN. 40411

July 6, 1979

Mr. Ralph Waldo, Manager
Harold's School Supply
842 Austex Street
Pharr, OH 40332

Dear Mr. Waldo:

We especially appreciated that fine order you placed with us April 8. We are glad, also, that you were feeling so prosperous and hopeful. When we did not receive your check after we sent your May statement for $186.90 and then when your June statement brought no return, we began to worry just a little. But we think we have the answer: with school starting and business booming after the vacation lag, you have been so busy selling that large order that you haven't had time to take care of our statement. We hope this is so and that after this little reminder you will send us a check today.

It isn't too early to be planning for the Christmas season. We have a specially designed assortment of Christmas wrapping paper with designs that are particularly appropriate for your customers. Under separate cover I am sending you our Christmas catalogue in which you will find a number of other attractive, new, fast-selling items.

May you continue to have a prosperous season.

Sincerely yours,

Willard Penn

Willard Penn
Collection Manager

As you can see, collection letters follow a pattern of increasing firmness and urgency. The number of reminders that are sent before a company threatens and executes legal actions varies from organization to organization; but regardless of the number, they are arranged in this order:

1. Routine monthly statement of amount owed.
2. Simple reminder that account is past due.
3. Firmer reminder.
4. Appeal for immediate action or explanation.
5. Threat of legal action.
6. Notification of legal action.

Figures 4-4 to 4-7 illustrate a series of collection letters sent by a credit department. Note how the letters progress from simple reminders to increasingly insistent requests for payment:

figure 4-5

Easy Way Paper Manufacturing Company
9305 Sunset Avenue
Ostego, IN 40411

August 1, 1979

Mr. Ralph Waldo, Manager
Harold's School Supply
842 Austex Street
Pharr, OH 40332

Dear Mr. Waldo:

I am enclosing this note in your monthly statement for $186.90 in order to point out that this bill is now nearly two months past due. This payment lag is not consistent with the prompt manner in which you have always handled your business with us in the past, and we do not believe that you really intend to be delinquent in your payments now. We hate to see you ruin your fine credit rating. So please, get your check in the mail at once.

Sincerely yours,

Willard Penn

Willard Penn
Collection Manager

figure 4-6

Easy Way Paper Manufacturing Company
9305 Sunset Avenue
Ostego, IN 40411

August 15, 1979

Mr. Ralph Waldo, Manager
Harold's School Supply
842 Austex Street
Pharr, OH 40332

Dear Mr. Waldo:

April 8 you placed a fine order for notebooks, paper, tablets, and other school supplies.

May 1 we sent you a statement for $186.90. No answer.

June 1 we sent you a second statement. No answer.

August 1 we sent you a third statement and a letter asking you please to care for this matter at once. Still no answer.

Don't you think we ought to hear from you? We are sure there must be a very good reason why you have not been able to pay, but we do not know what it is. Won't you please drop us a note and tell us what the problem is? Surely we can work something out. Perhaps you could pay fifty dollars now and the rest in three installments.

Please let us hear from you soon. We hate to have a good customer spoil his credit rating.

Sincerely yours,

Willard Penn

Willard Penn
Collection Manager

ASSIGNMENTS

I. On May 18 Howard Hardcastle, manager and owner of Hardcastle's Hardware Store, ordered eight dozen meat presses from Handy Kitchenware Company. The presses were listed in a sale catalogue as Number 84653. The sale was to close May 31. On May 25 Mr. Hardcastle received his order and was billed in invoice number 432-192 for the sale price. On June 3 he received an unordered duplicate order, invoice number 432-275, for

figure 4-7

Easy Way Paper Manufacturing Company
9305 Sunset Avenue
Ostego, IN 40411

September 1, 1979

Mr. Ralph Waldo, Manager
Harold's School Supply
842 Austex Street
Pharr, OH 40332

Dear Mr. Waldo:

It has been four months since you received the statement for $186.90 for your April 8 order. It has been fifteen days since I wrote and asked you to write us a letter of explanation or to offer us some plan for meeting your obligation. In all this time we have not heard from you.

We cannot let this matter run on any longer. On the other hand, we hate to subject you to the embarrassment and expense involved should we be forced to take legal action. However, if we have not heard from you by September 15, we shall place this matter in the hands of our attorney, Adam Huntley.

Sincerely yours,

Willard Penn

Willard Penn
Collection Manager

---

which he was billed the regular price of $9.25 per dozen instead of the sale price of $6.90 per dozen. The item was so popular that Mr. Hardcastle sold the second order also. Now he is writing the mail order manager of Handy Kitchenware Company, Mr. Arthur Allen, for an adjustment. Since the kitchenware company made the error, Mr. Hardcastle would like the second set of meat presses at the sale price of $6.90 per dozen. Write a letter from Mr. Hardcastle to Mr. Allen.

II. Write three answers to the above letter, one granting Mr. Hardcastle's request, one suggesting a compromise, and one refusing it. In the letter of refusal explain why you cannot grant the request and make some special effort to appease Mr. Hardcastle.

III. Mr. Hardcastle, following the adjustment letter which he receives from Mr. Allen, ignores his July statement and all following statements and communication. Prepare a series of five collection letters to be sent to Mr. Hardcastle.

The Job
Application Letter

Why is communication so important in the job application process?

The first direct step in your career is applying for the job you want. If you write a letter now applying for a job similar to the one you hope to hold when you finish your education, you can benefit from your instructor's objective criticism. If you are aware of the kind of experiences and aptitudes you will want to list in your letter of application in order to get the position you want, you can begin now to gain those experiences and abilities. Moreover, if you practice applying for jobs, even though the practice is in a classroom situation, you will gain confidence in the procedure. Many people are capable of holding much more important jobs than they are able to get. They lack both the knowledge of the techniques of getting a job and the confidence to use them. The object of this chapter is to help you acquire both.

What if there is a job application form?

Even though you write a letter of application, many companies may also require you to complete a job application form. Very often your application letter goes to one office and your application form, which contains more detailed information, to another. Do not approach the application form carelessly. It is an important record of many facts about you and your experiences, and it deserves close consideration.

Be certain you understand exactly what is being asked in each question of the form. Sometimes individuals fill in a certain bit of information and discover later that that information wasn't requested in the form or that they misread the question. A good policy is quickly to scan the form, determining what it asks throughout so you can better structure your answers. One problem with forms is that they seldom give enough room to answer adequately; thus you must plan your answers carefully.

If possible, type your responses onto the form that you are given. If this is impossible, write clearly or print. And use ink!

Figures 5-1 and 5-2 represent the front and back sides of an actual job application form. Study them. Be certain that you know the exact information that is being requested in each blank.

Why do you need a letter?

A letter is much more personal than the application form, and because you compose your thoughts in the letter it also reflects more of your personality. In most instances your first contact with a potential employer is via letter, even though he or she may subsequently send you a form for completion also.

Your letter, then, is your sales instrument. It should put your best foot forward, should reveal your most positive qualities. And since you are judged by your letter, it should be neat and orderly.

How should your application letter look?

You should exercise the greatest care in preparing your application. Type neatly on a good grade of white bond paper, $8^1/_2 \times 11$ inches. Never use company letterhead stationery, hotel stationery, lined paper of any kind, or colored, gilt-edged, or decorated personal stationery. Follow an accepted form for business letters. Before you mail your letter, double-check your spelling, grammar, and punctuation and be prepared to retype your letter or even to rewrite it if it is somewhat less than perfect.

Your application for a job will be in two parts: a letter of application, and a vita sheet[1] which gives an outline of your personal and professional background. The company may have a printed form on which they want you to describe your qualifications in a prescribed space, but you usually have no such form when you first write. If you

[1]A complete application folder is known as the *dossier* and includes the vita sheet, letters of recommendation, and any other important material.

figure 5-1

APPLICATION FOR EMPLOYMENT

with the
DALLAS COUNTY HOSPITAL DISTRICT

Social Security Number:

Answer every question completely. Be accurate. Any misstatement of a fact that would prevent original appointment will result in dismissal later.

Title of position you are applying for _____

Will you accept temporary work? ☐ _____

Part time work? ☐ _____

| Last Name | First Name | Middle Name | Address | | Phone Number |

Date of birth (Month) (Day) (Year)

Age _____ Mrs. Miss. Mr.

Color Hair / Color Eyes

Weight / Height

(Underscore) Married—Widowed—Single—Divorced—Separated

Number of Children: Ages:

How long have you lived in Dallas County _____ Are you a citizen of the U.S.A. _____

Have you any physical defect? _____ If so, what is it? _____

Have you had any serious illness, injury or operation in last 10 years? _____

Describe and give details _____

Were you hospitalized? _____ Dates _____ Hospital _____ Location _____

My health is: (Underscore) Good — Fair — Poor: If poor, why? _____

Give residential address for past 10 years; give length of time at each location (City and State):

Father's full name _____

Mother's full name _____

Full name of husband or wife _____

If husband or wife is employed, state where:

In case of emergency, notify _____

Have you ever been arrested for other than traffic violations? _____

If so, give records:

Date   Charge   Conviction or other disposition

Are you now, or have you ever been a member of any Communist organization? _____

Have you ever worked for the Dallas County Hospital District (Parkland or Woodlawn)? _____ If so, when? _____

What Position? _____ Reason for leaving _____

Do you have any relatives working for the Hospital District? _____ In what department? _____

Who are they and how are they related to you? _____

Have you ever filed suit against any of your former employers? _____ When _____

State details _____

70

figure 5-2

EDUCATION

High School Attended	CIRCLE LAST GRADE COMPLETED	DID YOU GRADUATE?	Give Date of Leaving or Graduation
	1 2 3 4 5 6 7 8 9 10 11 12	Yes _____ No _____	

	Years Attended	Major & Minor	Degrees Obtained	Give Date of Leaving or Graduation
College or University Attended				

	Years Attended	Course	Did you complete course? If so, when?
Business College, Trade School or Correspondence Course			

What professional or technical licenses, registrations, certificates, or memberships do you possess?

EXPERIENCE RECORD

Give complete information as to whom you worked for, the length of employment, and kind of work done. The time not employed must be shown. A complete record of your employment must be shown.

Date of Service			EMPLOYED BY			
From	To	Length of Employment	Name	Address	Salary or Wages	Nature of Your Work

May we communicate with your present Employer? _____
Use extra sheet when necessary to give complete employment record.

CHARACTER REFERENCES

Name	Mailing Address	Business or Occupation
1.		
2.		

MILITARY STATEMENT

Have you ever served in the Armed Forces of the United States? _____ Component or Branch of Service _____
Dates of Service _____ Service Number _____ Reason for Discharge _____
Type of Discharge _____ Highest Grade or Rank attained _____ Have you ever been court-martialed, fined, or disciplined under any Article of War or Uniform Code of Military Justice _____ If answer is yes, explain fully.

Are you receiving disability compensation, pension, or disability retirement from the Veteran's Administration? _____
If answer is yes, explain fully, the nature, type and severity of this disability. _____

TO BE COMPLETED BY RN'S, TECH. NURSES & LVN'S ONLY

School of nursing from which you graduated _____ Location _____ Year of Graduation _____
Current Texas License No. _____ Other states currently registered in & Number _____
For Registered Nurses Only: Are you a member of the American Nurses' Association through membership in District or State Association: _____ Are you a member of the National League of Nursing? _____

NOTE:

I REPRESENT AND WARRANT THE ANSWERS I HAVE MADE TO EACH AND ALL OF THE FOREGOING QUESTIONS ARE FULL AND TRUE TO THE BEST OF MY KNOWLEDGE AND BELIEF.

AND FURTHER in order that the officials of the Dallas County Hospital District may be fully informed as to my personal character and qualifications for employment. I refer to each of my former employers and to any other person who may have information concerning me, agreeing, as this information is furnished at my express request and for my benefit, to hold such persons harmless and I do hereby release them from any and all liability for damage of whatsoever nature on account of furnishing such information.

Signature of Applicant _____

Date _____

are asked to fill one out later, you can do so. Some duplication of information will emphasize your apparent worth rather than detract from it. Moreover, by arranging the facts of your background to point up your specific qualifications for the job in question, you can make your vita sheet do a better job of selling your skills than a standard printed form will do.

How do you make a vita sheet?

The vita sheet is usually divided into four sections with headings for each: (1) personal information, (2) education, (3) work experience, and (4) references. As you arrange and word your information, keep in mind the job for which you are applying. You should be concise and exact so that the reader can see at a glance what your experience has been. Naturally, your arrangement of data will be neat, uncrowded, and balanced on the page. The four sections of your sheet should be separated slightly, and the headings which introduce them should stand out. Under each heading arrange the data in order from the most important information to the least important, chronologically from the most recent to the least recent. In describing your experience, be brief, using phrases rather than whole sentences, but give complete and exact information. Do not flatter yourself or try to represent your ability as greater than it is. By the time your future employer is ready to make a decision concerning you, he or she will have investigated your references and background enough to discover any discrepancies between your statements and reality. Nothing will insure your failure to get the job so definitely as the implication that you are not completely truthful.

Personal information should include date of birth, height, weight, health, and marital status. If you have children, you may include the number if you wish. Including your place of birth, nationality, or race is a matter of personal preference; usually this information is not required. You can arrange the personal information as in Figure 5-3.

Your educational preparation is more important in securing the first job than it will be after you have had several years of job experience. Therefore, you should not be satisfied just to name the school from which you were graduated. List any colleges or technical schools which you have attended, the dates of attendance, and the degrees or diplomas which you obtained. Then give your major field of study and list the major courses which you have completed. If you had other courses which will make you a more valuable employee, name them even though they may not be directly related to the job for which you

figure 5-3

```
                        Charles E. Bates

PERSONAL

Address:  915 Hall Street                    Height:  5'11"
          Wilcox, Missouri 65502
                                             Weight:  160
Telephone:  816/522-9409
                                             Health:  Good
Date of Birth:  March 14, 1957
Marital Status:  Married, one child
```

are applying. Give the specific course title. "Income Tax Accounting" will give your employer a more definite idea of the content of the course than "Business II." Give the name of your high school and the dates of attendance. Name any of your courses which particularly increased your qualifications. List also any honors or awards you received in school.

Your employer will want to know if you have demonstrated any leadership potential, if you have had opportunities to develop social poise, and if you have broad enough interests to make you an interesting person. Therefore, you should list any offices that you held and name extracurricular activities, hobbies, and special interests. If an employer has to choose between a young person with a 2.85 grade point average and the experience of having managed a Little League baseball team, and one with a 3.00 average and no leadership experience at all, he or she may be inclined toward the Little Leaguer. The summary of your educational background might look like Figure 5-4.

figure 5-4

```
EDUCATIONAL BACKGROUND

Associate in Applied Science Degree, 1978.  East Valley Community
College, Wilcox, Missouri.  Major:  Business Administration
          Special Courses:  Managerial Accounting
                            Income Tax Accounting
                            Seminar in Auditing
                            Controllership

High School Diploma, 1975.  Walt Whitman High School, Wilcox, Missouri.
          Honors:  National Honor Society, 1975
                   Class Honors 1974, 1975.
                   Letter in Basketball, 1975
          Extracurricular activities:  Eagle Scout, 1973
                                       Business Club, 1973-1975
                                       Junior Community League, 1975
```

Even though you may not have had any work experience in the area in which you are applying for a job, the section which lists your job experience is still very important. The fact that you have held a job, any job, indicates to your employer that you have initiative and are industrious. If you held a job for some reasonable period of time and left for some good reason, your employer will know that you are willing to work, that you are dependable and conscientious, and that you have been able to make the necessary adjustment to a job. List every job you have ever held, beginning with the most recent and continuing in reverse chronological order. If you worked to help pay for your education, mention that. Show the dates for each job and briefly tell why you left. If you have had little experience working, do not omit this section or call attention to your lack of expereince. Almost everyone has done some work some time which could be summarized by writing, "While I was in high school, I did baby sitting," "mowed lawns," or "worked for my father in his grocery store." The summary of your vocational experience can be arranged as in Figure 5-5.

Applicants for a job are usually asked to give the names of three to five persons who can be asked for references. Three kinds of references are usually given: personal or character references, credit references, and vocational or professional references.

The person whose name you give for a personal or character reference should be a member of the clergy, or your family doctor, your family lawyer, or a teacher, someone who knows you well enough and who has enough experience in working with people to be able to make a reliable evaluation of your character.

For a credit reference you can name the bank where you have a savings or checking account or the name of some company where you have a charge account or a credit card. Your credit reference is important; your prospective employer wants to know that you know

figure 5-5

```
VOCATIONAL EXPERIENCE

1978–present:   Accountant.  Missouri Valley Grocers Association, South
                Plains, Missouri.  Duties:  Supervisor of accounts
                payable. Supervisor of three other accountants.  Salary:
                $9,000 per year.

1976–1978:      Accountant.  Gristede Bros. Grocery Store, Wilcox,
                Missouri.  Duties:  Supervisor of all accounts payable
                and receivable. Salary:  $575 per month.

1973–1976:      Accountant Trainee.  Gristede Bros. Grocery Store,
                Wilcox, Missouri.  Duties:  Routine account billing.
```

how to manage your financial affairs and that you aren't going to have to take time away from your work to entertain your creditors.

If you have had job experience, list one or two employers as references. If you have only recently finished your vocational education, you should also list one of your instructors, preferably one in your major field who knows your scholastic ability and preparation. Include the complete name, job title, and address of each reference. Your list of references may be arranged as in Figure 5-6.

Should you send a picture?

Many companies ask that the applicant include a photograph. Doing so may help you to secure an interview. Application pictures should be small, should have been recently taken, and should show you dressed appropriately. If you enclose a photograph, fasten it with a paper clip or staple to the upper right-hand corner of your vita sheet.

How do you write the application letter?

Now that you have organized your thinking enough to make a vita sheet, you are ready to write your letter of application. In making your vita sheet you have been concentrating upon yourself and your abilities, and you should have been doing so with an eye toward the job which you want. Your letter should be prepared with even closer

figure 5-6

```
REFERENCES

Personal:     The Reverend David R. Bishop, Rector, St. Justin Episcopal
              Church, 255 August Street, Wilcox, Missouri 65502

Credit:       Ms. Janice Irvine, Vice-president, South Plains State
              Bank, P.O. Box 800, South Plains, Missouri 65510

Vocational:   Mr. Robert K. Jacobs, General Manager, Missouri Valley
              Grocers Association, 2001 Greenville Highway, South
              Plains, Missouri 65510

              Mr. Alfonso Gristede, Owner, Gristede Bros. Grocery Store,
              7 City Hall Square, Wilcox, Missouri 65502.

              Professor Elisabeth Morgan, Chairperson, Department of
              Business, East Valley Community College, Wilcox, Missouri
              65502
```

attention to the desired job and the needs and attitudes of your prospective employer.

First keep in mind that this person is busy. Do not waste his or her time. Get to the point of your letter immediately. The first paragraph should state that you are applying for a position, what position you desire, and where you heard about the job. A direct statement such as one of the following will serve the purpose of saying what the prospective employer needs to know and of getting you started in your letter:

> I am applying for the job of machine tester advertised in the *Times* yesterday.
>
> I am interested in the position of staff artist advertised in the *Daily Observer.*
>
> Ms. Hilda Freed, placement director of Hilltop Business College, has recommended your company as one with excellent opportunities to rise in the field of transportation management. I would like to apply for a position as manager trainee.
>
> Please consider me an applicant for the position of receptionist advertised in today's *Journal.*
>
> I believe my qualifications for a position as a medical secretary will interest you, and I would like to come in for an interview.
>
> I understand from my friend Mr. Ronald Cummings that you have a position open for a salesman in your furniture store. I would like to tell you why I think I have the qualifications which you need.

The second paragraph of your letter should tell the employer why you are a desirable candidate for the position. You should attempt to show that you have an understanding of the requirements for success in the job and that you, by training or experience, are prepared to meet those requirements. These examples should give you an idea of how you might write your second paragraph:

> A summary of my qualifications is enclosed. My training at the Mercy Hospital School of Medical Technology was comprehensive and thorough. Because I was particularly interested in radiographic procedures, I not only took the regular course but also helped my instructor after classes on a special research problem in which he was engaged. Since your X-ray department is particularly well equipped for radiographic procedures, I am especially interested in working at your laboratory.
>
> At Bosworth Business College, where I took the medical secretary course, I consistently placed in the upper third of my class. Besides the classes in the usual courses, I also took classes in advanced accounting and business psychology. Because I took advanced courses in English and journalism in high school, I am proficient in composition and can compose letters as they are needed for collection and referral purposes. I can type 75 words per minute and take dictation in shorthand at 115 words per minute.

Although I have had no direct experience in furniture saleswork, I am especially interested in working in that area. Saleswork, however, is not new to me. Last winter I worked at the Free Stride Shoe Emporium and this spring I was hostess at the display houses for the Safe Way Construction Company. I majored in home economics, and last summer I took some courses in interior decorating at the L. E. Grant School of Design. My discussions with Mr. Booker Shelby from your Main Street store about the many interesting areas of the furniture business have convinced me that it is a business that I would enjoy.

The employer is not interested in your need for a job, so don't take time to discuss your financial problems or other difficulties. You will be hired not because you need the job but because the employer needs a worker and you seem to be the best-qualified applicant. Starting a new employee in a job costs the employer money. Someone must take time away from other work to teach the new worker, and the beginner will work more slowly at first and make more mistakes than one who has been on the job awhile. Therefore, the employer will feel that there is a smaller risk in hiring you if you can sincerely assure him or her that you are willing to learn and that you are genuinely interested in the job. Although you should not claim to have had more experience than you have had, you should not call unnecessary attention to your lack of experience. You might say something like the following:

Although many of the procedures and routines will be new to me, I shall work hard to learn my job as quickly and as well as I can.

I realize the importance of accuracy and attention to detail required in such a job, and I assure you that I shall do my best to do careful work at all times.

In spite of my inexperience I believe I can perform acceptably in this position. I learn quickly, remember what I learn, and enjoy the challenge of a difficult task.

The employer will not, of course, make a final decision on the basis of your letter alone. He or she will want to form a final estimation of your ability only after a personal interview. The last paragraph of your letter should ask that you be allowed such an interview. You should state when you can come in and how you can be reached or you can state that you will call the secretary for an appointment.

I shall be glad to come in for an interview at your convenience. I am available after 3:30 Monday through Friday and any time on Saturday. You can reach me to arrange an appointment by calling me at my home, 281-6633, or by writing me at the above address.

If you are interested in my qualifications, I should like to come in for an interview. I shall call your secretary next Tuesday morning to arrange a time convenient to you.

Place your letter and vita sheet in a plain, unprinted, matching envelope of good quality paper. Include your return address in the upper left-hand corner of the envelope. Follow the same neat and conventional style that you used in your letter and vita sheet.

Charles Bates's application letter will look like Figure 5-7 when he is through. Figure 5-8 is his completed vita sheet.

figure 5-7

---

                                                915 Hall Street
                                                Wilcox, MO 65502
                                                April 15, 1979
Mr. A. G. Schmitz, Manager
Royal Industries, Inc.
5421 Terner Road
Providence, MO 65521

Dear Mr. Schmitz:

        I am applying for the position of chief accountant advertised in the April 13, 1979 Kansas City <u>Star.</u> I believe that my qualifications and experience will interest you.

        You will notice from my enclosed vita that I am employed as an accountant at Missouri Valley Grocers Association in South Plains, Missouri. I am quite happy with my present job, and I wish to move only because I am attracted to the Providence area, which was for several years my home. My three years of work as an accountant for two grocery supply houses have made me aware of many of the merchandising and accounting problems that I am certain are shared by a specialty supply house. Supervision of other accountants for the last three years should also qualify me for the position of chief accountant, in which, I understand, I would be in charge of about ten accountants and the entire accounting department of your company.

        If you contact the references listed on the vita sheet, I believe that you will find that I have the ability to work well with others and the capacity to adjust easily to new procedures—both personal qualities which I assume are demanded of a chief accountant. I am particularly challenged by the idea of helping your firm make the transition to a data processing system of accounting.

        If you wish to contact me, please call me at my home: (816) 522-9409. I am willing to come to Providence for a personal interview at a time most convenient to you. Thank you for your time and consideration.

                                        Sincerely yours,

                                        Charles E. Bates

                                        Charles E. Bates.

---

figure 5-8

Charles E. Bates

PERSONAL

Address: 915 Hall Street   Height: 5'11"
          Wilcox, Missouri 65502   Weight: 160
Telephone: 816/522-9409   Health: Good
Date of Birth: March 14, 1957
Marital Status: Married, one child

EDUCATIONAL BACKGROUND

Associate in Applied Science Degree, 1978. East Valley Community
College, Wilcox, Missouri. Major: Business Administration
                          Special Courses: Managerial Accounting
                                            Income Tax Accounting
                                            Seminar in Auditing
                                            Controllership

High School Diploma, 1975. Walt Whitman High School, Wilcox, Missouri.
Honors: National Honor Society, 1975
         Class Honors, 1974, 1975.
         Letter in Basketball, 1975
Extracurricular activities: Eagle Scout, 1973
                             Business Club, 1973-1975
                             Junior Community League, 1975

VOCATIONAL EXPERIENCE

1978-present: Accountant. Missouri Valley Grocers Association, South
                Plains, Missouri. Duties: Supervisor of accounts
                payable. Supervisor of three other accountants. Salary:
                $9,000 per year.

1976-1978:   Accountant. Gristede Bros. Grocery Store, Wilcox,
                Missouri. Duties: Supervisor of all accounts payable
                and receivable. Salary: $575 per month.

1973-1976:   Account Trainee. Gristede Bros. Grocery Store, Wilcox,
                Missouri. Duties: Routine account billing.

REFERENCES

Personal: The Reverend David R. Bishop, Rector, St. Justin Episcopal
             Church, 255 August Street, Wilcox, Missouri 65502

Credit: Ms. Janice Irvine, Vice-president, South Plains State
             Bank, P.O. Box 800, South Plains, Missouri 65510

Vocational: Mr. Robert K. Jacobs, General Manager, Missouri Valley
             Grocers Association, 2001 Greenville Highway, South
             Plains, Missouri 65510

             Mr. Alfonso Gristede, Owner, Gristede Bros. Grocery Store,
             7 City Hall Square, Wilcox, Missouri 65502.

             Professor Elisabeth Morgan, Chairperson, Department of
             Business, East Valley Community College, Wilcox, Missouri
             65502

Perhaps your vita sheet will not be so long as that of Charles Bates. If you are making application for your first important job, your letter and vita sheet might look more like Figures 5-9 and 5-10.

What other letters might you need to write to your prospective employer?

Other letters may be required in connection with your application. If a decision is not to be made soon by the employer, you may want to write a letter in order to keep him or her aware that you are still interested in the position. A letter of thanks for the interview and a reminder of

figure 5-9

```
                                        1720 Dexter Drive
                                        Bristol Hill, NJ 07788
                                        May 3, 1979


        Mrs. Alice Ward, Manager
        Jean's Fashion Shop
        2808 Butler Parkway
        Jersey City, NJ 07311

        Dear Mrs. Ward:

                Please consider my application for the position of sales clerk
        that you have advertised on the college bulletin board.

                I am now finishing my freshman year at Towanda Community
        College, where I am enrolled in the mid-management curriculum.  In high
        school I had two years of home economics, and in my second year one of
        my dress designs won first-place awards at our annual style show. During
        this year I have learned much about meeting the public and running a
        small business.

                The people listed for reference on the enclosed data sheet will
        tell you that I am dependable and honest.  You will find also that I am
        always well-dressed and personable.

                If you are interested in talking with me, I would be happy to
        visit with you any afternoon.  Please call me at my home, 798-6549.


                                        Sincerely yours,

                                        Sarah E. Moore

                                        Sarah E. Moore
```

figure 5-10

Sarah E. Moore

PERSONAL

Address: 1720 Dexter Drive
Bristol Hill, NJ 07788

Telephone: 201/798-6549

Date of Birth: October 18, 1960

Marital Status: Single

Height: 5'5"

Weight: 124

Health: Good

EDUCATIONAL BACKGROUND

Freshman at Towanda Community College, Towanda Falls, New Jersey,
1978-1979.
        Major: Mid-Management
        Special Courses: Introduction of Accounting
                          Applied Communications
                          Business Procedures I

High School Diploma, 1978. Daniel C. Rogers High School, Bristol Hill,
New Jersey
        Honors: National Honor Society, 1978
                Scrivener's Award (for writing), 1977, 1978.
                Class Honors, 1975-1978
        Extracurricular activities: President of Senior class, 1978
                                  Secretary, National Honor
                                  Society, 1978
                                Co-captain, Women's Soccer Team,
                                  1977-1978.

VOCATIONAL EXPERIENCE

1978-present: Part-time assistant in Registrar's Office. Towanda
                Community College, Towanda Falls, New Jersey.

REFERENCES

Personal: Carolyn Raines, M.D., Medical Arts Building, Jersey City,
           New Jersey 07303

Vocational: Mr. Roger Peet, Registrar, Towanda Community College,
           Towanda Falls, New Jersey 07740

           Professor Anthony Ray, Instructor in Mid-Management,
           Towanda Community College, Towanda Falls, New Jersey 07740

           Ms. Mary Kay Schmitz, Instructor in English, Daniel C.
           Rogers High School, Bristol Hill, New Jersey 07788

some of the things you talked about is good strategy. If you are offered a position by mail, if the firm is out of town, or if you will not be reporting for work immediately, you should make your acceptance in writing. Remember that in some cases this letter might serve as a legal contract of employment. You should state briefly such terms of employment as salary and beginning date of work. If you decide not to accept such a job, write a courteous letter, giving solid, justifiable reasons for declining.

Figure 5-11 is an example of the letter you might write after you have been interviewed for a job.

To accept a position, you might write a letter somewhat like that in Figure 5-12.

If you cannot accept a position, a letter such as the one in Figure 5-13 is appropriate.

figure 5-11

```
                                    915 Hall Street
                                    Wilcox, MO 65502
                                    April 25, 1979


Mr. A. G. Schmitz, Manager
Royal Industries, Inc.
5421 Terner Road
Providence, MO 65521

Dear Mr. Schmitz:

        I wish to thank you for the opportunity of seeing you last
Monday. Everyone in your firm seemed so pleased and kind that I look
forward with greater anticipation to the possibility of working there.

        At your request, I have talked with Mr. Frank Bobsey, my present
supervisor. He said that I could leave my position here within a week
after I have given him notice rather than after the normally required
two weeks. Therefore I could come to work for you more quickly than we
originally thought possible.

        I hope that by this time you have had some response from my
other references, and I look forward to some early word from you.

                                    Sincerely yours,

                                    Charles E. Bates

                                    Charles E. Bates
```

figure 5-12

---

915 Hall Street
Wilcox, MO 65502
April 28, 1979

Mr. A. G. Schmitz, Manager
Royal Industries, Inc.
5421 Terner Road
Providence, MO 65521

Dear Mr. Schmitz:

    I am pleased to accept the position that you offer me of chief accountant. According to the terms set forth in your letter, I will report to work May 14, 1979, and my monthly salary will be set at $875 per month.

    This new position offers me a definite challenge and an excellent opportunity. I hope that I shall be able to perform according to your expectations.

    My wife and I shall move to Providence the week of May 6–12. I will call the office sometime during that week to see if there are any other instructions which I might need before reporting to work.

                  Sincerely yours,

                  Charles E. Bates

                  Charles E. Bates

Should you ask permission to name a person as a reference?

Answering inquiries about you from a prospective employer takes time. Consequently, you should ask the individuals whom you would like to name as references if they would mind your doing so. Not only is it courteous to give them the opportunity to refuse if they do not have time, but also you may save yourself the disadvantage of receiving a poor recommendation. If possible, telephone for such permission or ask the individual in person.

    Sometimes a former employer or teacher who should logically be consulted for information concerning your ability lives at some distance. To get permission to use that individual as a reference, you will

figure 5-13

915 Hall Street
Wilcox, MO 65502
April 28, 1979

Mr. A. G. Schmitz, Manager
Royal Industries, Inc.
5421 Terner Road
Providence, MO 65521

Dear Mr. Schmitz:

    I am sorry that I cannot accept the position of chief accountant with your company which you have offered me. The terms which you specified in your contract letter were especially attractive, and the challenges of the job were certainly inviting.

    My present employer, Missouri Valley Grocers Association, has made me an offer that permits me to finish my education, and I feel that I must not pass up such an opportunity. I will be given a two-year leave of absence, and the company will help me with some of my educational expenses.

    I do want to thank you for the time which you have personally given to my application. You were extremely helpful to me, and I looked forward to working with you.

Sincerely yours,

Charles E. Bates

Charles E. Bates

---

want to write a letter. Sometimes, however, you may not have time to write for permission and then to wait for an answer. Moreover, if this person has to write you a letter giving you permission, and then has to write another letter to answer the inquiry, he or she will have to spend twice as much time for you. Under these circumstances, be guided by your knowledge of the individual, the situation, and the urgency of your need. If you can, telephone to ask permission to use the individual's name as a reference.

Whether you telephone or write for such permission, the person can give a more helpful and favorable recommendation if you provide certain specific information. Discuss briefly the job you are trying to get, why you want that job in particular, and why you think you will do well in it. This information will allow the person who is writing the recommendation to focus on those qualities of yours which he or she has observed that will be especially important in this exact job. If you have not seen the person who is writing the recommendation for some time, you may make it easier for him or her to write the recommendation if you offer some current information on your vocational or educational activities. After you have been hired, you should write a letter of appreciation to anyone who helped you get the job.

A letter similar to that in Figure 5-14 is appropriate if you need to write to ask someone's permission to use his or her name as a reference.

Figure 5-15 is an example of the letter you might write to thank someone for recommending you for a job.

figure 5-14

```
                                      915 Hall Street
                                      Wilcox, MO 65502
                                      April 10, 1979


Mr. Alfonso Gristede, Owner
Gristede Bros. Grocery Store
7 City Hall Square
Wilcox, MO 65502

Dear Mr. Gristede:

        I am currently making application for a position as chief
accountant of Royal Industries, Inc. in Providence, Missouri.  Would
you please permit me to name you as a reference?

        The position which I seek will involve direct supervision of
several accountants, but the major task will be to update and program
the entire accounting system for the company.  You recall that when I
worked for you I had direct responsibility for all accounts payable and
receivable and that I helped initiate the computer programming of your
accounting office.  I feel that the experience I gained from that job
will be a definite asset to me should I obtain this new position.

        I hope that you will not mind my naming you as a professional
reference.  If I do not hear from you to the contrary, I shall submit
your name and address to Mr. A.G. Schmitz, Manager, Royal Industries,
Inc.  If you prefer that I do not use your name, please call me at
522-9409.

                                Sincerely yours,

                                Charles E. Bates

                                Charles E. Bates
```

figure 5-15

```
                                        915 Hall Street
                                        Wilcox, MO 65502
                                        April 28, 1979


Mr. Alfonso Gristede, Owner
Gristede Bros. Grocery Store
7 City Hall Square
Wilcox, MO 65502

Dear Mr. Gristede:

        I wish to thank you for recommending me to Mr. A. G. Schmitz of
Royal Industries, Inc.  I have just received word that I am to begin
work May 14 in the position for which I applied.

        Mr. Schmitz mentioned that you had given me an exceptionally
good recommendation and that I was given the position largely upon that
recommendation.  You were generous to take the time from your busy
schedule to write the letter for me.  I hope that I am able to live up to
the recommendation that you submitted.  Thank you again for your time
and personal attention.

                                Sincerely yours,

                                Charles E. Bates
                                Charles E. Bates
```

ASSIGNMENTS

    I.   You should begin now to learn as much as possible about your chosen occupational area by talking to persons working in such jobs and by reading books, periodical articles, and pamphlets. However, you must be careful. Remember that the people you talk to may be seriously biased either for or against a job or an employer, and that promotional literature always presents an overly optimistic picture. Assume that you have narrowed your job possibility to one specific kind of work and even perhaps to one specific company. Answer the following questions:

        1.   What is the demand for employees in this area? How many were hired in your city last year?

        2.   What are the minimum and maximum age limits?

        3.   Will you be asked to join a union?

        4.   What are the opportunities for promotion? How long will you work before you will be considered for promotion?

    5.   What is the average age of the persons now employed?

    6.   What is the average salary of the persons now employed?

    7.   What is the top salary paid at the level that most appeals to you?

    8.   What kind of insurance program is available? How much would it cost for you and your dependents?

    9.   What kind of retirement program is available? How much will it cost per month? When will it begin payment?

  10.   Are there any physical hazards closely connected with the work?

  11.   What is the policy for sick leave? How many sick days are you granted per year?

  12.   Do you get an annual paid vacation? How long?

  13.   Will you be expected to furnish any of your own supplies or tools? How much will this cost?

  14.   Will you be expected to wear a specified uniform or to dress according to a certain standard? How much will you have to spend to buy these clothes?

  II. Following these assignments is a set of four letters written in application for the same position. Each letter has errors both in mechanics and content. Read each letter carefully and then use a chart somewhat similar to that on page 92 to indicate errors.

III. The following assignments are to be done under the assumption that you are applying for a real job in your professional area. You will increase your interest in the project by finding a suitable job opening and directing your letters toward that specific project.

    1.   Find three advertised job openings in your area of interest. If possible clip the advertisements from the paper and staple them to a fact sheet to bring to class. Which job offers the best pay? Which has a comment about fringe benefits? Which one is in the best geographic location for your immediate needs? Arrange the three available positions in first, second, and third choice positions and be able to justify your preference.

    2.   Prepare a formal vita sheet, including listings for personal information, education, work experience, and references. Type the material neatly. Be certain to include all information that might help you secure the job.

    3.   Write a letter of application for the job that most interests you. Be specific and direct in your comments.

    4.   Write a brief note to one person whom you would like to name as a reference in your vita sheet. Advise the person of your wish and ask for permission to use his or her name.

    5.   Assume that you have been hired by your desired employer.

Write a brief letter of acceptance. Remember that in some cases this letter might serve as a legal contract of employment. You should briefly state such terms of employment as salary and beginning date of contract.

letter a

	915 Hall Street	1
	Wilcox, MO 65502	2
	April 15, 1979	3

915 Hall Street — 1
Wilcox, MO 65502 — 2
April 15, 1979 — 3

Mr. A. G. Schmitz, Manager — 4
Royal Industries, Inc. — 5
5421 Terner Road — 6
Providence, MO 65521 — 7

Dear Mr. Schmitz: — 8

    I hear that you are looking for a new chief-accountant and — 9
I would like to apply for that job. — 10

    I am working now at the Missouri Valley Grocers — 11
Association in South Plains, Missouri, but would like to move — 12
because I like Providence better. — 13

    I have had five years of experience as an accountant and — 14
if you think you might be interested in me I can give you some — 15
references. —

Sincerely yours, — 16

Charles E. Bates

Charles E. Bates — 17

letter b

```
                          915 Hall Street                    1
                          Wilcox, MO 65502                   2
                          April 15, 1979                     3


Mr. A. G. Schmitz, Manager                                   4
Royal Industries, Inc.                                       5
5421 Terner Road                                             6
Providence, MO 65521                                         7

Dear Sir:                                                    8

        I understand that you have a position open for a new 9
chief-accountant.  Let me apply for that job.                10

        For five years I have worked with grocery supply houses, 11
and I doubt that you could find anyone who is better qualified   12
than me to do your work.  I would be an honest, faithful worker. I  13
have not been sick but three days in the last five years; so I      14
would not lose time because of illness.                             15

        My salary at the present time is $9,000 per year.  Please   16
send me your salary list so I can see what you would pay.           17

        Also, what insurance company do you use for your            18
employees?                                                          19

        If you want me to, I will come to Providence next Friday    20
to meet you and talk about the job.                                 21

                          Sincerely yours,                          22


                          Charles E. Bates

                          Charles E. Bates                          23
```

```
                              915 Hall Street                    1
                              Wilcox, MO 65502                    2
                              April 15, 1979                      3


A. G. Schmitz, Manager                                           4
Royal Industries, Inc.                                           5
5421 Terner Road                                                 6
Providence, MO 65521                                             7

Dear Mr. A. G. Schmitz:                                          8

        You need a new chief—accountant, and I am the man whom you    9
are looking for.  I have been working in this kind of job for five   10
years and know all about it.  My boss here thinks I am the best      11
accountant that he has ever had——he told me so last week.            12

        The only reason I want to move is that Providence is my      13
home.  I went to school there before my family moved to Wilcox,      14
but I have always liked Providence the best.  I would like to buy    15
a home on the east side of town and settle down.  My wife and I      16
have saved a little money to use for a downpayment on the home,      17
and we think that we could move to Providence and live if I could    18
make a little more than I'm making now.  I'm making 9,000 a year.    19

        I went to high school in Wilcox and then took a business     20
administration training program at East Valley Community             21
College. I made good grades in my subjects.  You can see that I am   22
qualified.                                                           23

        If you are interested, call me and I will give you a list    24
of people who will tell you about me.                                25

                              Sincerely yours                        26
```

Charles E. Bates

```
                              Charles E. Bates                       27
```

```
                              915 Hall Street                    1
                              Wilcox, MO 65502                    2
                              April 15, 1979                      3


Mr. A. G. Schmitz, Manager                                       4
Royal Industries, Inc.                                           5
5421 Terner Road                                                 6
Providence, MO 65521                                             7

Dear Mr. Schmitz,                                                8

        I would like to apply for the position of Chief-Accountant  9
which you have advertised.  You will find that I am a dependable,   10
reliable worker.                                                 11

        I have had five years of experience in grocery supply   12
houses and feel that I have become familiar with almost every type  13
of accounting problem possible.  I now boss other accountants and   14
get along okay with them.                                        15

        The reason I want to move is that I like Providence so   16
much and would like to live there.                               17

        To learn more about me, you can write to Mr. Robert K.   18
Jacobs, General Manager, Missouri Valley Grocers Association,    19
2001 Greenville Highway, South Plains, Missouri; Mr. Alfonso     20
Gristede, Owner, Gristede Bros. Grocery Store, 7 City Hall Square,  21
Wilcox, Missouri 65502; or Professor Elisabeth Morgan,           22
Chairperson, Department of Business, East Valley Community       23
College, Wilcox, Missouri, 65502.                                24

        I would like to come to Providence to visit with you if  25
you are interested.  My telephone number is 522-9409.  I hope to    26
hear from you before very long.                                  27

                         Sincerely yours                         28

                         Charles E. Bates

                         Charles E. Bates.                       29
```

letter errors chart

Letter —————— (indicate by alphabetical reference)

Errors in Mechanics
(For each error, list the line number and identify the specific mechanical error; then show how the error should be corrected.)

Errors in Content
(Indicate material that should be included but is not present. Indicate also any unnecessary material present in the letter.)

Errors in Organization
(Indicate any errors in organization within the letter. Do all of the paragraphs perform their intended function?)

6

The Employment
Interview

Why is the employment interview important?

You have applied for a job with a particular company by writing a letter of application and completing the application form that was sent to you. What next? Chances are that the next step will be the job interview. If you appear to be a reasonably good candidate for the job (an employer would probably say that you "look good on paper"), then you will be invited to come for an interview.

You should not assume that you will get the job and that you can therefore relax. The interview is another very important step in the job-seeking process. An employer may receive dozens or even hundreds of applications to fill a particular job. The applications are evaluated, and a small group of qualified job candidates are invited to appear in person so the employer can determine in more detail how qualified they really are. Some of your first work experience—sacker at the corner grocery store or clerk at the neighborhood ice cream parlor—may have required very little in the way of a job interview. But as you move toward more demanding work assignments, the interview becomes a more important and demanding step.

The person who conducts the interview may be the company owner, a personnel director, or a member of management. Whatever his or her position, the interviewer is trained to find out much about you in a relatively short time. Chances are that you do have the essential skills that are wanted in the job; now the interviewer is examining to see if you have the sense of responsibility, degree of maturity, or whatever other personal traits may be considered necessary.

How do you prepare for an employment interview?

You are at the interview to sell yourself, at least an image of yourself, to the potential employer. You should decide ahead of time just what your good points are and then be certain to talk about them during the interview. Do not just sit there and answer questions. Ask questions too. Appear interested in the job and the company. Obviously you can do much before the interview to prepare yourself to answer anticipated questions and to phrase intelligent questions of your own.

Your task at the job interview is to sell yourself as the ideal candidate for the job. You cannot sell yourself unless you know your strengths and talk positively about them. Although selling yourself at the interview is not like selling your car, you can learn some important points from the following illustration.

Suppose you have decided to sell your ten-year-old Chevy so you can use the money for a down payment on a new car. You run an advertisement in the Sunday paper which one man answers. He talks as though he might be interested in buying your car, so you promise to drive it to his house so he can see it. At the appointed time you drive to his house, park the car in front, ring his door bell, and sit down on the front steps. The prospective buyer comes out. You motion toward the car and watch silently while he walks around the car, kicks the tires, checks the odometer for mileage, examines the worn spots on the upholstery, and opens the hood. You hope that he notices that the battery is only a month old and that two back tires are practically new, and you wish he knew that your car doesn't burn much oil and that it gets eighteen miles to the gallon of regular gasoline. But you don't say anything. Let him find out for himself. The car is a good buy. If he wants it, he can have it.

Will you make a sale? Possibly. But if you really want to sell the car, you won't risk losing the sale this way. You won't take a chance on his placing too much emphasis on the car's bad points or on his missing any of the car's good points. If you want to show him the car in the best possible light, you will give careful thought to the features of the car and plan how you can best present them to him.

First, you will consider the faults of the car: the scratches on the door, the worn places in the upholstery, and the short in the directional light switch. Perhaps you decide to repair the short. Since you are sure the prospective buyer will notice the scratches and the worn uphol-stery, you decide to point out that seat covers can be bought at the

Seato Company for twenty dollars and that you have considered that fact in setting the price.

Then you consider the car's strong selling points. The two back tires are nearly new. You try to make an accurate estimate of the number of miles on them so you can use this fact as a selling point. You decide to point out the economy of operating the car: the high gasoline mileage, the use of regular gasoline, and the small amount of oil that the car uses. You find the guarantee for the battery so you can show that there are twenty-three months left on it.

Then you consider what you know about the prospective buyer. He said he wanted the car as a second car for his wife to drive. Since he already has the expense of one car, he will be interested in the economy features of the car. You decide to mention the car's economy from that standpoint. Since his wife and perhaps his children will be riding in the car, he will be particularly interested in the car's safety. You will use that angle in mentioning the tires. Probably his wife will drive the children to school in the car. He will want the car to be dependable in cold weather; therefore, he will be glad to know the car has a nearly new battery.

When you have decided how to show your car to him, you are ready to meet him. Of course, you don't take a seat on his front steps and motion silently for him to find all these fine selling points for himself. You show him the car, enumerating the car's good features and describing them in the way that will have the most appeal to him.

Selling yourself to a prospective employer does require some of the same sales concepts that are needed when you sell your car. You cannot sit silently in the office of the prospective employer and expect him or her to discover all of the wonderful reasons why you will be a valuable addition to the company. You will have to decide ahead of time just what your good points are and why they are valuable to a potential employer; then at the interview you will have to talk up those good points.

Just as preparing to demonstrate your car to a prospective buyer would require you to analyze your car's good qualities from the standpoint of the buyer, so preparing to show your prospective employer that you have the characteristics he or she wants in an employee will require you to analyze your abilities from the standpoint of the employer. And you cannot know what qualities will be important to the employer unless you know something about the company. You should find out all you can about the company's history, size, policies, and product. Some of these things you can learn from your

Chamber of Commerce or the local chapter of your union. Your library will probably have some of the excellent reference books on American industries.[1] From employees of the company you can learn about working conditions, compensation, treatment of employees, and opportunities for promotion.

You will also want to learn as much as you can about the person who is going to interview you so that you can present the information about yourself in the best light. A college-trained individual will be more interested in your educational background. Someone who learned his or her skills on the job will be less interested in your education than in your actual experience. A technician will talk the language of a technical person and will expect you to be prepared to establish your technical qualifications and to show that you understand the technical angles of the job. If you and the interviewer have any background or experience in common, particularly vocational or educational experience, you can use this fact to establish common ground on which to begin the interview. If you know that he or she holds high standards for workmanship and you hold similar standards, you can find some opportunity in the interview to emphasize your standards. To find out as much as you can about this individual, you can ask employees of the company. If your local newspaper office keeps an index to back issues and your prospective employer is prominent in the community, you may find some information there. Your librarian may also be able to help.[2]

[1] *Thomas' Register of American Manufacturers* (New York: Thomas Publishing Co.). Lists manufacturers alphabetically by product and trade name.

Moody's Industrial Manual (New York: Moody's Investors Service). Lists 4,400 companies and their subsidiaries; describes operations, lists officers, products, size of company, and other data.

MacRae's Blue Book (Chicago: MacRae's Blue Book Co., issued annually). Classifies 40,000 manufacturers by type of product and trade names.

Industrial Research Laboratories of the United States, National Research Council (Washington, D.C.: National Academy of Science). Lists and describes nearly 3,000 laboratories, indicating personnel and outlining research activities and resources. Includes subject and geographic indexes.

Sources of Information on American Firms (Washington, D.C.: U.S. Department of Commerce). Describes local sources, mentions business guides, gives addresses.

[2] Two books that may be helpful are:

Poor's Register of Directors and Executives (New York: Standard & Poor's Corp., issued annually). Classifies over 26,000 American and Canadian firms by industry and products, gives officers and number of employees, includes brief descriptions of about 75,000 executives and company directors.

Directory of National Associations of Businessmen. Lists over 2,000 national associations, giving number of members, size of staff, name and title of chief executive, and mailing address.

How should you dress
for the interview?

Just as the package helps to sell a product, your appearance is important in selling yourself to your prospective employer. Moreover, you will feel more confident if you look your best. You should not appear for the interview dressed as though you were going to a party. A general guide to follow is that you should dress for the interview as you might dress for the actual job. If, for instance, a man applies for a job at which he will wear a coat and tie, he should wear a coat and tie to the interview. If the job permits casual clothes, then you may go to the interview dressed casually. But casually should not be interpreted as sloppily. Your clothes need not be expensive, but they and you should be neat. Just as your prospective employer drew some conclusions about you from the appearance of your letter of application, he or she will draw further conclusions from your appearance. If your shoes need polishing or the heels are run down; if your hair needs cutting, washing, or combing; if your face needs shaving or careful makeup; your nails need cleaning; or if your clothes need pressing, the interviewer will probably decide not to hire you.

What information should you
be prepared to give
at the interview?

Whether the interviewer asks you the question or not, your prospective employer will want to know why you want the job for which you are applying. He or she may think you will adjust to the job more quickly, work better, and stay satisfied longer if you take the job for some special reason than if you will merely accept any job you can get. Moreover, you will seem to be a more desirable job candidate if you can afford to look for a particular job. You will do your best work, enjoy your job more, and satisfy your employer better if your particular abilities and aptitudes match the requirements of the job. Analyze your personal and professional qualifications and decide why this job is the one you want and why you are especially well qualified to hold it. Then be prepared to convince the interviewer.

Of course, you don't want to appear conceited. But facts are facts. If you can type 75 words a minute with a minimum of errors, you would be lying to claim a poorer speed; and if you neglect to mention your typing speed at all, you may be omitting information the interviewer needs. If you have had experience that should prove valuable in this job, that experience is a fact that the interviewer won't know if you don't reveal it. If you honestly know that you have the ability to put people at ease and to deal with them tactfully, that ability is also a fact and one that you should mention.

Should you apply for a definite job?

Obviously, since it is important to convince the interviewer that you are especially well qualified for one particular job, you should not say that you are looking for just "anything." Nobody is exactly suited to do "anything." If you really don't know exactly what kind of work the employer has available, describe your qualifications for the two or three jobs you think you can do well.

Sometimes after hearing you outline your capabilities, the interviewer may decide you are better qualified for a different job than the one you have in mind. The interviewer may be right. On the other hand, he or she may be describing the second job to test you, to see if you will change your analysis of yourself to prove that you are just the person for this second job as well. The only insurance you have against such a trick is your own sincerity. If you have made an honest self-analysis in the beginning, you will not misrepresent yourself to get either job.

Remember if you get the job, you have to work at it. If you are not really suited for it, you will not be happy in it. You may have heard stories about people who bluffed their way into jobs for which they were not prepared but in which they made good, but you do not hear about the nerve-racking days they spent while they were learning the job and covering up their ignorance. Nor do you hear about the bluffers who do not make good, or who succeed in their work but are unhappy because they are not psychologically suited for the job.

What should you say about your past jobs?

Your prospective employer will want to know why you left other jobs you have held. You can volunteer the information or you can wait to be asked. If you wait to be asked, the interviewer may get the impression that you lost the jobs for some reason you would rather not mention. Don't wait. Give a complete history of your work experience, job by job, including your reasons for leaving each one. Since you are probably not perfect, you may have left some of these jobs for reasons that are not flattering to you. Don't criticize your past employers or try to place the blame on others. The interviewer knows that complaining workers do not change their habits with their jobs. He or she probably has enough gripers on the payroll already and is not looking for more. If you were wrong and deserved to lose your job, admit it and explain what you have learned from the experience. Everyone makes mistakes, but not everyone learns from them.

Have the facts and dates of your past employment memorized and ready to give as you discuss your experience. You may have sent these facts to your prospective employer already, so the interviewer may have them at hand during the interview. The interviewer, then, will notice any discrepancies between what you wrote on your vita sheet and what you say. There is no need to lie about your age or about any of the periods of time involved in describing your past experiences. Interviewers are trained to put two and two together quickly and accurately enough to estimate actual facts.

What should you do about your weak points?

If you were honest in the self-evaluation that was part of your preparation for the job interview, you discovered that there are weak spots in your experience and ability. You hope that your prospective employer will not also discover these weaknesses, but discovering them is one of the purposes for interviewing you. As you answer questions, the interviewer will seek to uncover these defects and estimate how they might cause you to fail if you are hired. In your preparation for the interview you should consider your weaknesses carefully so that you can concentrate on your strong points and make your weak points seem slight in comparison.

How should you conduct yourself during the interview?

Throughout the interview be courteous and pleasant. Greet the interviewer with a pleasant smile and tell him or her why you are there. Do not offer to shake hands unless the interviewer makes the first gesture. Stand erect and wait for an invitation to be seated. Take the chair offered you and sit erect but relaxed. Do not prop your knee against the desk or slouch in your chair. You don't want to appear lazy, bored, or in need of medical attention. Try to keep your hands folded calmly in your lap; but if you can't keep them still, put them out of sight. You may find it difficult to appear calm when your stomach is full of butterflies, but use your will power to do so. If you can give the appearance of confidence, the interviewer will give you credit for having more ability than if you look as though you are afraid some awful secret of yours will be uncovered. Although you want to appear confident, though, you don't want to seem cocky. There is a difference between productive aggressiveness and objectionable boldness. Look directly at the interviewer and answer questions without hesitating. Do not interrupt while the interviewer is talking; look interested in what he or she is saying.

Even if the interviewer does not treat you courteously, you have nothing to gain by acting rudely. If you remain unruffled and respect-ful, the interviewer may use a different approach. He or she may purposely be testing your self-control, trying to determine how flexible you are in an unpleasant situation.

When the interview comes to a conclusion, leave as pleasantly as you entered. You will probably not be told at this time whether you have the job; the interviewer may have several candidates to talk with. Probably you will be told that you can expect to hear from the company within a certain time. Thank the interviewer for seeing you and then leave.

If you should be told at that time that you will not get the job, do not become hostile or argumentative. There may be reasons for your not being selected that you cannot immediately see, and you may in the future apply to the same company again. Try to be just as positive and confident as you leave as you were when you entered.

What does the interviewer want to know about that he or she does not ask?

The answers to many questions the interviewer will ask you may already be in your application letter or vita sheet. Perhaps, some questions may not seem relevant to you at all, but your prospective employer, listening to your answers, may be hearing responses to questions that were in his or her mind—questions that were not asked directly. Will you get along with other workers? Will you be a good team worker? Will you be loyal to the company? Will you be able to grow and advance with the organization? The interviewer will also reach some conclusions about your work habits. Are you alert and observant? Are you open-minded and flexible? Are you able to learn? Do you have common sense? Do you take a real interest in your work and a pride in good workmanship? Do you do your work promptly and thoroughly? Do you have initiative and enthusiasm? He or she will also listen for answers to questions concerning your character and personality. Are you honest and trustworthy? Are you reasonably mature and well-adjusted? Are you able to control your emotions and your actions? In short, are you a person who will be an asset to the company?

How will the interviewer find the answers to these questions? They will be found as he or she examines the details of your personal appearance, observes the way you respond physically to the stress of the interview, and listens to you describe your educational and vocational experience, your relationships with your past instructors, employers, and fellow workers, and your plans and hopes for future work.

Will anyone else gain important impressions of you during your interview?

You will probably come in contact with several people employed by the company in connection with your interview. You may talk to the secretary of your prospective employer when you arrange for the interview, and you will certainly meet the receptionist in the outer office when you arrive for the interview. Other employees may enter the outer office while you wait or may come into the office while the interviewer talks to you. The prospective employee may show you around some area of the company and introduce you to some of the workers. Before they come to a decision about hiring an employee, many employers like to have someone else's opinion. So your prospective employer may ask the secretary's opinion of you, or may ask the opinion of someone you were introduced to, or even of someone you didn't even notice. Obviously, then, you ought to treat everyone you meet with the same courtesy, respect, and pleasantness as you treat your prospective employer. Some of them may have a very important influence on whether you get the job or not. And if you do get the job, the good impression you have made will be still more important because these people will be your fellow workers.

ASSIGNMENTS

I.   You will be more relaxed during your interview if you have carefully planned some of your responses. Make a list of the most important facts which you might use in an interview. Include, for example, summary statements about your training, experience, and qualifications. What weak spots do you have that might affect your prospective employer's decision?

II. Your instructor may invite to class employers from the community who represent several occupational areas. These individuals will interview several members of the class in exactly the same manner that they would use in a legitimate interview. If you are one of those interviewed, put to use the ideas you have gained from this chapter. If you simply watch others being interviewed, be prepared after the interview is completed to discuss both the strengths and weaknesses the applicant demonstrated.

III. A good way to prepare for an interview is to think what types of questions you would ask if you were on the other side of the desk. Work with another student in your class and prepare a five-minute interview dramatization. Be realistic. If you are the interviewer, ask questions that seem really important. If you are the applicant, answer as seriously as you would at an actual interview.

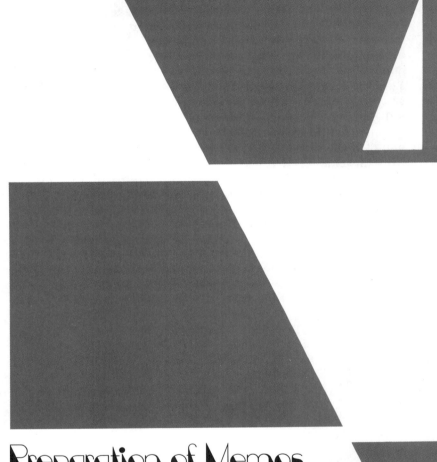

Preparation of Memos and Short Reports

Why do you need to know how to write reports?

Reports of all types—long and short, formal and informal, technical and general, offset-printed and handwritten—help to keep the business world turning. It's hard to think of a single job at which you would not be required to do some writing. The nurse keeps charts, the auditor summarizes records, the mechanic presents a diagnostic report to the car owner, and the sales clerk maintains a daily sales record.

Some of these reporting jobs are admittedly formulaic: the writer is given a prepared form and blanks to complete. But even many of these blanks require sentence and sometimes paragraph responses. You may need to prepare the minutes from a departmental committee meeting, write a memorandum to the shipping department, post a notice on the bulletin board, deliver a report on a meeting or convention you attended, dictate a letter containing your recommendation for the new salary scale, prepare a detailed cost breakdown on the proposed expansion of the sales office, or issue a progress report to your immediate superior. All this communication can be classified as report writing. Most reports will remain within the company; sometimes they will not leave your immediate department. But the fact that the public doesn't see a report doesn't mean that such intracompany communication isn't important. The smooth operation of your company or department will depend upon clear and accurate communication within your department and between your department and other departments. No longer is the average company so small that requests, recommendations, and reports can be passed on by word of mouth. They must be carefully worded, filled out on a prescribed form, recorded in triplicate, stamped and approved by someone in the various offices through which they pass, and stored safely in some official's filing cabinet. Modern businesses are so large that the chain of command through which an employee report must pass may be very complicated.

When thousands of dollars are at stake, a company cannot afford to act on the basis of vague verbal reports and hurriedly jotted notes. The expert who has been asked to record the present state of a department, or the recommendations for the new year has applied all his or her professional knowledge to the gathering of accurate information. The ability to communicate these findings with appropriate accuracy and clarity is just as important as the ability to gather the information. Somebody will read the report and base a decision on it. That somebody can understand that report and decide wisely only if that report is written well. Yet according to a survey made recently among prominent American organizations, the handicap that keeps most industrial engineers from advancing is their failure to communicate their ideas effectively—and there is no reason to suppose that engineers have more communication difficulties than members of other professions.

What form is used for the communication of information?

Your communication of information will normally take the form of a report. Reports fall roughly into two kinds: informal and formal. Both kinds of reports contain the same basic parts, the chief difference between them being length. The informal report may be only a paragraph long or it may be as long as two pages. Longer reports are usually more formal in structure and writing style.

What is a memorandum?

A common type of informal report is the memorandum or memo. Each company has its own memo style and many have printed memo forms. All memos contain four essential items of information, which are usually given in the heading of the form: (1) the date; (2) the name of the person to receive the memo, referred to here as the addressee; (3) the sender; and (4) the subject of the memo. Figure 7-1 provides examples of three different types of memo headings.

figure 7-1

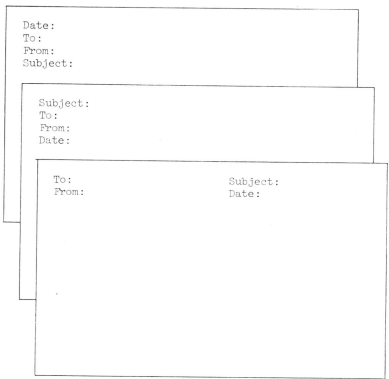

```
Date:
To:
From:
Subject:
```

```
Subject:
To:
From:
Date:
```

```
To:              Subject:
From:            Date:
```

figure 7-2

```
                        Memorandum


Date:       October 18, 1978
To:         Joe B. Bush
From:       Al J. Clark
Subject:    Purchase order #1332


        Three items were omitted on the first order:  AX 20485,
AX 21120, and B2 1158.  Please have a new order made out including these
items.  Get the signature of the department manager and have the order
on my desk to be signed for a rush order by Wednesday.
```

Such a form may be filled in on the typewriter, or it may be handwritten. It may be sent to another employee by special messenger, carried through interoffice mail, or sometimes posted on a departmental bulletin board. If the memorandum is important enough and contains information needed by a number of employees, it may be mimeographed and sent to each one. A memorandum may be destroyed as soon as it has served its purpose, or it may be filed for future reference.

What other kinds of reports are made on printed forms?

Many companies require specialized reports for which printed forms are used. The form and content of these reports vary from company to company. The most common ones are accident reports, travel expense reports, supply requisitions, sales reports, operation expense reports, and progress reports. The purpose of all such reports is to give information in a uniform, easily read, easily understood form.

What are the most common kinds of reports not made on a printed form?

Letters, which of course use standard business letter form, as well as handwritten notes are also common kinds of informal reports. Although they are not written on a printed form with labels for the four essential pieces of information, that information is still included. Examine the short handwritten note in Figure 7-3 to see how closely it resembles the memorandum in Figure 7-2.

What are the main parts of the message of the report?

Although the message carried by reports is brief, each contains some of the basic parts of all reports: introduction, summary, body, conclusions, recommendations, and appendix. Notice how the contents of this brief note break down into three of these parts:

Introduction   About that purchase #1332 for Oct. 15.

figure 7-3

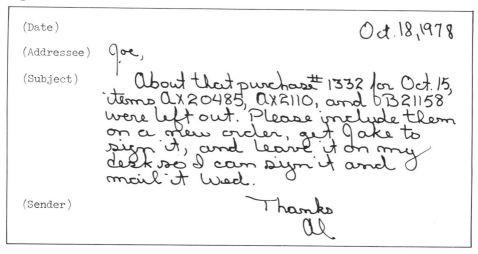

(Date)   Oct. 18, 1978

(Addressee)   Joe,

(Subject)   About that purchase # 1332 for Oct. 15,
              items AX 20485, AX 2110, and B2 1158
              were left out. Please include them
              on a new order, get Jake to
              sign it, and leave it on my
              desk so I can sign it and
              mail it Wed.

(Sender)   Thanks
                                  Al

Body	Items AX 20485, AX 21120, and B2 1158 were left out.
Recommendations	Please include them on a new order, get Jake to sign it, and leave it on my desk so I can sign it and mail it Wed.

An informal report may omit some of the basic parts, may combine some of them, or may contain all of them, or may contain all of them separately. In this case the conclusion—that these items should have been included on the order—is implied by the statement of the problem and by the recommendations. No summary is needed in such a brief report.

Later in the chapter we will look at a longer report containing all of the basic parts.

What are the stylistic requirements of report writing?

Writing short reports, whether they take the form of memos, of letters, of notes, or of longer reports, should not create any problem. The form and content requirements are simple enough and are frequently identified for you on the sheet or blank provided for that purpose. But an examination of some of the memos and directions that pass through the interoffice mail of any large company will reveal that many people who write such informal reports do not find the task easy at all.

An analysis of a large number of these reports reveals that the writers have a real problem in communication. They know what they want to say, and they would know how to say it in simple, straightforward English if they thought that simple, straightforward English would do the job. But somehow they have an idea that company memos and directives should be written in some kind of special gobbledegook that is at best misunderstood, at worst completely unintelligible. Such communication, or lack of communication, must cost American industry thousands of dollars yearly because those who receive it don't know what they are expected to do after they have received it.

Figure 7-4 is a memorandum that was issued with some urgency and evidently considered important; but, unfortunately, it is not clearly written. If the writer of this memorandum had thought through exactly what he wanted the department inspectors to do and had tried to

figure 7-4

```
To:      All Department Inspectors          Date:  February 6, 1979

Subj.:  Processing of G.I.A.'s

There seems to be some confusion as to whom is to clear final operation
complete, and going forward stamping applicable G.I.A. operations in
subsequent stations as instructed in the G.I.A.

This is evident in Pre-Delivery Station when G.I.A.'s are ran prior to
going to customer.  Approximately 80 to 90 percent of ships arriving in
this station have one or more operations open.

Effective immediately, all inspectors that release ships from one
station to the next less shortages or whatever, will stamp these
operations as such.

Two other problems are also evident.  (1) Stamps not legible and dated,
(2) Ship numbers not entered on appropriate bottom block of operation
clearance form.

Effective immediately all inspectors' stamps will be legible and
dated. The inspector will be responsible for seeing and placing ship
number on operation clearance form.

                                          S.R. Hardy
                                          Supervisor,
                                          Flight Inspection
```

describe those operations clearly and simply, he might have written something like the memo in Figure 7-5.

What kinds of words should you avoid in a report?

Proper word choice is important for the exact kind of writing required for instructions and reports. For one thing, you should avoid emotionally loaded words. Remember that some words call highly personal pictures to the reader's mind, and such pictures may not be the same as those *you* connect with the the same words. Such words will not help you to write clear instructions that will be followed without error.

Remember also that emotionally loaded words may cause the reader to react in an emotional way just when a clear head is most needed. Theoretically, a lawyer examining prospective jurors tries to select individuals who have no preconceived ideas concerning the guilt or innocence of the defendent and who also have had no personal experiences that might cause them to feel emotionally involved in the outcome of the trial. Such an impartial attitude is also needed by the secretary recording the actions of the school board, the policeman gathering the facts about the need for a stop sign at Highway 83 and Plaza Boulevard, and the researcher establishing the relationship between the use of tobacco and the common cold.

Just as such individuals should try to keep open minds, they should

figure 7-5

```
To:      All Department Inspectors        Date:   February 6, 1979

Subj.:   Processing of G.I.A.'s

         Eighty to 90 per cent of the ships that reach the Pre-Delivery
Station are incomplete.  All inspectors releasing ships from one
station to the next are responsible for the following:

         (1) Stamping each incomplete operation legibly on the operation
             clearance form that accompanies the ship.
         (2) Dating the stamp accurately.
         (3) Entering the ship number in the appropriate bottom block of
             the operation clearance form.

                                         S.R. Hardy
                                         Supervisor
                                         Flight Inspection
```

describe their findings with words that allow the reader to remain equally objective. The reader of the police report should not be able to tell whether the writer wants the stop sign installed or not; but the reader should know how many vehicles use the streets, whether traffic is heavy at certain hours, whether school children use the intersection, and how many accidents have occurred at the corner. The tobacco-common-cold researcher should write a report that gives no hint as to how many packs he or she smokes a day or whether he or she is employed by American Tobacco Company or the American Medical Association.

What kind of words should you use in a report?

You will also communicate more accurately and effectively if you choose words that mean exactly what you intend them to mean. Some words have meanings very close to those of other words and yet they suggest a fine shade of difference which you need to be aware of it you are to communicate effectively. *House* and *home* might identify the place where you live, but *home* conveys the notions of family, love, warmth, etc. that the word *house* does not. *Residence* is more formal, as is *dwelling. Mansion* not only describes the size of the house but suggests wealth, power, or prestige. *Shack* intimates the opposite. Can you see the shades of difference in the following groups of words:

   a. common, ordinary, vulgar, pedestrian, everyday, conventional
   b. get, attain, achieve, secure, receive capture, take, procure
   c. freedom, liberty, independence, liberation, emancipation, release
   d. book, volume, tome, publication, manual, treatise, encyclopaedia
   e. messenger, envoy, emissary, legate, delegate, herald, go-between

Because some words have several meanings, they can lead to misunderstanding. If you declare that the day is *nice,* that your neighbor's daughter is not a *nice* girl, and that your mother looks *nice* in her new hat, you may know what you mean, but others might be confused. *Overlook* means both to inspect or survey and to neglect or pass over without criticism. *Peculiar* has a number of meanings that appear unrelated: belonging to an individual, privately owned, not common, characteristic or distinctive, different from the normal or usual, singular, special, particular, queer, or eccentric. If you think that any of your words may be minunderstood by your reader, define your terms.

Some words are so overused that they have relatively little value in helping you communicate what you want to. *Good, beautiful, nice, great, bad, lovely,* and *fantastic* are just a few of the words which are fairly ineffectual. How well did you describe a movie or a book when you said, "That was a *good* movie," or "That was a *great* book"? And, today everything is "beautiful," from broccoli soup to sunsets in the Rockies. To be an effective communicator you must train yourself to be on the lookout for empty words. You can start by listening carefully to other people's speech and writing. Note the effective words and the ones that really communicate nothing. Then note your own speech and writing. Make an effort to rid your speech and writing of those words that say little or nothing and to concentrate on using precise, meaningful words.

Will the arrangement of the words in your sentence help you to write more accurately?

The arrangement of words in a sentence is very important if you are to say exactly what you mean. If you write, "Still he stood by the window," your meaning is quite different than if you write, "He stood still by the window." The sentence, "The little boy nearly walked ten miles" actually means that the little boy came very near to taking a walk ten miles long but he did not really walk at all. If in fact he walked nine and a half miles, the sentence should read, "The little boy walked nearly ten miles."

Note the differences in the following pairs of sentences:

Almost everyone had finished eating when the band began to play.
   (Most people had finished eating, but some had not.)
Everyone had almost finished eating when the band began to play.
   (Probably no one had finished eating, but everyone was nearly finished.)
People who exercise frequently keep physically fit.
   (Frequent exercise promotes physical fitness.)
Frequently people who exercise keep physically fit.
   (Exercise commonly promotes physical fitness.)
The student council met to discuss vandalism in the student center.
   (The vandalism occurred in the student center.)
The student council met in the student center to discuss vandalism.
   (The council met in the center. There is no statement concerning the site of the vandalism.)

Sometimes such poorly arranged sentences can be almost amusing:

The judges presented the trophy to the owner of the horse which had been engraved in gold.

The car can be seen at the garage which was in the accident.

The float moved slowly down the street with artificial flowers covering the top and sides.

There was loud applause when the speaker said he was in favor of the program at the back of the hall.

He returned the coat to the store that didn't fit.

We have a booklet on our new underground sprinkler system which we will send you on request.

You will also fail to say what you mean if you leave out necessary words. Be especially careful in your use of pronouns. Notice how confusing these two sentences are:

Mr. Hartley told Joe that he needed to complete the filing before he made out the paychecks.

The bookkeeper showed her assistant the office in which she would be working.

Directives and instructions are frequently indirect and hard to follow because they are written in the passive voice. Compare the directness and clarity of these two sentences:

When you answer the phone for someone else in the office, your name should be stated for identification.

When you answer the phone for someone else in the office, identify yourself by stating your name.

Here is a summary of the above suggestions for clear and accurate report writing:[1]

Use the most accurate and exact word you can find.

Avoid words that don't say anything or that repeat other words.

Arrange the order of your sentences so that they say what you intend them to say.

Don't leave out anything your reader needs to know.

Don't suppose that your reader will know what the words *this, which,* and *it* refer to if you don't make the intended meaning clear.

Do not use passive verbs unless you can't avoid them.

---

[1]Additional examples of style and usage can be found in the Handbook section of this text.

How can you achieve brevity?

Your writing will not be clear if you clutter it up with words that don't say anything or that just repeat other words. Find the simplest, shortest, most direct way to say what you have to say. Notice the difference in the following pairs of sentences:

57 Words

It is the responsibility of each and every department head to make the arrangements necessary to provide personnel replacement in order to ensure the efficient continuation of operation in his or her area in the case of absenteeism resulting from the illness of any salaried employee ordinarily involved directly in the activities of his or her department.

11 Words

Each department head is responsible for hiring substitutes for ill employees.

Should you always use the fewest words?

Although your statements should be direct, you will not communicate clearly if you do not include all the necessary details. The sentence "The man entered the building" really doesn't give much information. The following are much more specific:

The rookie staggered into the bar.
The burglar pried open the window and crawled into the jewelry store.
Santa Claus slid down the chimney.

If the plumber who asks someone to hand him a small tool really has in mind a ⅝-inch socket wrench, a screwdriver simply will not do. If a friend of yours promises to send "a small momento" from a trip to Europe, you might be disappointed with a postcard. Cooks once baked cakes by using a pinch of baking powder, a smidgeon of spice, several eggs, flour, and enough milk to hold the batter together; but today's cooks would rather measure with graduated spoons and cups and prefer to use a tested recipe. Brevity does not work if it fails to convey the exact meaning that is intended.

What special problems will you meet in writing instructions?

Writing instructions that can be followed correctly requires using all of the techniques of good technical writing. You will also need both forethought and discipline. Before you start to write, think through exactly what you have to say and decide on the best order in which to say it. If you have to back up and explain something that you should have said earlier, you will only confuse your reader. Moreover, don't try to tell your reader too much at once. The more complicated your material, the more you must break it down into small, simple parts. Finally, don't make your instructions any more complicated than necessary. If the operation is relatively simple, keep your instructions simple. Don't expect the reader to read your mind, but do give credit for some common sense.

Compare the following statements of instruction to a firm's new employees.

Because of the excessive amount of paperwork and the problem in scheduling, it has become impossible for us adequately to process your insurance papers in our usual way. Those desiring insurance should report to Ms. Lyons, Office 257-B, on either Monday or Tuesday of next week (March 20-21). You will assume responsibility for the satisfactory completion of your own papers.	New employees are responsible for filing their own insurance application forms in Ms. Lyons' office (257-B) on either March 21 or 22.

A typical problem in writing instructions is presenting too much material at once, thereby confusing the order of action. Notice how confused the instruction at the left is, compared with the one at the right.

To start a fire in your new home grill, place the charcoal on the grill floor and make certain that the grill vents are all open. After soaking with charcoal lighter, ignite with a match, and then wait five to ten minutes before beginning to cook.	To prepare your new home grill for cooking, first open all of the vents on the bottom and the sides. Then place charcoal evenly on the grill floor and apply a small amount of charcoal lighter evenly over the charcoal. Wait five minutes, and then light with a match. Let the charcoal burn five to ten minutes before beginning to cook.

How do you handle abbreviations and figures in report writing?

Writing reports frequently involves the use of more abbreviations and figures than ordinary writing does. Although different businesses have their own rules for using figures and abbreviations, there are certain practices that are standardized throughout much of the business community. A rather complete listing is given in the Handbook section of this text. Consult it if you have questions.

How are longer informal reports written?

Figure 7-6 is a longer informal report on the findings of the committee that investigated the problem of the employees' cafeteria. Notice that it contains all of the basic parts of a report but that it is short enough to be classified as an informal report. Notice also that the body of the report states and analyzes the problem, locates the causes, and suggests and examines the solutions. The order in which each part of the problem and each part of the solution are handled is consistent.

ASSIGNMENTS

I. Prepare the following memoranda:
   1. A memo from you to your school librarian requesting permission to keep two books out a week longer than is normally allowed. Give the specific titles and call numbers of the books.
   2. A memo from you, acting as secretary for a club on campus, announcing a meeting. Be certain to indicate the name of the club and the time and place of the meeting.
II. Write the following brief notes:
   1. A note from you to your communication instructor asking that he or she remember to bring you a specific book from the downtown library.
   2. A note from you to your employer (real or imaginary) asking that you be permitted to have next Saturday off. Cite the exact date. Give a brief reason for your request.
   3. A note from your employer responding to your note and giving permission for you to take the requested time off.

figure 7-6

```
Date:      December 4, 1978
To:        B. R. Frederick
From:      Lynda Rothberg
Subject:   Findings of the special committee
           authorized to investigate the
           employees' cafeteria.
```

(Summary)

All information indicates a need for purchasing a new oven for the bakery, remodeling the cafeteria cold room, and opening two doors into the serving area.

(Introduction)

This report will give the findings of the committee authorized by B. R. Frederick to investigate the causes for the complaints concerning the food and service in the employees' cafeteria.

(Body:
Analysis of
the problem:
baked goods,
salads, service)

The complaints lodged against the food in the employees' cafeteria chiefly concern the quality of the hot breads and baked desserts, the temperature and freshness of the salads, and the slowness of the food service.

(Cause of the
problem: old
outmoded oven,
cold room, poor
arrangement
of entrance to
serving deck)

Investigation of the cafeteria facilities reveals that the bakery ovens were purchased in 1952 and that the thermostatic controls and timers are inaccurate and undependable. The cold room, measuring 6 by 8 ft., was built in 1948 when the cafeteria served 300 employees. It is inadequate today when an average of 750 employees are served daily. The present serving area is crowded and inefficiently arranged. The waitresses replenishing the steam deck must pass through the dishwashing area and through the same door as the busboys returning from the dining area with trays of dirty dishes. The resulting bottleneck slows the progress of food to the serving deck.

118

figure 7-6 continued

(Solution: Repair of the oven thermostatic
 buy new ovens,   controls and timers seems impractical as the
                  cost would be only slightly lower than the
                  replacement of the ovens with newer and more
                  efficient equipment.

 enlarge cold   A consultant of the ColdWay Commercial
 room,   Refrigeration Company recommends enlarging
                  the cold room to 6 by 18 ft. Two rows of
                  shelves down the center as well as along the
                  back and sides of the room would not only take
                  care of present needs but would also be
                  adequate for any expected increase in
                  personnel.

                  Space for the enlarged cold room
                  could be taken from the adjoining dishwashing
                  area which is larger than necessary now that
                  new and more compact dishwashing and drying
                  equipment has been installed.

 rearrange   Two new double doors cut into the wall
 entrance to   behind the steam deck would allow for efficient
 serving deck)   service in that area.

(Conclusion)   It is the conclusion of the com-
                  mittee that the complaints concerning the caf-
                  eteria food are justified and that the prob-
                  lems responsible for these complaints can be
                  solved by purchasing new ovens for the bakery,
                  enlarging the cold room, and making two double
                  doors behind the steam deck.

(Recommendation) It is the recommendation of this
                  committee that these actions be taken as soon
                  as possible.

(Appendix)   Here is a sketch of the proposed cold
                  room and the reduced cleanup area. A
                  breakdown of the necessary costs follows.

4. A note from your employer denying you permission to take the requested time off.

III. The following memo is wordy and unclear. Completely rewrite it so that the writer's purpose will be accomplished.

```
To:  All day-shift employees          Subject:  Personal Claims

From:  David Barnum                    Date:  January 15, 1979


        In regard to recent inquiries as to whether the personal
equipment in your work areas can be replaced by company insurance should
it be stolen, you are advised that by reason of the fact that it is
impossible for us to inventory all such personal belongings it then
becomes impossible for us to cooperate and insure them.

        However, our insurance company is willing to issue each of you
on an individual basis a policy for your own belongings; the cost of
this coverage may be deducted from your monthly pay check.

        Attached hereto is an application form and a sheet for your
inventory list of items you wished to be insured.  If you will fill out
both of these instruments with all pertinent information, every effort
will be made to have your policy in force by the end of January.

        Your forms should be submitted to my office no later than the
end of your work shift Friday, January 19, 1979.  Place them in the
special drawer on top of my desk that is marked "Insurance-Urgent."
```

IV. Work with a group of your fellow students and identify an important local problem, related either to your campus or your local community. Identify what you feel to be the issues and then address a formal report to the appropriate governing body. Structure your report similarly to the one in Figure 7-6.

Serving on the
Problem Solving
Committee

Why are committees appointed?

Almost every organization—businesses, churches, schools, etc.—have occasion to appoint committees to carry on certain aspects of the organization's purpose. Some committees are appointed for one particular task and are disbanded after that task has been completed. Other committees are appointed to serve longer periods of time and are given much broader responsibilities. Whatever the assignment given to a committee, the members placed on that committee are the ones who will most often determine success or failure. Committees are appointed to further the work of the parent organization in some manner, and assignment to a committee must be accepted with an awareness of the responsibilities that go along with effective committee work.

Why do you need to learn how to serve on a committee?

You may find that much of your work time will be spent in committee meetings and that some of your most important work will be done at a conference table. For all that has been said against them, committees often work successfully. Two heads are better than one in problem solving, and a committee of three or five or seven ought to be even more effective.

Certainly the multiplication of heads produces a multiplication of opinions. Committee members take sides and discussion becomes heated. Discussion takes time, but it is part of the democratic process by which American institutions operate. Mature individuals do not always expect everyone to agree with them. Certainly if all those on a committee always agreed with each other there would be no need for the committee. One person could make all of the decisions for the group.

A committee room is not an arena for a verbal free-for-all, however. There are well-established, generally accepted rules by which business is conducted. And there are certain skills and attitudes that will help you become a more valuable employee because you work well with others.

On what kinds of committees will you serve?

Committees, conferences, and similar meetings are organized to solve problems. Some committees are *temporary,* called to handle one specific problem. Others are *standing* committees that exist to deal with all the problems of a certain type with which the organization is concerned. There are also *executive* committees to which the top administrators of the organization belong. Such committees make decisions of policy and delegate other committees to handle problems in various areas. You may serve on a committee because the person in your particular job always serves on that committee, because you have some needed specialized skill, or because you are thought to have clear judgment.

What are the requirements for a committee member?

Problem solving requires, first of all, informed thinking. The problem facing the committee may be a new one in which you have no background at all, or you may have had considerable experience with similar problems. Since no two problems are exactly alike, in either case you will need all of the information that can be gathered on the subject.

Sometimes the chairperson or someone appointed by the chairperson will bring the necessary information to the group. Sometimes a number of such reports will be necessary. Although you can usually count on being filled in on certain aspects of the problem, you ought to do some work in preparation for the meeting yourself. When the meeting is not a regularly scheduled one, you will probably be notified of its purpose. For regular meetings an agenda or list of matters to be discussed is usually sent to the committee members before the meeting. The chairperson may inform you ahead of time of the subject of committee business, in order to give you time to think about the subject and perhaps learn something about it on your own. If you think the information you have gathered about the subject before or during the meeting is not enough for you to make an intelligent judgment, say so and ask that any action on the problem be postponed until more facts can be learned. Members of the committee may then be assigned to make further investigation and report to the committee at a later meeting. Never let a committee on which you serve act upon inadequate information just because the hour is late and the members are tired.

The second requirement for problem solving is an objective mind. Facts are worthless if the people who examine them have already made up their minds about what they think and what they intend to do before they know those facts. You may not be able to do much about the prejudices and preconceived ideas of other members of the group, but you are responsible for your own objectivity. Examine your own ideas and thoughts honestly. Recognize your biases and try to guard against their influencing your decisions. Don't be manipulated by emotionally charged words, and don't use them to manipulate others. A free discussion is not a debate or a power contest. You should want the group to find the best answer to its problems more than you want to persuade it to do something your way.

What kinds of problems are solved by committees?

Three types of problems are handled in discussion: problems of fact, problems of value, and problems of policy.

problems of fact

Obviously the best method for solving problems of fact is to consult experts who have already investigated the matter or to assign the best-qualified members of the group to investigate it. Your group should not waste its time discussing a question which could be settled by referring to an almanac, a government bulletin, or a personnel officer's survey.

Usually the problems of fact that are brought to committee contain several parts; in other words, the information sought is made up of many separate facts. The committee may decide what individual facts are needed; or they may, because of their different backgrounds, be able to supply these various needed facts. Problems of fact include such questions as these: Will the present steam deck in the employee cafeteria be adequate if the lunch hour is decreased ten minutes? What are the causes of the decrease in production in the X-ray department? What changes in process will have to be made if the top of the hygroflam bottle is made of plastic foam? How much will such changes cost? Solving a problem of fact is frequently the first step in solving one of the other kinds of problems.

problems of value

A problem of value is similar to one of fact except that it allows for some difference of opinion. Facts may be the basis of the discussion, but the question will be settled finally by the judgment and preference of the group. The best decisions of value are reached when the group withholds judgment and remains uncommitted until its members have heard *all* the facts. Such a situation is ideal and exists more often in textbooks than in groups made up of real people. You can help your group to make fair judgments by guarding your own objectivity and by making a tactful suggestion if the decision seems to be affected by personalities.

Problems of value concern questions such as these: Is one twenty-minute coffee break more valuable for employee morale and efficiency than two ten-minute breaks? Will changing the color of the top of the hygroflam bottle from navy blue to seafoam green increase consumer appeal enough to offset the temporary increase in production costs?

problems of policy

Many of the problems that face your committee will be problems of policy. Problems of policy concern the actions that might be taken to meet a given situation. In any business, circumstances are constantly changing, and such changes create problems. Solving those problems may require other changes. When a committee faces a problem of policy, it must consider all of the possible solutions and decide which one is best and most practical. Problems of policy are as varied as the businesses and committees that consider them. The variety of the solutions considered is limited only by the imagination of the group dealing with the problem.

What is the most informal type of problem-solving committee?

One of the most productive ways of approaching the problem of policy is the "brainstorming" session. Such a session is quite unconventional in its organization since the one who calls the group together is not looking for obvious or conventional answers. The purpose of the session is to bring out every solution that pops into the minds of the inventive men and women invited to the meeting. At a brainstorming session everyone is expected to speak out without inhibition or restraint. The point is not to consider the merits of the suggestions at the moment, but to try to think of everything even distantly connected with the problem. No solution should be considered too impossible or ridiculous to suggest.

The group will probably have no leader. Someone will be needed to take down all the suggestions, preferably on a blackboard, since the sight of what has already been suggested may stimulate other ideas. Usually none of the ideas is evaluated or discarded at this meeting. Each member of the group may be assigned a certain portion of the suggested solutions for investigation. No solution should be discarded as foolish or impractical until it has been examined carefully. After a complete examination and fair evaluation, an answer which originally sounded quite silly may turn out to be the best one. Therefore, give each idea a chance, What good are fresh ideas without fresh minds to consider them?

Although this kind of meeting is not usually very orderly, it stimulates originality and draws ideas from many who are otherwise too shy to let anyone know how creative they can be. Such meetings frequently yield new and workable solutions and are therefore grow-ing in popularity among progressive organizations. If after an active brainstorming session the problem still seems insoluble or soluble only by some faulty method, you and your colleagues will know that at least you gave a fair hearing to every possible solution.

What do you do when you are a committee member?

An ordinary committee meeting has a chairperson and is conducted a bit more formally than a brainstorming session. At a fomal meeting, as at any other discussion group, you should observe the ordinary rules of courtesy. You will listen to what others say, really listen, taking care to hear exactly what is said and to understand what is meant. You should even develop the habit of taking notes so that you can keep in mind the different points that are made. Of course, you will not interrupt a speaker or talk to those about you while someone else is speaking.

When it is your turn to speak, don't talk as though you had all the answers and don't start an argument or take sides in one somebody else has started. You are not there to get your way, to show how stupid someone else is, or to impress others with your powers of public speaking, reasoning, or sarcasm. You are there to help solve a problem which can be solved more easily if everybody stays cool and objective.

The ability to be tactful when you disagree is a trait that will help you in both your professional and personal life. Use expressions such as "I would like to hear more on this subject" or "I may be wrong but it appears to me. . . ." Assume that other speakers are as intelligent and are striving as sincerely for objectivity as you are certain you are.

Don't think, on the other hand, that you have fulfilled your purpose on the committee just because you have answered to roll call, looked intelligent, and refrained from insulting anybody. The strong, silent committee member is frequently sitting there shyly worrying what others would think if he or she really said something. After the meeting this person may voice his or her opinions loudly and critically, but they will serve no useful purpose then.

Consider the problem before the committee to be your own problem. Face it thoughtfully. If you have a thought that is pertinent and has not already been expressed, ask for recognition in whatever manner is customary in the group and speak loudly enough to be heard, without mumbling, droning in a monotone, or gesticulating wildly. Don't worry about what others will think about your ideas. You like them, and you are there because somebody in authority thought your ideas worth hearing.

But you don't have to speak on every question. Sometimes your opinions will be the same as those already expressed by others. Sometimes it is possible that you honestly have no preferences in the matter. Every group usually has at least one member who has an opinion on every subject. Frequently it is the same opinion. He or she may even express it in the same words. Another unpopular member is the one who talks too long, who has trouble staying on the subject, and who can't tell a relevant fact from one that is completely beside the point. If you notice that your fellow committee members frequently grow restless when you rise to speak, review what you said and what others said before and after you spoke to see if any one of these faults is yours.

What do you do when you are the chairperson of a committee?

If you are the committee chairperson, you have a very important job. Whether or not the group accomplishes its purpose will be largely up to you. As committee chairperson, you send out an agenda to the members of the group a few days before the meeting so that they can come to the meeting prepared to discuss the questions at hand. Give reasonable attention to matters which other members ask to have considered as well as to those which you feel are important. If some special information will be needed, secure it or ask some other member to do so. You should also take care of any other preparations, such as announcing the meeting, arranging for a meeting place, preparing ballots, making minutes of past meetings available to the members, and seeing that a record will be made of this meeting.

At the meeting you will introduce topics to be discussed according to your agenda and you will lead the discussion. Although you will allow anyone to speak who asks for permission in the customary way, you should exert some guidance in keeping the discussion on the problem and moving toward a solution. To be fair, you must see that everyone is allowed free expression, but you should not allow a troublesome or fervent minority to take over the whole meeting. Naturally you will never use your office to gain special advantage for your desires or ideas.

How is the business of a committee conducted?

In small, informal committees decisions may be made by general consent. Sometimes no formal vote is necessary, although informal opinions may be voiced. The business of larger committees, however, is conducted more formally and according to standard parliamentary procedure. In such meetings you or someone else may suggest a decision or an action. You should ask that the proposal be stated as a formal motion. The person who made the suggestion, or perhaps someone else, will then say simply, "I move that . . ." Another person must then say, "I second the motion." If no one seconds the motion, then no one except the person who made the motion is in favor of it, and the motion dies for want of a second. After the motion has been seconded, you will restate the motion or, if its wording is difficult,

128

have the secretary read it. Then you will ask if there is any discussion of the motion. When no one has any more to say about it, you call for a vote, taking care that everyone understands the motion. The vote may be taken by a simple *yes* or *no* given in unison, by a show of hands, by roll call, or by secret ballot. The manner of voting depends upon the importance of the question and the customs of the group. You will always restate the motion three times: before you call for discussion, before you call for the vote, and after the motion has been voted.

The kind of motion that concerns the usual business of a meeting is referred to as the *main motion.* Two main motions cannot be handled by a group at the same time. After a main motion is made and seconded, the group must accept, reject, or in some way dispose of the motion before another main motion can be considered.

improving or changing a motion

If there is a motion to change or amend the main motion, it must be discussed and voted upon before attention is returned to the main motion. Be sure to state the motion to amend a motion three times: before the discussion, before the vote, and after the vote. It is especially important that everyone understands that it is the *motion to amend* the main motion and not the main motion that is being considered. After the motion to amend the motion has been accepted, the main motion can be discussed and voted upon in its new form. The motion to amend a motion is amended by a similar procedure, but usually it is simpler if the person who made the original motion withdraws that motion and the group starts over.

referring a problem to some other group

Sometimes someone in the group may feel that the problem involved in a motion requires further study or action by some smaller group that can give the problem more specialized attention. This person will *move to refer* the matter to a standing committee or to a special committee. The motion may name the standing committee, or it may describe the kind of new committee desired: "I move that the question be referred to a committee of five members to be elected by this group and that the committee report its findings at the next meeting." A majority vote is required to pass this motion. Naturally, if it passes, no further attention is paid to the original motion at this time.

These three motions—the *main motion,* the *motion to amend* a motion, and the *motion to refer* the question—are the principal ones used in most meetings. There are, however, a few other motions which you may need to know about. These motions are all subsidiary motions because they pertain to main motions which have been made and seconded and which are before the group at the time.

postponing a motion

A *motion* may be made *to postpone* a motion until some definite, stated time. Such a motion is usually made to allow the members of the group time to give more thought to the matter and to get some more information. This motion is a fair and useful one because it can be discussed, and it does not keep the matter from being considered again at an appointed time. This motion requires only a majority vote.

A motion may also be made to postpone a main motion indefinitely. The purpose of this motion is to kill the main motion. The opponents of a main motion may also use this method to test the popularity of the main motion. This motion is a fair one because it can be discussed. Only a majority vote is required to pass it.

reconsideration of an indefinitely postponed motion

At some later time a motion that has been posponed indefinitely can be brought up for reconsideration. Someone who was present when the main motion was postponed moves that this main motion be reconsidered. The *motion to reconsider* requires a second, it can be discussed, and it passes with a majority vote.

If someone who was not present when the motion was made to postpone a motion objects to that postponement, he or she cannot move to reconsider the motion. The person can, however, move that the postponement motion be rescinded or taken back. A two-thirds vote is required to pass the *motion to rescind.* To keep from confusing these last two motions, remember that you can't move to reconsider a motion that you didn't consider in the first place.

another way of postponing a motion indefinitely

A rather unfair motion—and one that is frequently misunderstood—is the *motion to table* the main motion or to lay the main motion on the table. This motion requires a second, but it cannot be discussed. It requires only a majority vote to pass. An undebatable motion kills free discussion, which is important to the democratic process. Therefore, a motion to postpone indefinitely is a much fairer motion and one which serves a similar purpose.

A motion which has been placed on the table can be returned to consideration only after other business has intervened. Anyone can move to take the motion from the table and return it to consideration. A second to the motion and a majority vote are required.

keeping a motion from vote

A motion may be kept from vote in two ways. Someone may *move to object to consideration of a question or motion.* This motion requires a second. It is not debatable. If it passes with a two-thirds vote, the matter is closed indefinitely. If a motion has been made but not discussed, someone, frequently the person who made the motion in the first place, may say, "I move that the motion to . . . be withdrawn." No one need second this motion, and no vote is required. But if the original motion has been discussed at all, the *motion to withdraw* must be seconded, voted upon, and passed by a majority vote.

closing the discussion

After a motion has been under discussion for some time, someone may think that those discussing the matter are repeating themselves or each other or wasting time. Someone may wish to bring the question to a vote before it loses some of its support. The person may say, "I move to close the debate." Someone must second this motion. Discussion of the motion must be allowed. And the *motion to close the debate* must pass by a two-thirds vote.

motions concerning parliamentary procedure

There are two motions that concern parliamentary procedure. Someone may *move to suspend a rule* of the organization. A two-thirds vote is required to pass such a suspension. Clauses of bylaws of the constitution of the organization cannot be suspended.

If someone thinks that a mistake is being made in the procedure with which a motion is being handled, this person makes a *motion on point of order.* The chairperson may accept or reject the point. No second, discussion, or vote is necessary, but the chairperson's ruling may be appealed.

The *motion to adjourn* must be considered and seconded whenever it is made, regardless of what business is already before the group.

Since only a majority vote is required to pass it and since it must be voted on when it is made, it should not be used as a means to close a discussion or prevent fair consideration of a problem. The *motion to fix the time* for the next meeting has priority over even the vote to adjourn.

Most organizations have their own methods for nominating officers and the procedures are specified in their bylaws. If they are not, a motion suggesting procedure is necessary. Nomination may be made by a committee, from the floor, or both. Nominations do not require a second. A motion to close nominations requires a two-thirds vote and should not·be used to restrict the rights of the members. A motion to reopen nominations requires only a majority vote.

The various types of motions are outlined for you in Figure 8-1. Reference to this chart will familiarize you with the types of motions, when each may be used, and what vote is necessary for passage.

figure 8-1   A simplified chart of parliamentary procedures

Principal Motions		
Type of Motion	*Comment*	*Vote to Pass*
Main Motion	Concerns principal business before the group; only one main motion may exist at a time	simple majority
Motion to Amend	Adds to or changes the main motion; must be voted before returning to main motion	simple majority
Motion to Refer	Refers a main motion to a committee or some other group for further study; must be referred to a definite group	simple majority
Subsidiary Motions		
Type of Motion	*Comment*	*Vote to Pass*
To Postpone	Postpones action on principal motion until another time; may postpone until a designated time or indefinitely, but must state which; may be discussed	simple majority

figure 8-1 Continued

Type of Motion	Comment	Vote to Pass
To Reconsider	Brings up for reconsideration a motion which has been postponed or referred; must be made by someone present when motion was postponed; may be discussed	simple majority
To Rescind	Rescinds a motion which has been postponed; used by someone not present when motion was postponed; may be discussed	simple majority
To Table	Postpones a principal motion indefinitely; may not be discussed	simple majority
To Object to Consideration	Objects to further discussion and voting on main motion; may not be discussed	two-thirds
To Withdraw (before discussion)	Withdraws a motion from any further action	no second; no vote; motion automatically withdrawn
To Withdraw (after discussion)	Withdraws a motion from further action; must be seconded	simple majority
To Close Debate	Ends discussion on a motion and calls for immediate vote; discussion allowed	two-thirds
To Suspend Rules	Suspends a rule temporarily, usually to get faster action; may not apply to bylaws	two-thirds
To Call Point of Order	Questions procedure of another member or of chairman	no vote; ruled on by chairman
To Adjourn	Adjourns the meeting; must be considered as soon as made	simple majority
To Fix Meeting Time	Sets time for next meeting; must be voted even before a motion to adjourn	simple majority

What attitude toward committee work and rules is helpful?

At first, all this discussion of motions and procedures may seem a bit complicated. If you reread it, however, and give the matter a little thought, you can see that most of the rules of parliamentary procedure are matters of common sense, courtesy, and justice. They are designed to ensure order and democracy. If you frequently serve as chairperson of committees or as an officer of an organization or if you are placed on the constitution committee of a new organization, you will find a book explaining parliamentary law in greater detail to be quite helpful.[1]

But don't allow natural timidity or awe of procedure to keep you from being an active, contributing member of the groups and organizations in your professional and personal life. Although you should not use your membership in such groups merely for your own personal advancement, you will find that if you sincerely try to make a real contribution when you are asked to serve on a committee, you will benefit both in your professional prosperity and in your personal satisfaction.

ASSIGNMENTS

I. Make arrangements to sit in on an actual committee meeting in your school, neighborhood, or city. You might receive permission to be a spectator at a departmental meeting at your school, you might attend a committee session at your church or at work, or you might visit a session of your city council's open meeting. Your purpose in attending the meeting is to be an observer of both proper and improper committee activities, of both proper and improper personal behavior. Be observant; take notes if necessary. Be prepared to discuss with your classmates what you have seen and heard. The following questions will guide your observations, but you will probably discover additional points of interest as well.

    1. Did the chairperson appear to be organized and in control of the session?
    2. Did the chairperson unfairly manipulate issues and speakers so that the "oppositon" had little chance to present its views?

[1] A very helpful book is *Sturgis Standard Code of Parliamentary Procedure,* by Alice Sturgis (New York: McGraw-Hill Book Company, 1966).

3. Was there evidence that the chairperson and committee members had done outside preparation for the meeting?
4. Was there a printed agenda for the session? If so, was it followed?
5. Were correct parliamentary procedures followed throughout the meeting?
6. Did you feel that anyone at the committee meeting was speaking on almost every issue just to hear himself or herself speak?
7. Did committee members treat those with opposing views fairly? Did they appear to listen attentively to the opposing arguments?

II. Most committees meet to solve a problem, and the solution to that problem is usually presented as a report to the individual or group that authorized the committee. The following assignments, done in order, will take you through the usual tasks of committee work.

1. Assume that your class is an organized body of some type and that it is presently involved in working toward the solution of some important problem. Elect one person from the class to function as chairperson. This person should be someone who has some definite leadership ability and who can devote some extra time to this special assignment.
2. The chairperson should lead the group in a discussion to select a topic. The following suggestions are given as guides, but perhaps you have a more pressing problem to suggest.
   a. The college library should be open longer hours.
   b. Students should not be required to take a general orientation course.
   c. The fee for the use of the Student Center should be lowered.
   d. The college should sponsor a book exchange at which students may trade texts between semesters.
   e. Some changes need to be made in the existing structure of the student government.
3. After you have selected a subject, your chairperson should conduct a group discussion aimed at identifying the specific problems involved. This discussion should also lead to the development of a list of persons or sources which should be contacted for information.
4. The chairperson should appoint subcommittees with responsibility to conduct interviews and research to gather needed information. These subcommittees will probably need to

meet, select their chairpersons, and plan the exact course of their business.

5. At a later meeting the chairperson should ask for reports from the various subcommittees. Conflicting evidence will probably be presented and will have to be discussed.

6. After sufficient discussion, someone should propose a motion which contains the statement of the problem and the proposed solutions. Vote on the major motion.

Solving Problems
Logically

What is a problem?
A solution? Logic?

You may define a *problem* as any unsatisfactory or undesirable condition that needs to be corrected. That undesirable condition is placing a hardship on someone or something—a person, persons, or the company. Problems in business might range from job discrimination to loss of profits, from cafeteria food to lack of proper supplies.

A *solution* is anything that remedies the unsatisfactory or undesirable condition without causing an even greater difficulty. The hardship caused is relieved: cafeteria food is improved; adequate boxes are provided for shipping, and so on. Often a solution may not be permanent or even conclusive; it may be just the best remedy for the time. At any rate, when you solve a problem, you do relieve the unwanted situation to the benefit of most people concerned.

Solving problems *logically* means using solid, reliable, and verifiable information and sound reasoning to arrive at your conclusions. You present your case clearly and forcefully, keeping emotion out of it. When you have finished your argument for or against something, your reader feels that you have "made sense" and that your solution to the problem "sounds good and reasonable." The most difficulty you will have in trying to arrive at solid, logical solutions will be keeping personal feelings or preconceived ideas out of the reasoning process. If you are asked to work on a problem that involves a close friend of yours, you might be tempted to glide over some facts that you might not disregard if the person were a stranger. In a case like that it would be very difficult for you to keep the objectivity needed for sound reasoning.

What is the first step in solving a problem logically?

The first step in solving a problem logically is to find the problem. This may sound silly since you don't go around looking for problems; normally the problems will find you soon enough. Moreover, you know what the immediate problem is since it was brought to your attention or to the attention of a committee on which you are serving. However, the immediate, referred problem may not be the real one. It may be merely a symptom of the real trouble. For example, suppose you are on a committee at your plant that is asked to investigate employee complaints about food in the cafeteria. Merely knowing that the food in the company cafeteria is bad is not knowing the real problem. Tasting the food may show that there is a problem, but you don't sit in the committee room and complain about the food and then take a vote asking the dietitian to improve it. In trying to arrive at a solution logically, you and the committee would have to gather information about the entire cafeteria operation. That information is evaluated, and the committee can then focus upon the real trouble and arrive at a satisfactory answer.

Some individuals on the committee—maybe you—must gather all the information relevant to the case, not just the facts that are easiest to find. You don't, for instance, go down to the kitchen and talk to the cook. You talk to others as well. You gather information from as many other sources as you can. You find out if the equipment in the kitchen is adequate and efficiently arranged. You may have to call in an expert to give an opinion. You may have to talk to both the dietitian and the personnel director to find out if there are enough people working in the cafeteria, if they are properly trained, if they work well together. If there are not enough employees, perhaps you can find out why. Maybe the budget for the cafeteria is too small to allow for enough workers. You might also investigate the wholesalers who sell to the kitchen. If the dietitian is buying a poor grade of produce or meat, find out why. As you investigate, you will uncover other questions that you must answer before you will have all the facts. But you must have all the facts before you or the committee is ready to evaluate them and come to a decision about the real problem.

What is the second step?

Recognizing the problem may be all that is necessary in order to find a solution. Usually, however, there is more than one solution to the problem, and the best solution is not necessarily the first one that comes to mind. All the possible solutions must be thought through and evaluated before the best one will be found. The second step, therefore, is to consider what all the possible solutions are.

Suppose, for instance, that you or the committee find that the problem is inadequately trained personnel, but they find also that the wage scale by which the workers are paid is good. One solution would be to fire all workers, or at least the poorest ones, and start over with a new group. Another solution might be to start an in-service training program with increases in pay as the employee advances through the training offered and demonstrates proficiency in the job. Perhaps the final solution will be a combination of these two: firing the poorest workers and beginning a program to train the others.

What is the third step?

After you have identified all the possible solutions, the third step is to evaluate them. It is important that you withhold judgment on any one solution until all the possible solutions have been identified and all the facts involved in each solution gathered. A solution that at first appears to be impractical or even ridiculous may, upon investigation with an open mind, prove to be the best.

Having an open mind is essential if you are to weigh all the possible solutions fairly. You shouldn't try to persuade yourself or anyone else that one solution is the best because it will be more convenient for you or because you happen to be the one who thought of it. You are looking for the best solution, not some solution that will further your own personal interests.

Examining the solutions may require as much gathering of information as was required to locate the problem. It may require more. But you won't be ready to evaluate the solutions until you have gathered that information so that you can consider all the facts.

What is the last step?

Solving a problem involves making changes. Changes take time, cost money, and create personnel problems. Some people don't want to change their work patterns; they prefer the status quo. Before you ask employees to change their habits and the employer to spend money, you must test your solution by these questions:

- Is the problem great enough to justify all that is involved in making the changes required by the solution?

- Will the solution work, and is it practical and realistic?
- Are you certain that the solution will not create more problems than it will solve?

In the light of these questions you may find that the ideal solution isn't the one that should be chosen at this time or that some compromise must be made. You may even find that although the problem can be solved, solving it is so costly or difficult that matters will just have to remain the way they are for a while.

Thus, you can see that problem solving involves four steps:

1. Locating the problem.
2. Locating all the possible solutions.
3. Evaluating the solutions.
4. Choosing a solution.

How do you evaluate the information you gather?

The first three steps require you to gather information. All four steps require you to evaluate that information. Statements of facts can be checked to see whether they are true or false; the truth of a statement is not a matter of opinion or judgment. However, evaluation of the facts after you have gathered them *is* an act of judgment. To make a judgment, you draw a conclusion from the facts. Facts do not vary, but judgments vary because the people who draw the inferences from the facts vary in the manner in which they examine the facts and draw their conclusions.

There are two ways of drawing inferences: by deduction or by induction. Therefore, we say there are two kinds of reasoning: deductive and inductive.

What is deductive reasoning?

When you use deductive reasoning, you are thinking by classes. That is, you are working from a general idea about everything in one particular class to a specific statement about one individual thing within that class. The term *deduction* itself comes from two Latin words meaning to lead from something to something (specifically, from a general statement to a conclusion).

Suppose that a friend calls and tells you that he or she has just bought a new car. The friend may talk about the car's color, engine size, or special equipment, but it would be unnecessary for you to be told that the car had four tires. You have seen other cars, and they all had four tires on the ground. It is natural, then, for you to assume that all cars have four tires. You assume your friend's car is a normal car; therefore it must also have four tires. You have reasoned from the general statement to a specialized application. The movement of your thought process can be grouped into a series of classes, each becoming more specialized. Class I includes all things with four tires. Within that class is a subclass, automobiles. And within that subclass is the specific car that your friend has purchased. A sketch of the deductive scheme looks like Figure 9-1. In each instance in the process, the smaller class must be capable of being fitted into the larger and being one of its component parts.

Perhaps you are an avid jogger. If so, you jog because you think it is good for your health. Other exercises are also good, but jogging is the specialized one you have selected. Your deductive process might be sketched to look like Figure 9-2. What you are saying, in effect, is that exercise is good for your health, jogging is a form of exercise, thus jogging is good for your health. You would have violated the deductive process of thinking by classes had you thought as follows: exercise is good for your health, eating is good for your health, thus eating is a nice form of exercise. Look at the sketch in Figure 9-3. Obviously eating cannot be fitted into the circle that includes exercises. Both are a part of Class I, "things good for your health," but each is a member of a separate division within Class I. In the first example about your friend's new car, you cannot begin by thinking about things that have four tires, examine Class II, and then decide that what your friend bought was a car *because* it has four tires. Your friend may actually have bought a lawn mower or even a toy wagon. Deductive reasoning

figure 9-1

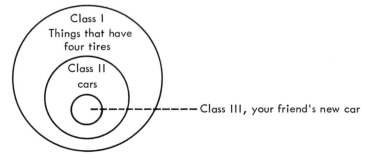

demands systematized organization of classes within their appropriate groupings.

Throughout each day you make evaluative statements about persons and things. Many of these are made on the basis of knowing traits of the general group and then applying those traits to your specific object. Be certain, as you make these decisions, that your classes are in their proper order.[1]

figure 9-2

What is inductive reasoning?

In deductive reasoning you apply a general statement to a specific case. To reason inductively, you reverse the process. You examine one specific case, several specific cases, or many specific cases to reach a conclusion. There are three kinds of inductive reasoning: reasoning to reach a generalization, reasoning from analogy, and reasoning by considering causal relationships.

figure 9-3

[1]The formula for deductive reasoning is the *syllogism,* but it is not the purpose of this text to review its complicated structure in detail. A good book on logic will provide further information if you are interested.

What is reasoning
to reach a generalization?

The deductive reasoning that you have just been considering begins with a *major premise*. A major premise is a general statement. In order for that general statement to be true, it must be universally true as it is stated or implied in the syllogism. Universally true major premises are not so plentiful as is sometimes supposed. It is easier to take the statement of a major premise as truth than to question it and check it out, especially if you have heard it repeated often enough. Consequently you may be ready to base your deductive reasoning on statements such as these: "All redheads have quick tempers," "All fat people are jolly," "People from (Peoria, Russia, the South, Addis Ababa) are (civic-minded, enemies, religious, ignorant, irresponsible)," or "People who (drink, smoke, wear beards, vote Republican, go to church) are (stupid, irresponsible, wicked, enemies, good)."

But your major premise was first arrived at by a type of inductive reasoning called *generalization*. Generalization is the process of examining a number of individual cases, finding that a certain fact is true of all of them, and stating that fact as a generally true conclusion. To make the perfect, absolutely infallible generalization, you would have to examine every case—everywhere in all time, past, present, and future. Obviously the opportunity to make such a generalization doesn't occur very often. Normally you will have to be satisfied with something less than a total count.

You will rely on examining a number of selected samples, drawing a conclusion, and then applying that conclusion to the whole. All political, sociological, and scientific examination is based on this method. The method has its limitations, however—limitations that you don't always recognize when you see figures and statistics. The percentages and *alls* and *mosts* that you hear the experts toss about so glibly are not based upon an actual count of all the doctors, decayed teeth, or upset stomachs under discussion. Such a total survey would be impractical if not completely impossible.

How do you test a
generalization?

If you are a careful researcher, you must observe two rules in selecting and examining your samples and in drawing your conclusion. First, you must examine a large enough sample. How large is large enough will depend upon what you are measuring. If a certain antibiotic placed on a dozen plates of bacteria under carefully controlled conditions kills all of the bacteria, the scientist might be justified in deciding that under those same conditions the antibiotic would always destroy the bacteria. The scientist would, however, need hundreds of tests before he or she could draw a conclusion about how the antibiotic would act on bacteria found in a human being. There is a greater difference in the physical makeup of people and the conditions under which they are living when they receive the antibiotic than there is between the plates in a carefully controlled environment. The researcher would need a larger sample when drawing a conclusion about people simply because there is more room for variation. You can safely say that the larger the number of variables or differences between the individual members of a class, the larger the number that must be examined before a generalization can be safely made.

The second thing that you must be careful about is that the samples you examine are typical of their group. If you talk about the percentage of children with no dental cavities and your test group included children who have never been permitted to eat sweets, you have an invalid sampling and your figures are unreliable.

If you examine a sample which is too small or which is not typical, you have made the fallacy known as *hasty generalization.*

Whenever you, in your research for information, draw a conclusion about any group of people or class of materials, or whenever you read or hear such a conclusion, you are probably not handling an absolute fact but a generalization. Test it by asking two questions:

- Did the researcher examine a sample which was large enough to allow for the variables in its class?
- Is the sample typical of its class?

What is an analogy?

A second type of inductive reasoning is *reasoning by analogy.* Analogy means similarity. When you reason by analogy, you infer that if two things are alike in several important ways they will also be alike in certain other respects.

The members of the committee that was looking for an answer to the problem of the poor food served in the company cafeteria all bring to that problem experiences they have had with similar problems elsewhere, and they may reason that because a solution worked for a similar problem, it will work for this one. One man, for instance, remembers that when he did KP duty in the army, he observed that the food was poor because many of the workers didn't care whether they did a good job or not. He suggests that probably these kitchen workers serve poor food because they don't care. Another man says that he hasn't eaten in the company cafeteria very much but that he complains about the food his wife serves at home whenever the meal contains food left over from another meal. He suggests that perhaps the dietitian is buying and cooking food in too large amounts and that warmed-over food or rehashed hash is what the employees are complaining about. One woman says that in a company where she worked once there was a similar problem which was solved by getting a new dietitian.

All these persons are reasoning by analogy. They all see similarities between the present problem and other problems they have met. They are wise to do so. Few problems are completely unique. Each experience you meet is in some ways like some other experience, and you reason that the manner in which you handled the earlier experience successfully will be equally effective this time. If you handle this experience the same way you did the last one and the method doesn't work, you compare the two experiences to see how they are different as well as how they are alike.

How do you test an analogy?

To a baby, the dissimilarities between the objects that are good to eat and the objects that are not good to eat are not as evident as the similarities. But the baby is learning what to eat and what not to eat by reasoning by analogy. He or she tests the inferences in analogies with the same question that the committee members will ask in testing their analogies:

> Are the two things (marbles and candy, household bleach and milk) similar in the characteristics that are important for this analogy?

While no situation is unique, no two situations are exactly alike either. In other words, there are no perfect analogies. The first committee member must remember that the men on KP might have lacked interest in their work because they had drawn KP duty as punishment, whereas the cafeteria workers can quit and get other jobs if they dislike kitchen work. The second committee member should investigate to find out if the cafeteria serves leftover food. The situation in the cafeteria and the situation at his home might be similar in that food is bad in both places, but quite dissimilar in the way it is bad. The situation the woman describes is analogous only if the fault for bad food in this cafeteria lies with the dietitian, as it did at the other company cafeteria.

Finding a solution for a problem by analogy is a very useful method, but it is not perfect. You should always test the analogy to be sure that the two cases are analogous in the ways that matter in this situation. To make such a test you will have to gather information and use some of the other kinds of reasoning.

What are the kinds of causal relations?

Reasoning according to *causal relations* is another very useful kind of inductive reasoning. In this type of reasoning you relate two events to see if one caused the other. In solving problems you might reason by considering causal relations in three kinds of problems:

1. Two conditions exist that suggest that one may in some way be responsible for the other, and you need to find out if they are so related:

    You pushed the button of the dashboard, and the glass cover fell off.

    There is a $5,347 error in last month's audit; and last Monday the bookkeeper, who makes $125 a week, traded in his ten-year-old jalopy on a new luxury car.

    The cafeteria food is poor, and the equipment for the kitchen was bought in 1955.

2. A condition exists, and you need to find out what caused it. Here you know the result or effect, and you are trying to find the cause. You are reasoning from effect to cause:

    Mr. Sparks is lying dead on the floor in front of his open library wall safe. What killed him?

    The electricity is off in the cafeteria's refrigeration locker. What is wrong?

    There is a bottleneck in the shipping department. What is responsible for it?

3. A condition exists and you need to know what will be the probable result. Here you know the cause, but you are trying to find the result or effect. You are reasoning from cause to effect:

    Old Moneybags is dead. Will his step-nephew inherit his money?

    The electricity is off in the cafeteria's refrigeration locker. Will the food spoil before the current can be restored?

    There is a bottleneck in the shipping department. Will the special government order go out in time?

Sometimes you will find a whole chain of causes and effects so that there will be several steps in your reasoning. An effect of one cause becomes a cause of another effect and so on until you have a long line of such causes and effects:

Bill Dennis overslept last Monday;
Therefore he was late leaving for work;
Therefore he ran a red light on the way to work;
Therefore his car was hit by a truck at the intersection;
Therefore he was injured;
Therefore he is in the hospital;
Therefore he has not worked in the shipping department this week;
Therefore there is a bottleneck in the shipping department;
Therefore the special government order probably won't go out on time.

A *sufficient cause* is one which can produce an effect without the aid of any other factors. You may find more than one sufficient cause operating at the same time. You may also find several causes, none of which is sufficient when found alone, but which can produce the effect when they occur together. In either case, you could express this relationship with the following equation:

$$A_1 + A_2 + A_3 + A_4 \rightarrow B$$

You can test your reasoning concerning causal relationships by asking a few questions:

1. Is it possible or even probable that the cause you are considering could produce this effect unaided?
2. Could the cause you are considering be one of several causes which, operating at the same time, could produce this effect?
3. Does some condition exist which could alter the relationship that you would normally expect between the causes and effects which you are considering?

Are the kinds of reasoning usually found alone or in combination?

Although there are two kinds of reasoning—deductive and inductive—and three kinds of inductive reasoning—generalization, analogy, and causal relation—you will not often employ any of these methods alone. You might make a survey from which you make a generalization. Then you might use this generalization as a basis for your deductive reasoning. Generalization is frequently used in reasoning from cause to effect or from effect to cause. When you test your causal reasoning to see if the cause you are considering could be responsible for the effect in question, you will weigh the possibility on the basis of past experience. If you have a large number of experiences from which you have drawn the conclusion that a certain cause could produce a certain effect, you will probably form a generalization. If your experience has been more limited, you will probably use analogy as the basis for judging the relationship.

But whatever kinds of reasoning you use, you should be certain that you have gathered all the facts. Then as you organize those facts to arrive at your conclusions, you should test each step of your reasoning with the appropriate questions.

ASSIGNMENTS

I. Following the format of the sketches in this chapter, use circles to structure the deductive reasoning process suggested in the following examples:
    1. All part-time personnel will get a raise. George is working part-time. George will get a raise.
    2. All merchandise bought during the January clearance cannot be returned. I cannot return the desk pad I bought on sale in January.
    3. I am depressed because I have to work overtime, and you know that working overtime always depresses me.
    4. Only authorized personnel are allowed to use company stationery. I guess I cannot use the company's stationery.

II. Find the faulty deductive reasoning process in the following examples:
    1. All executives are well-prepared for their jobs. Katherine is always well prepared. Katherine is an executive.
    2. All good workers are well paid. John is well paid. John is a good worker.

III. You are constantly reasoning by analogy, and sometimes you are guilty of setting up a false analogy. Point out the false analogy in the following examples and prepare to discuss in class:
    1. Why shouldn't the telephone company get a 4.7 percent rate increase this year? The gas company got a 5 percent rate increase last year.
    2. I don't know why the company doesn't hire more people for the billing department. They hired three last week in shipping and two in the secretarial pool. If they can afford to hire in those departments, then they can afford to hire in billing.
    3. Both participating in and watching sports can teach you much about the game of life.

4. Who needs to study anyway. Look at great men like Einstein and Faulkner. They both failed school.

5. Running an office is just like running the government. If everyone knows his or her place, all will run like clockwork.

IV. List three or four specific instances where you have reasoned by analogy and briefly state why the analogy was or was not a good one.

V. Qualifying words like *some, few, all, only, most,* and *almost* are important to generalizations. Look at a recent newspaper or issue of a popular magazine and find examples in which the use of a qualifier makes a generalization acceptable. Find examples, too, in which the generalization is either invalid or questionable because no qualifier is used. Clip these examples, tape them to a full-sized sheet of paper, and bring them to class. (*Hint:* Advertisements and commercials are a good place to start.)

VI. A danger in causal reasoning is the assumption that one cause alone is responsible for one effect. Indicate an incident where you have been guilty of falsely reasoning that *A* alone caused *B*. Show that *B* was really caused by numerous factors, and list them. Set up an equation similar to the following.

$$A_1 + A_2 + A_3 + A_4 \rightarrow B$$

Avoiding
Common Fallacies

What is a fallacy?

Not all information that you might have for solving a problem is good information, and not even all good information is used properly. When you combine or present information in such a way that an incorrect conclusion is reached, you have committed an error in reasoning or a *fallacy.* Such reasoning is called *fallacious reasoning.*

Sometimes fallacies are made intentionally by someone who is trying to manipulate others either through false information or through the improper use of valid information. More often than not, though, fallacies are made unintentionally. Some fallacies, particularly those committed by clever manipulaters, may be very subtle and therefore difficult to detect. In the hands of less experienced users, fallacies are usually more easily recognized. It is important that you learn to recognize some of the most frequently used fallacies so that you can avoid being misled by someone else's fallacious argument and, also, so that you can evaluate intelligently the information that you use in your own arguments.

In the last chapter you learned that the first three steps in solving a problem require you to gather information. Some of this information you will find is contradictory. Some will be hard for you to believe. Some will be obviously untrue. Some, after careful study and research, you will find to be only partly true. You need to know how to evaluate this information so that you won't be fooled either by those who deliberately want to fool you or by those who have been fooled themselves. The reports that you bring to committees, give to your superior, or pass on to clients will be of value only if you are able to examine your material and identify and remove any information or conclusions that are false or misleading.

What are the most common fallacies?

Of the many fallacies listed in logic textbooks, the most common ones—those most often used by propagandists and those which you might be inadvertently guilty of yourself—are listed here:

Hasty Generalization
Name Calling
Glittering Generalities
Plain Folks
Bandwagon
Card Stacking
Poisoning the Well
Red Herring
Transfer
Testimonials

What is the hasty generalization fallacy?

As you will remember from what was said in the chapter on problem solving, the ability to make generalities about whole classes of objects is essential if you are to deal efficiently with the individual sample. The shoemaker labors under the assumption that most people have two feet; the bricklayer, that mortar made by a given formula will hold most bricks together; and the department store manager, that most people will buy an assortment of toys, knickknacks, and baubles at Christmas time. But the *hasty generalization,* the generalization which is made before a large enough sample has been examined carefully and objectively, causes you to deal with the individual too quickly; you reach a conclusion about the individual sample without thinking about it. This fallacy, which was described at length in the previous chapter, can be made honestly by the careless or untrained researcher. But it can also be made honestly by the careless or untrained researcher. But it can also be made deliberately by the propagandist who hopes you will accept the concept of "all" without questioning the means by which he or she reached such a generalization.

What is the name calling fallacy?

Sometimes you draw a hasty conclusion because you have reacted automatically and emotionally. Feeling is easier to do than thinking, and feeling is even easier to do when you have been patterned or conditioned to feel a certain way in response to certain symbols or labels. George Orwell's book *1984* depicts a society which set aside a period of time each day known as the "Two Minutes Hate." Each day the workers gathered together before a screen on which were flashed pictures and words pertaining to the enemy of their country. The group responded with a wild demonstration of hate which lasted for two minutes. The enemy changed from time to time, but the reaction remained the same. The viewers didn't stop to analyze the pictures or the words or to remember that this year's enemy was last year's ally. They were conditioned to respond with hate to the verbal symbols and they responded according to that pattern.

The only difference between the "Two Minutes Hate" in *1984* and your set responses to certain words is that the people in the book had a warning that they were expected to respond in a particular way to certain words. Propagandists, advertisers—and even you when you aren't thinking—use certain words and labels to get expected responses. The labels change, but the response remains the same. You hate what you in your generation have been taught to hate, and you identify it easily and quickly by its label. This propaganda device is called *name calling.*

During the Victorian period any word suggesting that people were created male and female was labeled immoral, and people who used such words were regarded as lusty, sinful people. The emotional reaction against such words was so strong that the taboo was extended to include any words that referred to human anatomy. Thus women had *bosoms* rather than *breasts* and *limbs* rather than *legs;* even the parlor table wore a long skirt to cover its offensive appendages lest some lecherous male in the presence of both table and lady should be reminded that ladies, like tables, had legs.[1]

In wartime, emotions must be stirred if citizens are to enlist, buy war bonds, face personal inconvenience, and support the national cause. During World War I feelings against the enemy were transferred to any item or word that was Germanic in origin. The names of streets were changed, men who had inherited German names found it

[1]Henry Louis Menken, *The American Language* (New York: Alfred A. Knopf, Inc., 1960) II, 650.

154

difficult to get jobs, and it was unpatriotic to call wieners and sauerkraut anything but Hot Dogs and Liberty Cabbage. In World War II the label *Nazi* suggested not only the enemy but the enemy's concentration camps, its totalitarian denial of human rights and liberty, and its torture chambers, gas showers, and crematory ovens.

During the McCarthy Senate investigation of un-American activities in the 1950's the labels *Red* and *Communist* could keep an individual from getting a job, cause those so accused to lose a job already held, and alienate friends and voters. Labels are always used in political campaigns, and the reaction to the labels varies according to a person's political philosophy. Some labels that are used today to brand candidates and ideas are *reactionary, right wing, left wing, radical, conservative, labor, capitalist, racist,* and *rebel.*

How can you detect the name calling fallacy?

Propagandists engage in name calling because they know that most people, without thinking, make an immediate emotional connection between the label and a whole set of distasteful ideas. To those who have been conditioned to make the connection, the labeled individual or idea stands accused and found guilty of all the unpleasantness that the label implies. Because the accusation is implied rather than spoken, the person so labeled has no opportunity to deny it. The propagandist wants people to react without thinking, so they can be manipulated into acting as he or she wants them to act. Unless you want to be a puppet who moves whenever some clever name caller pulls verbal strings, you should learn to spot the labels that are used. When you meet such a label, stop and analyze the situation. Ask two questions:

1. What does the label really mean, apart from the suggestions that popular opinion has taught you to attach to it?
2. Is the label in either its real sense or in its popular enemy-branding sense important or correct?

What is the glittering generalities fallacy?

Just as labels can be used to signal that certain people and ideas should be avoided, they can also be used to secure approval for people and ideas. In either case, they cause people to act hastily without proper evaluation of the situation.

Words that are used to secure blanket, automatic approval are called *virtue words.* To use them in place of careful reasoning and analysis is to commit the fallacy of *glittering generalities.* Virtue words are not so much subject to fads and temporary conditions as are the labels used in the propaganda device of name calling. Americans are generally in favor of patriotism, liberty, God, motherhood, the girl next door, and apple pie, and they can be depended upon to execute whatever action is called for in honor of these sacred institutions. Office seekers, commencement speakers, and dedicators of park statuary can string together terms like *noble, forefathers, progress, achievement, this modern age, our homes, the man of tomorrow,* and *the common man* for thirty minutes and be certain to be rewarded with approval and applause. Such words are calculated to be translated from the notes of the speaker into desirable action by the hearers without any mental activity on the part of either. Parrots can learn to say such words; dogs can learn to roll over at command; and Americans will stand, cheer, die, or vote for anything draped in a flag, topped by a cross, or suggested in the name of Dear Old Ivy.

How do you detect the glittering generalities fallacy?

The questions that you ask when you hear a virtue word and feel your eyes blinded by a glittering generality are the same as you ask when you spot an enemy-branding label:

1. What does this label really mean?
2. Does it have any importance here?

What is the plain folks fallacy?

The propagandist uses one particular group of virtue words so well that they deserve a separate heading of their own, *plain folks.* The labels of "plain folks" are implied as often as they are stated. Americans favor people who use simple language, even make a grammatical error now and then; who come from poor but honest, hard-working parents; and who eat beans and potatoes for supper, fried chicken on Sunday, and hot dogs and hamburgers on picnics and at baseball games. These people are just plain folks like you and me. You can trust them. They understand you. They won't try to put something over on you like those people who use big words with a stilted accent and order food from a French menu; people who don't know what it is to work for a living; people, in short, who aren't like you and me.

Americans honor the hometown boy or girl who made good, the dime store clerk who became a movie star, and the little boy who grew up in a log cabin and became President. The poor person's success is part of the American tradition, one with which everybody identifies. So no one admits to being lower class or upper class in America today. We fall into the lower-middle income bracket, the upper-middle, or the middle-middle.

How do you detect the plain folks fallacy?

When you meet an appeal on behalf of a person or idea that is dressed even slightly in words or symbols that remind you that this candidate deserves your support because he or she is just an ordinary person, ask yourself two questions:

1. Is the plain folks label sincere?
2. Would the individual or idea have your approval without the plain folks label?

What is the bandwagon fallacy?

The ordinary American favors a leader who is "a representative of the common people" because it is easy to identify with such a person's success. This individual has risen through difficulties to success, and his or her rise encourages the voters to believe that they could do the same if they wanted to. Nobody, however, wants to identify with a failure. The propagandist appeals to this natural desire to be a winner when he or she invites you to hop on *the bandwagon* and go along with the crowd.

The bandwagon fallacy appeals also to another basic human desire, the desire to belong, to be one of the group. The person who disagrees with the crowd stands alone and is lonely. Few have the courage to be lonely. You feel safe when you are part of the crowd, when you vote with the majority party, attend the largest church, belong to the most popular club, watch the television show with the highest ratings, brush your teeth with the tooth paste preferred by nine out of ten, and wear your skirts and hair at the length that is in style.

The bandwagon device is used to encourage you to take a certain action because "Everybody's doing it." Thus it is natural that the propagandist using this device sees you not as an individual with individual tastes and opinions but as a member of groups that already exist for other purposes. As a member of an organized group, you have characteristics and interests in common with other members, you have a loyalty to your group and its interest, and you have a strong desire to act in accordance with other members of your group so that you can maintain your membership and acceptance by that group.

So the propagandist appeals to you as a student or teacher; as a Catholic, Protestant, or Jew; as a black or white; as an American; as a member of a party, profession, or union; but never as a member of the human race. The propagandist flatters you that members of your group are superior and then arouses your prejudices, your hatreds, and your fears against those who do not belong to your group. They must remain inferior if you are able to remain superior. Since such superiority lies with the group that is in power and thus can designate which group is superior, you are invited to vote for the candidate who is sure to win, to attend the show that everybody is talking about, to read the book that is on the best-seller list, and to listen to the song that is in the "top ten."

What is the card stacking fallacy?

The propagandist who uses *card stacking,* he stacks the cards in favor of the idea, product, or person the propagandist is trying to sell. He or she may be satisfied with overemphasis of the facts that favor his or her side and underemphasis of those on the other side, or may distort the evidence completely, using lies and censorship of truth to make sure that the picture the public sees is one that will make it seem unreasonable for anyone to favor the opposite cause.

What is the poisoning the well fallacy?

The fallacy of *poisoning the well* is one form of card stacking. The propagandist using this device states a proposition in such a way that the listener takes sides against the opposition without thinking. When the businessman is favored in an election because he is not "a dirty politician," when you are asked to vote against a bill that will "allow gambling and syndicated vice in your fair city," or when you are asked to buy a product because it will protect you from upset stomachs, heel marks on your kitchen linoleum, or bad breath in dogs, the propagandist is poisoning the well by the subtle assumptions that politics and dishonesty go together, that syndicated vice must accompany legalized gambling, and that we lie awake at night worrying about our digestive systems, kitchen linoleum, and dog's breath.

What is the red herring fallacy?

The *red herring* fallacy is the introduction of information that really is not relevant to the question at hand but which the propagandist hopes will catch your attention so completely that you will miss the real issues. The propagandist tells you that the other candidate is divorced, is wealthy, or belongs to some unpopular church. He or she reminds you that his or her product is "imported." The propagandist hopes that you will be so distracted by this startling but wholly irrelevant information that you won't get around to asking the very logical question, "So what?"

What is the transfer fallacy?

The propagandist who uses the *transfer* fallacy relates the person or item being promoted to something which already has your respect or favor. An advertisement might picture a handsome young man offering his girlfriend a cigarette or admiring her hair color; the hope is that you will assume that you might buy romance in the advertiser's package. Before stricter laws made such presentations illegal, many television advertisements for medicines were presented by kindly persons in white smocks, similar to those doctors wear. Politicians like to be photographed in front of a church so viewers will think they are religious.

The transfer fallacy can also be used against an individual or idea. The "enemy" may be shown leaving a controversial political meeting or sitting in a local bar drinking. You may be told through transfer that wearing a certain brand of cologne will not get you a goodnight kiss.

What is the testimonial fallacy?

The *testimonial* fallacy is really an abuse of a legitimate form of evidence. This is an age of specialization in an ever-increasing number of highly technical fields. You will never have the training or the time to become well-informed in all the many areas that are related to your professional and private life. You must rely upon authorities who have the education and experience to give you the information you need about their particular fields. You should, however, learn how to evaluate the authority of the individual who gives the information so that what he or she says won't influence you more than it should. When you are faced with disagreement between two authorities, you should be even more careful to examine their backgrounds, qualifications, reputations in their fields, and personal prejudices.

How do you evaluate a testimonial?

When information comes to you from one who claims to speak as an authority, you should examine that authority by asking two questions:

1. What is the background of education and experience upon which this person is basing his information or judgment?
2. Will your acceptance of this person's information or judgment benefit the person in any way?

If you make the effort to learn the identity and background of the individual who is offered as an authority, you will usually place the proper emphasis upon the person's testimony. The propagandist, however, doesn't want you to make such an effort but hopes you will be so impressed by the importance of the celebrities used to endorse the particular ideas and products that you won't ask whether these celebrities qualify as authorities on the question at hand. Sometimes an individual who has gained prominence and fame in one field will express an opinion in another area in which he or she is no more an authority than any other person on the street. The nuclear physicist has a right to an opinion on religion, the war hero to his or her own ideas about American education, and the famous surgeon to a personal attitude toward our foreign policy. The propagandist is trying to mislead you when he or she expects you to accept these ideas, opinions, and attitudes as being important because of the people who hold them. Frequently such people have spoken as private individuals with no thought of having their personal ideas accepted as authoritative, but the propagandist has used the words and the prominence of the speaker to support a prejudiced cause.

Frequently, however, the celebrity has been paid directly or indirectly to endorse the product or idea. Dazzled by a famous athlete, you fail to wonder why this person is a better judge of the taste of a brand of orange juice, diet beverage, or cigarettes than ordinary mortals.

Sometimes you even accept anonymous testimonials: "authorities have found," "a leading laboratory has proved," and "a prominent health journal has published the facts." In the face of such convincing proof, who are you to quibble about identity? You dose yourself with the approved pain killer, scrub your bathroom with the acceptable disinfectant, and start your days with the recognized corn flakes, serene in the knowledge that every move in your daily routine bears the stamp of the Better Businessman's Bureau, the Good Housekeeping Institute Seal of Approval, and the blessing of the National Council of Dental Hygiene.

A famous authority and prominent American writer once said that there is no limit to how far a person will go to escape thinking. Propaganda plays such a prominent part in the modern world that you need not go very far to find such an escape. But if you want to reach your professional and personal goals, down the roadway of sound judgment, you will learn to recognize the propaganda escape hatch as the trap that it is—so say nine out of ten leading propaganda detection experts.

ASSIGNMENTS

I. Explain briefly the fallacious reasoning in each of the following:
    1. Buying a foreign car is un-American.
    2. That's just the kind of remark a hippie would make. What can you expect from those long-haired weirdos?
    3. I ate at Lim's Restaurant yesterday and got sick. That's really a bad place to eat.
    4. I didn't do well in high school English because the instructor didn't like me.
    5. You just can't tell Jack anything.
    6. What's good for General Bullmoose is good for the U.S.A.
    7. United Star Life Insurance . . . people working for people.
    8. I would never buy anything from that store. You know their son was arrested on a drug charge last week?
    9. You're only twelve years old. What do you know?
    10. I would never own a Mercedes. You know, it was Hitler's personal car.
    11. Well it's got to be good. I saw it advertised on television.
    12. The entire family works extremely hard all week, and then they spend all day Sunday at church. I'm going to buy my stereo from their store because I know they wouldn't cheat anybody.
II. An interesting source for arguments, many of them fallacious, is

the local newspaper. Begin reading letters to the editor and editorials in your local paper. Study ideas set forth by popular syndicated columnists. Bring clippings of your material to class and be prepared to discuss and label any fallacies.

III. Advertisers often use the propaganda devices described in this chapter to sell their products. Look through several recent magazines and find at least ten advertisements that use these devices. Clip these and paste each on an individual sheet of paper. Mark the words and items in the pictures that are propaganda and label the device. Bring your clippings to class for discussion.

Collecting Data

What are the sources for collecting data?

As you have seen, to locate a problem and investigate all the possible solutions, you must gather all the related information you can. You can gather information from four sources: on-the-spot observation, personal interviews, public speeches, and written material. Sometimes you may need to use only one of these methods, but if you are a thorough worker, you will usually gather information from many sources. Some people can't see the facts even when they are right under their noses; but the person who locates the real problems and finds the best solutions is the person who leaves no source of information unexamined.

How do you gather information on the spot?

How you will conduct on-the-spot observation depends upon the kind of problem you are considering. The medical researcher observes the action of bacteria, viruses, drugs, and vaccines on the specimens in the laboratory. The social scientist studies the conditions in an area and the actions of its inhabitants. The anthropologist lives in a primitive village and observes the customs of the natives. The motion study expert follows the progress of a product through a factory and notes the movements of the workers involved in the manufacturing process. But regardless of the methods used by researchers, these individuals all have three habits in common: (1) They are alert to all that occurs. (2) They keep an open, objective mind; they draw no conclusions until

164

they have gathered all the facts, and they don't try to arrange the facts to lead to a desired conclusion. (3) As they observe, they take careful and complete notes. They don't depend upon their memories. They know that nobody can remember everything and that their personal biases may cause them to forget something because they don't want to remember it or because they thought at the time it was unimportant. If their notes are complete, later when they reread them, they may see a relationship between the facts that they didn't see at the time.

How do you gather information from an expert?

If you talk to people to gather information from them, you should exercise the same caution you would in on-the-spot observation. Don't overlook anyone who might have information or a valid opinion. Sometimes you will gather information from an individual during an informal chat. At other times the person is a stranger to you, has a tight schedule, or is generally unavailable. When any of these conditions exist, you should make an appointment for a more formal interview.

What preparations should you make for an interview?

If you interview such an expert, you should make some preparations before you arrange the meeting. Read all the information available on the subject. Naturally, you should take notes. It may be that you will learn everything you want to know in this way. If not, you will have the basic information and can concentrate when you talk with the expert on the data which he or she has that you could not find anywhere else. Never take the time of an expert until you try to get information that is freely available elsewhere.

If you don't know the individual, find out his or her particular qualifications and prejudices. It may be that the person you planned to ask for information is really qualified in a slightly different field and is not the best person to approach for what you want to know. If you find that the individual is able to help you, surveying his or her background before you meet will enable you to know how to phrase your questions in a diplomatic way and how to evaluate answers. Some careful researchers include even the hobbies and avocational interests of the person to be interviewed in their preparation. They believe that finding any common interest with the expert may result in better conversation and, thereby, a more worthwhile interview.

How do you arrange to interview someone?

When you have decided that a particular expert has information you need and can't obtain from published material, call for an interview. Introduce yourself; give your company, the project on which you are working, and your qualifications for doing so. It may be that you can find out all you need to know in a telephone conversation.

A face-to-face interview is necessary when the information is complicated, when you will need to be shown something or to show something, or when there is a possibility that the person won't want to release the information to you. When any of these circumstances exist, you will, of course, ask for an appointment. Don't quibble over time. If at all possible, take the hour offered you, making note of whatever time limits are set. Unless the matter is confidential or there is some possibility that your party may not want to help you, be certain that he or she understands ahead of time what you wish to know. The interviewee may save time by gathering certain facts or papers before your arrival.

Sometimes it is better to write for an interview. If there is a possibility that the person won't see you, or if you need to establish your qualifications at any length, it may be better to write, stating the nature of your investigation and mentioning other similar work you have done.

Joe Quickly and Anne K. Pable were separately engaged in research that required them to examine some rare manuscripts that were in the possession of Dr. Centrik. Joe wrote a pleasant letter identifying himself and his project and asking to see the manuscripts. He received no answer at all. Anne wrote, enclosing the unfinished typescript of the section that related to Dr. Centrik's manuscripts, an explanation of why she needed to see the collection, and a copy of an article she had published on a similar project. Dr. Centrik replied immediately, offering Anne the use of his library and his time and enclosing a copy of an article he had written on a related subject.

How do you plan an interview?

After you have made your appointment, you will still have some preparations to make. Decide exactly what questions you should ask in order to find out what you need to know. Memorize the questions. Think about all you know about the person and about the subject. If you try to plan now for the possible turns the interview might take, you will be able to use the time of the interview better.

You should arrive for your interview exactly on time or perhaps five minutes early. If you are meeting at an office and you have to wait, use the time to observe your surroundings. Pictures, diplomas, maps, or charts on the wall, the furnishings of the room, books and magazines on the tables and shelves, and the general atmosphere of the waiting room may give you some clue to the person's personality that will help you to communicate more effectively.

How do you conduct an interview?

When you meet, it isn't necessary to engage in social pleasantries such as commenting on the weather or admiring the view of the trees from the office window. The individual you are interviewing is probably busy and is accustomed to attacking problems directly. Of course, if he or she begins a conversation about something else, try to engage yourself readily in that topic. Sometimes a person being interviewed likes to use this tactic for a few minutes in order to determine some important facts about the other person.

The interviewee can help you better if you briefly state what you are doing, what general or specific information you need, and how you expect to use it. Then you can use your questions to get the necessary information you wish. Although you have planned your questions and memorized them, you need not phrase them exactly as you planned. Try to work them into your conversation easily and gracefully. As a carry-over from their school days, many people are made uncomfortable by a steady stream of formal questions.

The interviewee may answer many of your questions without your asking them directly. Perhaps, in spite of your careful forethought, he or she will open up areas that are entirely new to you. You may find this new information vital. On the other hand, it may merely be a distraction from what you need to know. You will have to judge hastily whether to allow the person to continue talking about this new area or to try to bring the conversation gently and politely back to the problem.

How do you take notes?

If the information is too detailed to remember, ask if you may take notes. Even if the interviewee agrees, he or she may be disturbed if you write constantly. Therefore, you should write as inconspicuously as possible, keeping your eyes on the person's face as much as possible. Certainly you won't try to take dictation. When you begin to write, the interviewee may begin to talk less freely. If this happens, you will have to stop taking down any but the most difficult material. More than likely, however, he or she will know that you need to be accurate and will be glad to help you get the facts straight. If any of the information is so complicated that you are afraid you didn't record it accurately, ask if you may read it aloud to check for accuracy. Your notes should be dated and documented with the name of the person interviewed, his or her title or position, and the place in which you conducted the interview.

How do you close the interview?

When you have taken as much of the person's time as you were promised, bring the interview to a close, thank the person for his or her time, and leave. If the secretary didn't tell you how much time you could take, judge how busy the interviewee is from the number of people waiting for appointments and the number of phone calls and interruptions, and limit your interview accordingly. Even if the interviewee seems relaxed and unhurried, don't stay more than half an hour unless the interviewee personally urges you to stay. Even if this happens, you still shouldn't stay much longer.

What do you do with your notes after the interview?

Immediately after the interview you should go over your notes, completing by memory any information which seems fragmentary. As soon as possible, work your notes up into the form in which you will use them for your report or project. You should be very careful in this writing to keep the meaning and purpose of the person's remarks accurate. If you are writing an article in which you use the person's name and quote either directly or indirectly, you may wish to send the person a copy for approval before you submit your article for publication. File the notes from the interview with the notes which you took during your preliminary reading.

ASSIGNMENTS

    I.   In Chapter 1 you were asked to gather information about your occupational area by visiting with someone presently employed at such a job. For that first interview you were given some general questions to guide you, but these questions were related more to the importance of communication skills than to the more detailed aspects of the work itself.

You should now conduct another interview with a different person employed in your occupational area. This time you should find out as much as possible about the exact nature of the jobs performed, specific working conditions, and opportunities for advancement. If some other subject for an interview has come out of your committee work or your preparation for your formal report, you may want to use this assignment to gather material relevant to that subject. The following assignments are directly connected with this second interview:

1. Prepare a set of at least twenty questions that you want answered. Remember, though, that a good interview is much more than just a question and answer session.
2. After your interview, sit down with your own question sheet and see if you can answer all of your questions.

II. Think of some problem-related situation on campus. Perhaps students want the lunchroom opened earlier; maybe the book store is not carrying an appealing list of casual books for reading. Identify a person on campus who should be able to give you some valid information regarding the problem, and make an appointment to see that individual. Before your interview, prepare a list of approximately twenty questions that you want answered. After your interview, see if you can answer all of your questions. Remember, your purpose is to get information relative to your interviewee's knowledge of the problem and his or her attitude toward it.

III. Select the information you gather in either Assignment I or II above, and organize the material into a carefully unified 500-word theme.

Gathering
Information at Seminars
And Meetings

Why are meetings a valuable source of information?

When you begin to work at your chosen job, there will inevitably be meetings for you to attend. You may be asked to attend training sessions or workshops sponsored by the company for which you work, and you may have the opportunity to attend seminars or conventions sponsored by the professional or vocational organization of which you are a member. These types of gatherings will offer you one of the best possible ways for keeping up with latest developments in your chosen field. The information gained at these meetings is frequently well in advance of what you might be able to get from other sources.

The world moves so fast that you can't keep up with the latest knowledge in any given field if you rely entirely upon books and other published material. By the time a new machine or product or process has been researched, reported, and published in a book and that book has been purchased by the library, accessioned, and made available on the shelves for examination, your alert competitor may already have made use of the new information, having learned about it months earlier by attending a meeting.

Not only is the information gained at meetings often more up to date than that found elsewhere, but it may also be more directly related to your needs. Other companies have faced problems similar to those your company faces, and they have found solutions. As you hear them discuss these solutions, you may find some of the answers you are seeking. Sometimes your company will send you to a meeting in order to find the answer to a specific problem. Sometimes you will go just to learn about the most recent developments in your field. What you learn at a meeting may be of no immediate use to you, but sometime in the future what you have learned may become important. In none of these cases will you want to depend upon your memory. You may need to recall what you have learned to make a report to some individual, committee, or larger group. At other times you need the information for your own immediate use in a large report or paper. You will also want to record information to keep in reserve for future, undefined use. For all these purposes you will want to know how to gather the most useful information in the most efficient way.

What preparation should you make before attending a meeting?

If you want to gather useful information efficiently, you must prepare for the occasion. Usually you know something about a meeting before it is held. When the organization to which you belong holds its annual meeting, you will receive a brochure listing the speakers, their topics, and the time for their addresses. If the meeting is local, your newspaper will have an article announcing it. You will read all this material carefully; but you shouldn't stop there. If the meeting is important enough for you to attend and for your company to finance, you will want to go prepared to get the maximum benefit.

After you have studied the program and selected those meetings which you think will be the most valuable to you, you should try to learn as much as you can about the speakers and their subjects. All the material that you read before you attend a meeting should be examined with two purposes in mind: (1) to give you the background you need in order to understand and benefit from the material which will be presented; (2) to allow you to evaluate what you hear with an informed and unbiased mind.

If you are attending a training session sponsored by your company, think seriously about how that session may improve your worth to your employer. What are you expected to gain from attending? What do you know about the topic already? What questions do you hope will be answered for you by the speech or demonstration? Will you be expected to share the information that you gather with employees who work with you in your department? Go to the meeting with some definite objectives in mind.

Apply some of the same principles if you are attending a seminar or convention. If you have already learned as much about the subject to be discussed as you can, you should be able to add to that general knowledge the finer, less well-known points that the speaker may give you. Sometimes, unfortunately, the speech will be little more than a rehashing of the information you have already gathered. Sometimes you can foresee this kind of performance and use your time more valuably by attending some other meeting held at the same time, by meeting some speaker who has especially interested you, or by visiting some of the exhibits. If the speaker is an active, alert individual who is still making real contributions in his or her field, and not some old-timer who has been asked to speak because of a twenty-year-old reputation, he or she will probably have some information beyond what you have been able to learn. And you will be able to make better use of it if you have taken the trouble to get a thorough background in the subject.

How do you evaluate what you hear?

You don't go to workshops and conventions to swallow completely all that is dished out to you. Frequently, you will find that the speakers disagree with each other, with what you heard at a similar meeting elsewhere, or with what you already know. You should therefore be prepared to evaluate intelligently what you hear. As you listen, you should examine the logic of the speaker's reasoning; you should also be on the alert for propaganda devices. Whether the speaker employs these devices intentionally or unintentionally, you shouldn't be fooled by them. If you learn as much as possible about the speaker before the meeting, you will be able to make a better judgment about what is said. What is his or her professional background? The speaker may be identified in the brochure that announced the meeting. If he or she is prominent enough, you may find a brief biography in *Who's Who* or in a specialized *Who's Who* for your profession or section of the country. An issue of one of your professional journals may identify the speaker in some way. Has he or she written any books or articles? Find and read them if you can. As you read, make some judgment of the writer. Does the article approach the subject objectively or is there an inclination to oversimplification, excessive enthusiasm, or oversight of some pertinent facts or considerations? Is there anything in the speaker's background or present position that could logically cause a bias in attitudes? Unless you are aware of his or her prejudices, a dynamic speaker can persuade you to accept ideas that are not completely sound. Your employer may spend money on the basis of your report of the speeches. The employer, then, has a right to expect you to weigh carefully what you hear. Even if the speaker is a famous authority in the field, you should know what other authorities have thought and written about the subject. There may well be some valuable aspects of the matter that your speaker has overlooked, or there may be another reasonable, though less popular, side to the question. Naturally, you will take notes on this background material. You may need to summarize this background briefly in your report. Moreover, you can review your notes quickly before you attend the meeting.

How should you listen to a speech?

To get the most from a public speech, you should arrive a few minutes early and find a seat near the front. Try to sit where you will not be disturbed by latecomers or by groups who use such gatherings to visit with old friends. Attend the meeting alone or with someone who is also serious about gaining from what is said. Don't worry about how you can leave early. Meet that problem when it comes. For the time being concentrate on the speech.

Spend the few minutes before the speech in rereading your notes on the speaker's subject or in reviewing in your mind what you have learned about it. Then when the speaker begins, you will be ready to tune in on his or her wavelength at once because you will already be thinking with the speaker. While the speaker is acknowledging the introduction and engaging in a few opening pleasantries, compare the individual you see and hear with what you already know of him or her. But don't be misled by the speaker's presentation. You aren't here to be entertained. Unless you are attending a convention of comedians or toastmasters, there may be little relationship between the speaker's ability to hold an audience and the speaker's professional knowledge. The people in the audience are there presumably to learn something which the speaker knows, and there is no need to resort to tricks in order to hold their attention.

The problem of attention is your concern, and it isn't always an easy one. One of the reasons that listening is difficult is that you are capable of thinking many times faster than the speaker can talk. While he or she is explaining to you why alphodiesel engines are inclined to coagulate when operated under high pressures and at low altitudes, your mind has time to wander. Those mental wanderings might be fine if you could always be certain that your mind would get back in time. Since you can't, it would be better if you confined its wandering as closely as possible. If you must think of something else while the speaker discusses the coagulation tendencies of the alphodiesel engine, you might make a brief review of what you already know about alphodiesel engines, about coagulation, or about any other fact that seems relevant. Your mental wanderings will then aid your understanding of the speech rather than interfere with it.

While you listen to what the speaker is saying right now, try to connect it to what has already been said. Summarize the speech to this point and try to anticipate what will follow. If the speaker draws the conclusions which you expect, you will understand them better because you have drawn them yourself. If he or she does not, you can listen for an explanation or be prepared to reexamine what you have heard to see why the conclusions are different from yours. Remember, your physical presence is not enough. You are there to listen to what is said. Intelligent listening isn't an oral sponging-up process. You can benefit from what you hear only if you listen actively, questioning and evaluating what you are told, measuring it by what you already know, and applying it to the problems and questions that you have already found. On the other hand, you should suspend complete judgment of the material the speaker is presenting until the speech is finished. It may be only later, when you are reviewing your notes in your room, that the full impact of what has been said will reach you. Be careful, also, to hear what the speaker really says and not what you think was said or what you think should have been said.

How should you take notes on what you hear?

You will listen better if you take notes on the speech. You will also need notes to prepare your report. Even if no report is expected of you, you should have some record of what you have heard since you don't always know what pieces of information you will need later.

Probably your notes will be more useful to you if you take them on full-sized typing or notebook paper. Such sheets will fit well into a folder in your filing cabinet and can be filed with other material on the same subject. Arrange the material on the page to show the relative importance of various items and their relationship to each other. If you take notes in a small pocket notebook or on file cards, you may be tempted to take less than complete notes. Your purpose here is to cover one lecture as a complete unit, and you don't want to break up information into bits and pieces. Later, if you want to extract various ideas or facts from your notes to be used in a paper or report, you can do so more accurately if you have a complete resume of the lecture to draw from. Since the notes will go into your file, the first thing you should write down is the date, the occasion, the place, the name of the speaker, and the title of the speech. Then if you use the material at some later time, you won't have to depend upon your memory.

Some speakers are well organized. You can almost hear the *I* and *II* and the subheads *A* and *B* that must be in their notes. In this case, take your notes in outline form with proper indentations for subheads. If you are able to take most of your notes in outline form, don't be disturbed if occasionally there is a block of material which you prefer to summarize with whole or nearly whole sentences. If the lecture isn't organized well enough for you to take your notes in outline form, you may still be able to indicate by indentation that certain material seems to fit under certain headings. Perhaps the speaker will indicate with the words *second* and *third* a pattern of organization, and you can number some items. If he or she indicates by voice, gesture, or repetition the importance of some term or fact, you can underline it.

Leave a wide margin on the left-hand side of your page for additional comments that may occur to you or for anything you might want to add to make your notes more useful. Don't fill up the margins or corners with aimless doodling that distracts you as you take your notes and will distract you as you use them.

Don't try to write down everything the speaker says. Many speakers tell stories as illustrations, repeat certain points in different ways for emphasis, or even include information that is just padding. Your notes will be more valuable to you than a transcript of the speech because you will have omitted such unnecessary material and preserved only the real meat of the address. For this reason it isn't wise or necessary to try to take the speech down in shorthand or to employ a tape recorder. A tape recorder is useful at a convention to catch an address which you are unable to hear, but it can't take the place of your notes. If you rely upon your tape recorder, you will have to listen to the lecture again in order to pick out the most pertinent information, so instead of saving time, you will have to spend more time in listening to the lecture twice. Furthermore, you won't listen as well the first time if you are relying upon a machine.

ASSIGNMENTS

    I. Contact a local employer who hires persons in your field of interest. Determine when the employer plans to conduct an in-service training session for employees and ask if it would be possible for you to attend. If you can attend the session, be prepared to share with your classmates the following information:

1. When and where was the session held?
2. Who arranged the session's program?
3. Who was the speaker (or speakers)?
4. Was the format lecture, demonstration, or a combination of both?
5. What seemed to be the attitude to the audience: interested, excited, challenged, bored, etc.?
6. Did the presentation seem worthwhile to you? What facts did you learn that you did not previously know?

II. Find the answers to the following questions. (You may have gathered some of the information called for here in an earlier assignment.)
   1. What is the name of the most important national organization in your field?
   2. When and where does this organization hold meetings?
   3. Who may attend these meetings? What fees are charged?
   4. What are the names of any regional, state, and local organizations within your field?
   5. When are their meetings held?
   6. Who may attend these meetings What fees are charged?

III. Perhaps now or some other time during the semester your instructor will ask you to attend a nearby meeting. If so, you should submit to the instructor the following information:
   1. When was the meeting held? Where? What dates?
   2. What organization was the sponsor?
   3. How many persons were in attendance?
   4. Was the program largely composed of general sessions with important speakers, or was it a workshop program with smaller study groups?
   5. Exactly what sessions of the meeting did you attend?
   6. Who was the keynote speaker?
   7. What are his or her qualifications?
   8. Write a brief summary of the speaker's important statements.
   9. Write a short reaction to the statements. Did you agree with the speaker? Did you find him or her convincing? Did you find him or her interesting?
   10. If you attended any small workshop groups, indicate the subject discussed.
   11. Who was in charge of the workshop group? What are his or her qualifications?
   12. Was the subject treated in a panel discussion, with a debate or forum, or in a general discussion by everyone present?

13. Write a brief summary of the discussion within this workshop group.
14. Write a brief evaluation of the discussion. Did the subject receive fair treatment? Did any opposition present have an adequate voice? Was the subject handled in such a way that it gave you any new ideas or changed any that you already had?

IV. Perhaps it will be impossible for you to attend an actual meeting. If so, obtain a set of written reports (often published in a professional journal) from a recent meeting and answer as many of the questions in III (above) as possible.

Using the Library

Why do you need to learn how to use the library?

In the fast-moving professional world you are about to enter, knowledge in each field is changing and multiplying so fast that you will constantly find that much that you know is no longer valid. Of course, you will do your best to learn all that you can about your field while you are in school, and you will also try to keep up with the advances that are made later. Nevertheless, you will soon realize that you can't know everything about your field and that you need to be able to locate the information that you don't have.

If you become really successful in your profession, libraries will play an important part in your life, not only in college but throughout your career. This is true even if you haven't chosen one of the professions usually considered to be "bookish." Once you learn to use a library and to depend upon its facilities, you won't think you have adjusted to a new community until you have become acquainted with its local library. Fortunately, once you have learned to use one good library well, you will find you know how to use other libraries also, for they all have their materials organized in a similar manner.

How is a library arranged?

Whether they are located in an abandoned armory or on a university campus, most libraries divide their facilities into three groups. There will be a corner, a section, a room, or a floor devoted to *periodicals;* a section or room where *reference books* are found and used; and a section, room, wing, or floor reserved for the rows and rows of books which are normally referred to as the "stacks."

How are the books arranged?

The area of the stacks may be closed to public admission. If so, you will have to ask for the book you want at the desk reserved for that purpose. The library may have "open stacks" so that you can go among the shelves of books, find your own book, and perhaps even sit down at a desk close by to use it. Some libraries allow their patrons free access to fiction books and biographies but maintain "closed stacks" for other books. Whether you find your own book or ask the librarian for it, you will need to understand the way books are arranged in a library so they can be found.

All the books in a library are arranged according to one of two systems. The *Dewey Decimal System* divides knowledge into ten divisions, easily subdivided by decimals. Its main divisions of subject classification are as follows:

000–099	General Works	500–599	Pure Science
100–199	Philosophy and Psychology	600–699	Applied Sciences
		700–799	Fine Arts and Recreation
200–299	Religion	800–899	Literature
300–399	Social Science	900–999	History, Travel,
400–499	Languages		Collected Biography

Fiction in English may be classified under *F* and arranged alphabetically according to author, or it may be under the appropriate number in the 800's. Individual biography may be classified under *B* and arranged alphabetically according to the name of the subject, or it may be arranged under the numbers appropriate to the subject's field. Public and high school libraries are more likely to use *F* and *B* headings than are college and university libraries.

The *Library of Congress System* uses letters for general headings and offers twenty-one categories. Although the Dewey System has been in general use longer than the Library of Congress System, more and more libraries are converting to the Library of Congress System as they increase their holdings and need more subdivisions to locate one book among hundreds of its class. Here are the main divisions of the Library of Congress System:

A. General Works (including Encyclopedias)
B. Philosophy and Religion
    BD.   Metaphysics
    BF.   Psychology
    BJ.   Ethics
    BL.   Religions

BM.   Judaism
BR. and following   Christianity
C. History (General, including Civilization, Genealogy)
D. History—Old World
    DA.   Great Britain
    DC.   France
    DE.   Classical Antiquity
    DF.   Greece
    DK.   Russia
    DS.   Asia
    DT.   Africa
E. American History and General United States History
F. American History (Local) and Latin American
G. Geography, Anthropology, Folklore, Sports, and other
H. Social Sciences
    HA.   Statistics
    HB.–HD.   Economics
    HF.   Commerce
    HG.–HJ.   Finance
    HM.   Sociology
    HQ.   Family, Marriage, Home
    HV.   Social Pathology (Alcoholism, Criminology, Penology)
J. Political Science
K. Law
L. Education
M. Music
N. Fine Arts
    NA.   Architecture
    NB.   Sculpture
    ND.   Painting
P. Language and Literature
    PA.   Classical Language and Literature
    PB.   Celtic Languages
    PC.   Romance Languages
    PD.   Germanic Languages
    PE.   English Languages
    PN.   Literary History and Collections
    PQ.   Romance Literature
    PR.   English Literature
    PS.   American Literature
    PT.   Teutonic Literature
    PZ.   Fiction and Juvenile Literature
Q. Science
    QA.   Mathematics
    QB.   Astronomy
    QC.   Physics
    QD.   Chemistry
    QE.   Geology
    QH.   Natural History

QK. Botany
QL. Zoology
QM. Human Anatomy
QP. Physiology
QR. Bacteriology
R. Medicine
RD. Surgery
RS. Pharmacy
RT. Nursing
S. Agriculture, Forestry, Animal Culture, Fish Culture, and Hunting
T. Technology
U. Military Science
V. Naval Science
Z. Bibliography and Library Science

Each book in the library has a Dewey number or a Library of Congress number and, below it, a "book number" consisting of a code number for the author's last name followed by a digit or digits and a small letter. Below the book number may be the date of the book if the library has more than one edition and the copy number if the library has more than one copy. The Dewey number or the Library of Congress number and the book number make up the complete *call number.* The complete call number belongs to only one book in the library and is, consequently, the most accurate designation of that book in a library. You will use it to call for a book at the library desk or, if the library has open stacks, to locate the book for yourself.

Where are the books listed?

All of the books in the library are listed in two places. The *shelf list* is a catalog of the books as they stand on the shelves. Books are entered on 3 × 5-inch cards arranged in trays. Because the books are arranged on the library shelves by numbers assigned them according to their subjects, the shelf list, which is arranged by these numbers, can also be used as a subject catalog. You won't use the shelf list often; but when you do need it, you will find it useful.

Usually you will locate books in the *card catalog.* This catalog also consists of cases of trays containing 3 × 5-inch cards. The cards here are arranged alphabetically; a label on the front of the drawer indicates the alphabetical range of that tray, and guide cards indicate alphabetical divisions within the tray.

Within the trays are three kinds of cards: *subject cards, author cards,* and *title cards.* Figure 13-1 is an example of these cards:

figure 13-1

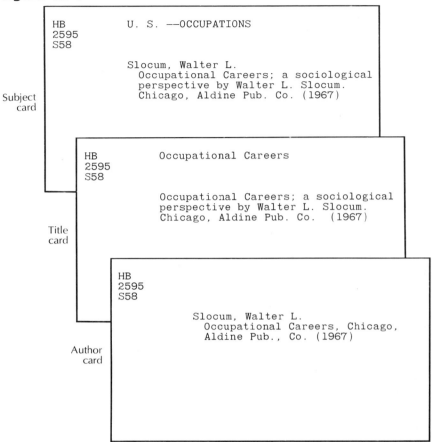

You will notice that the only difference between these cards is that the title or subject has been inserted above the author's name on the title or subject card. Don't be confused when the title or subject is also the name of a person. Notice that the inserted titles or subjects are typed in on the cards, but the rest of the information is printed. The subject heading is in capital letters. The subject heading and the title heading are indented, but the author's name is not.

Cards for books written by one author and cards listing that author as the first of several authors are filed before cards that list him or her as a second or later author. For identical words or names, the filing order is person, place, title.

Hudson, William Henry
Hudson, N.Y.
The Hudson and Its Moods

There are a few other practices followed by libraries in filing cards that you should know:

Alphabetizing is done word by word rather than letter by letter.
North America
North Sea
Northanger Abbey
Northern Ireland
Northern Rhodesia
The Northerners
Abbreviations and numbers are alphabetized as though they were spelled out: Dr. Johnson as Doctor Johnson, St. Louis as Saint Louis, U.S. as United States, 18th century as eighteenth century.
Personal names beginning *Mac, Mc* and *M'* are all filed under *Mac.*
A, An, The, and their foreign equivalents are ignored when they occur initially in alphabetizing.
The foreign prefixes *de, van,* and *von* are ignored, and the card is filed as though the name were *Winkle* not *van Winkle.*
But French surnames beginning with *La, Le, Dela, Du,* and *Des* are treated as though the prefix were joined to the next word.
Saints, Popes, Kings, and common people are filed in that order by name and not by title.
Although subjects are subdivided alphabetically, history is divided chronologically.

What are some standard reference works?

You will often save time in your research if you first consult the appropriate standard reference works. There are general works that contain information about a broad range of subjects; then there are specialized works that contain information about limited subject areas.

Below are presented some of the most useful reference works, both general and specialized:

GENERAL REFERENCE WORKS

Ayer's Directory of Newspapers and Periodicals. 1880. Current edition published in 1978.
BESTERMAN, THEODORE. *A World Bibliography of Bibliographies.* 2 vols. plus index. 1947–49.
Book Review Digest. 1906 ff. A standard source for critical reviews.

Book Review Index. 1965 ff. Monthly index to reviews appearing in more than 200 periodicals.

Cumulative Book Index. 1898 ff.

MURPHEY, ROBERT W. *How and Where to Look It Up: A Guide to Standard Sources of Information.* New York: McGraw-Hill, 1958.

New Serial Titles. A Union list of periodicals in the U.S. and Canada which began publication after December 31, 1949. Listed monthly, cumulated yearly. Cumulation 4 volumes. 1950–70. Washington, D.C.: Library of Congress.

Readers' Guide to Periodical Literature, 1900 ff. 1905 ff. The most standard magazine index. Author-title-subject index.

SHEEHY, EUGENE P. *Guide to Reference Books,* 9th ed. 1976. Annotated list of reference books which replaces Winchell as the standard one-volume guide to various reference sources. Classification by subject.

Ulrich's International Periodical Directory, 15th ed., 1973. A listing from over 7,500 periodicals, grouped by subject.

WINCHELL, CONSTANCE M. *Guide to Reference Books,* 8th ed. 1967. Annotated list of reference books classed by subject.

GENERAL DICTIONARIES

The American College Dictionary, rev. ed. New York: Random House, 1967.

The American Heritage Dictionary. Boston: Houghton Mifflin, 1975.

Funk and Wagnalls Standard College Dictionary. New York: Funk and Wagnalls, 1973.

MURRAY, JAMES A.H., et al., eds. *Oxford English Dictionary.* 12 vols. Oxford: Clarendon Press, 1933. Supplement. Excellent etymological dictionary.

Webster's New Collegiate Dictionary, 8th ed. Springfield, Mass.: G. & C. Merriam, 1974.

TECHNICAL DICTIONARIES

Chamber's Technical Dictionary. Revised and supplemented in 1948 by C. F. Tweney and L. E. C. Hughes. A good all-round technical dictionary.

Computer Dictionary. 1966. Identification, classification, and interpretation of terms and concepts important to electronic data processing.

A Dictionary for Accountants. 1970. Alphabetized accounting terms and definitions.

Dictionary of Science and Technology. 1971. A good technical dictionary with concise definitions.

Dictionary of Scientific and Technical Words. A convenient book with definitions of some 10,000 words. Now out of print.

Dictionary of Technical Terms. 1970. Terms commonly used in aeronautics, architecture, woodworking, building trades, painting, and television.

Encyclopedia Dictionary of Electronics and Nuclear Engineering. 1959. An excellent dictionary for terms in electronics and nuclear engineering which was designed for scientists, technicians, and students.

Electronics and Nucleonics Dictionary. 1967. Definitions, abbreviations, and synonyms for over 13,000 terms.

McGraw-Hill Encyclopedia of Science and Technology. 15 vols. 1977. The most current general encyclopedia in the field.

Modern Dictionary of Electronics. 1972. Analysis of words and their meanings as determined by common usage.

A Short Dictionary of Architecture. 1953. A useful dictionary of terms used in architecture, with excellent illustrations.

BIOGRAPHY

American Authors 1600–1900; British Authors Before 1800; British Authors of the Nineteenth Century; Junior Book of Authors; Twentieth Century Authors. 1938. A series edited by Stanley Kunitz and Howard Haycraft.

Asimov's Biographical Encyclopedia of Science and Technology. 1964. Biographic sketches of 1,000 scientists from the Greek Era to the Space Age.

Biography Index. 1947 ff. Index to sources which provide sketches of particular individuals (both historical and current), published quarterly and annually.

Chamber's Biographical Dictionary. 1968. International listings.

Contemporary Authors. 24 vols. 1978. Guide to twentieth-century authors and their works.

Current Biography. 1978. Contemporary Americans, with photographs.

Dictionary of American Biography. 1958. A multivolume work containing biographic sketches of Americans no longer living. Frequently referred to as DAB.

Dictionary of American Scholars. 4 vols. Sketches of scholars in history, English, speech, and drama; foreign languages, linguistics, and philology; philosophy, religion, and law.

Dictionary of National Biography. 1965. British equivalent to the DAB. Frequently referred to as DNB.

Dictionary of Scientific Biography. 1970–75. The most authoritative set of biographies of scientists from antiquity to the nuclear age.

The International Who's Who. 1935 ff. An annual list of basic biographical information on prominent world figures.

McGraw-Hill Encyclopedia of World Biography. 12 vol. 1972. An excellent source for information about deceased world figures.

National Cyclopaedia of American Biography. 1898–1946. More than 50 vols. to date, containing a broad coverage of American historical biography.

New Century Cyclopedia of Names. 3 vols. 1954. Over 100,000 proper names with short biographical sketches.

Notable American Women, 1607–1950. 3 vols. 1971. Contains biographical sketches of women deceased prior to 1950.

Webster's Biographical Dictionary. Brief data of famous persons.

Who's Who. An annual listing of prominent living British persons, with abbreviated biographical data. *Who Was Who* is a separate list of the biographies of persons now deceased, with date of death. Pub. 1964.

Who's Who in America. A biennial equivalent of the British work, with the companion volume *Who Was Who in America.*

AERONAUTICAL AND MECHANICAL

Aeronautical Engineering Index. 1947 ff.

Aeronautical Reference Library. 1943. Now out of print.

Applied Mechanics Reviews. 1948 ff.

Aviation and Space Dictionary, 5th ed. 1974. A very good current dictionary of aviation terms.

Glenn's Auto Repair Manual. Revised annually and back-dated eleven years. A standard source for repair information.

GROGAN, DENIS J. *Science and Technology.* 1973. Introduces readers to different types of scientific literature such as handbooks and encyclopedias.

A Guide to Information Sources in Space Science and Technology. 1963. Excellent bibliography for recent developments in the space industry.

Handbook of Astronautical Engineering. 1961. Handy reference aid.

McGraw-Hill Dictionary of Scientific and Technical Terms. 1974.

PARSONS, STANLEY. *How to Find Out About Engineering.* 1970. A basic guide to engineering sources.

Van Nostrand's Scientific Encyclopedia, 5th ed. 1976.

WALFORD, ALBERT J. *Guide to Reference Sources.* Vol. 1, *Science and Technology.* 1973.

BUSINESS

American Business Practice. 12 vols. 1933. Now out of print.

Black's Law Dictionary. Defines terms and phrases in legal use in America and England.

Business Information: How to Find and Use It. 1955. A valuable bibliographic guide to business.

Business Periodicals Index. 1958 ff. Guide to articles on business, trade, finance. Issued monthly, cumulated yearly.

Business Reference Sources. 1971. A basic guide for use of business libraries which was intended for use of students at Howard University.

Encyclopedia Dictionary of Business Finance. 1961. Gives detailed explanations of terms in finance.

Encyclopedia Dictionary of Business Law. 1961. Defines legal terms in nontechnical language.

Encyclopedia of Banking and Finance, 6th ed. 1962.

Encyclopedia of Business Reference Sources. 2 vols. 1970. Contains basic information on both monographic and periodical sources needed by the student or businessman.

How to Use the Business Library, 2nd ed. 1957. Contains a bibliography of business information classified by fields and heavily annotated. Now out of print.

Sources of Business Information, rev. ed. 1964.

PARAMEDICAL

Black's Medical Dictionary, 31st ed. 1976. The standard medical dictionary.

BLAKE, JOHN B., and CHARLES ROSS. *Medical Reference Works.* 1976, with supplements. Lists basic reference works in the field.

Current Clinical Dental Terminology. 1974. Basic definitions and terms.

Darland's Illustrated Medical Dictionary. 31st ed. 1976. A basic medical dictionary and, along with Black, a standard in the field.

Encyclopedia and Dictionary of Medicine and Nursing. 1972. Work for nurses and practitioners in other paramedical fields.

Index Medicines. 1960. A series which began in 1879 and has continued to serve as a comprehensive index to the world's medical literature.

LINGEMAN, RICHARD. *Drugs from A to Z,* 2nd ed. (New York: McGraw-Hill, Inc. 1974). Designed for the lay person.

Physicians' Desk Reference. 1947, revised annually. Basic information about pharmaceutical products.

SCIENCE AND ENGINEERING

American Scientific Books. Annual list of scientific, technical, and medical books.

Applied Science and Technology Index. (Before 1958 published as *Industrial Arts Index.*) Subject index to periodicals in engineering, science, technology. Very helpful to undergraduate students. Issued monthly, cumulated annually.

Engineering Encyclopedia, 3rd ed. 1963. Condensed encyclopedia and mechanical dictionary.

Engineering Index. 1892–1919; 1920 ff.

A Guide to Science Reading. 1963.

Guide to the Literature of Mathematics and Physics. 1958. Excellent source, includes related works on engineering science.

Harper Encyclopedia of Science. Important multivolume work.

Industrial Arts Index. 1913–57. Indexes more than 200 technical journals. Issued monthly, cumulated annually.

New Technical Books. 1915 ff. Ten issues per year. Excellent annotations of recent works.

Technical Book Review Index. 1914–1928; 1935 ff.

I. You should be able to find the material required in the following exercises in your own school library.

  1. Locate a standard bibliography for your occupational file. Copy five of the entries that interest you most.

  2. Find what information is available about the authors you listed in the exercise above. For each author make a brief list of important biographic facts and a notation of your source.

  3. Find the etymological derivation of at least five terms that are important to your specialized area. How old are the terms? What did they mean when they first came into the English language?

  4. Assume that you are going to prepare a paper on changes in your vocational area. Make a bibliography that contains at least three very early references and three more recent ones to your field.

  5. List the journals in your school library that apply directly to your field. For each journal answer the following questions:

     a. When was the journal first published?

     b. How often is it published?

     c. Who is the present editor?

     d. How many pages are in a typical issue?

     e. What is the format? Is it largely a collection of essays about the field? Is it filled with pictures and charts? Is it written for the professional or the lay person?

     f. What volumes are in your school library?

II. A good student finds that he or she often makes use of more than one library to find all the information that is needed for an assignment. The following set of exercises relates to library facilities in your community other than those at the school where you are studying.

  1. How many public libraries are in your community?

  2. Where is the central library located? When is it open?

  3. Where is the branch library nearest to your home? When is it open?

  4. What other college libraries are close enough to be used conveniently? What are their hours?

  5. Answer the following questions with specific reference to the branch library nearest your home:

     a. What standard unabridged dictionaries are available?

     b. Do they have a complete file for *Readers' Guide to Periodical Literature?*

c. Make a list of at least five popular magazines and determine how far back the files go for each.
d. Do they have a collection of popular records? If so, how long may you borrow these?
e. What materials are available in their pamphlet file system? Is there anything in this material that relates directly to your field?
f. What journals do they have that relate to your field? How far back do these files go?
g. What are the three most recent books representing your field? Copy author, title, and date of publication for each.
h. Find out the general operational procedures of the library. Who is eligible to check books out? Must you pay a membership or registration fee? How long may you keep books? What is the fine for returning a book late?

Effective
Reading
and Note Taking

How do you effectively use information from a book or periodical?

Many individuals have huge libraries in their homes but they are not particularly well read themselves. The fact that you have an expensive encyclopedia set does not necessarily make you educated. You have to know how to locate appropriate information in those encyclopedias if you are going to use them effectively. Similarly, you must also know how to use in an efficient manner the books and periodicals that you need for research purposes. You will not always have your books or periodicals with you when you need information, and you do not always have time to relocate what you vaguely recall. Therefore, efficient readers often like to take notes of important facts as they read; then those notes serve them long after the book or periodical has been laid aside. If you are going to take usable notes, you will find that certain reading and study techniques are helpful.

How do you preview a book?

Before you begin to read a book, a chapter, or an article in a periodical, preview the material to save time and prepare for more effective reading. To preview a book you plan to read for information, look first at the title page of the book. Who wrote it? Is there any identifying information about the author there? Where is the book published? Does the place of publication or the name of the publisher give you a hint as to where the research behind the book was done? What is the date of publication? Does the book represent recent scholarship? Is

193

this an older book that has proved its value in the demand for several editions? What is the exact name of the book? Does a subtitle give you a hint as to what to expect?

Now turn to the preface. Perhaps you do not usually read the preface, but here the author explains his or her purpose in writing the book. By reading this statement about purpose you may find out if the book will meet your purpose. Look at the table of contents. Perhaps the title of one of the chapters will seem to indicate to you that one chapter is all you really need to read. If so, you will certainly want to read that chapter; but don't neglect to study the other chapter titles and to investigate any chapters or parts of chapters that might possibly contain relevant material.

Even though you may have selected only a part of the book to read, look through the entire book. Read the introduction or the first few pages. Notice the style and the general tone of the book. Is the author writing objectively or is he or she writing propaganda? Is the writing to convince or to persuade? What is probably the reason for doing so?

Finally, read the conclusion of the book. Now you should be able to see any part that you read in its relation to the whole.

How do you read the chapter effectively?

As you read the chapter, turn the individual sections and paragraph headings into questions for which you will seek answers. This process may sound time-consuming and complicated, but once it becomes a habit it will take no longer than your old method, and your reading will be more rewarding.

If you are studying the material with an eye to remembering it for a later examination, stop at the end of each paragraph or section, ask yourself the question implied in the heading, then look away from the book to see if you can answer it. When you have finished the chapter, review the questions formed from the section headings to see if you know the answers; then ask yourself the question formed from the chapter title.

If the book is yours to keep, you may mark those words or phrases which form the center of each answer so that you can reread more quickly the answers that you have forgotten. Do not mark too much, however, or you will have to reread the whole thing. If your instructor lectures so that you can follow along in the book and frequently mark words and sentences which are stressed, you may want to use a different color ink in order to tell the instructor's stress from your own.

If you jot down your instructor's comments on the text in the margin beside the pertinent material, when the time comes to prepare for the examination, you can correlate the attitudes and information of the instructor and those of the author of the text.

This study method is one that has been followed successfully by many excellent students. It has been taught at numerous specialized army schools for accelerated students and at expensive speed-reading workshops. It should work for you.

How do you read when you want to take notes?

If you are reading a chapter or article to gather information for some purpose, you will still preview and read as outlined here; but you won't, of course, attempt to learn any of the material in this way. Your purpose is different, and your method is different. Previewing the article allows you to find out quickly if the article contains information you need, how much of it you need, and perhaps how it will serve your purpose. You may want to read the whole article or only part of it. After you have read the article or the parts that you need, you may need to make some notes on what you have read.

What kind of notes will you take?

Your notes may take the form of a *synopsis,* a *paraphrase,* a *summary,* or a *direct quotation.* A synopsis is a summary of the plot of a story. In college your principal use for the synopsis is in literature courses as a study aid and as part of the content of reviews and critical papers on novels, plays, and short stories. A paraphrase is a restatement of the ideas and thoughts of the original in your own words. The paraphrase may be as long as the original because it includes all the facts, illustrations, or other material of the original. A summary is just what its name suggests—a highly condensed version of the original. It focuses on the major points of the original but does not necessarily deal with all of the minor details. Your purpose in taking notes will determine which form you will use, and sometimes the form is dictated by the nature of the original material itself.

How do you take a note that is a quotation?

A quotation is the easiest kind of note to take because you just copy somebody else's words. You must be very careful, however, that you copy them exactly. After you have copied a quotation, compare what you have written with the original to be certain that you have everything exactly as in the original. If you misquote the original source, you may have a piece of misinformation that will seriously affect you finished product. Sometimes you may for legitimate reasons need to make some changes as you quote material. Some types of alterations can be made, but you must notify your reader that you have made them.

Sometimes you may want to omit part of the material because it is too lengthy or because it is irrelevent for your purpose. You must be careful, however, that your omissions do not in any way misrepresent what the author says. You could leave out words and phrases here and there to make the author appear to be saying anything you want, but you wouldn't really be quoting and you would be dishonest to pretend you were. If you do need to delete certain portions of the quotation and you can do so without altering the writer's meaning, use three spaced dots (. . .), called an *ellipsis,* to take the place of one word, a phrase, or any portion of a sentence. It can be used at the beginning of a sentence, in the middle, or at the end. If it is used at the end of the sentence or at the end of material that is followed by some mark of punctuation, the ellipsis is used and then the punctuation mark. If as much as a sentence is omitted, close and reopen your quotation marks to indicate that you really have two separate quotations. Here are some examples of quotations using ellipses; the material quoted is taken from this chapter:

> "You could leave out words and phrases here and there to make the author appear to be saying anything you want, but you wouldn't really be quoting. . . ." (3 dots for the ellipsis, 1 dot for the period)
> "If you do need to delete . . . you can do so . . . ," (3 dots for the ellipsis, comma taken from the quotation)
> ". . . compare what you have written with the original. . . ." (3 dots for the ellipsis, 1 dot for the period)

Sometimes when you copy a quotation, a pronoun or other reference to person, place, or time is not clear because the thing referred to is named in a portion which you do not want to include. Sometimes you may want to supply a date or place name to clarify some less definite term. Here again you must be honest. You must not distort or misrepresent the writer's meaning, and you must let the reader know what you have done. To insert such information, you should use brackets. You do not change the original term; you copy it and then clarify it with whatever explanation you think will help the reader. This is the way you handle such an explanation:

> "It [the ellipsis] can be used at the beginning of a sentence, in the middle, or at the end."
> "At the time [1892] Eldredge was still living in Boston."

Occasionally, you may want to quote a portion of a sentence which you work into a sentence of yours, not, of course, because you wish to alter the writer's meaning, but because you want to use his or her phrasing. Sometimes the tense of a verb does not agree with the tense you need in your sentence. You may change the tense of the verb to the appropriate one if you place brackets around the altered verb. Sometimes in material you want to quote you find a fact that you know is inaccurate or a word that you know is misspelled. You can't correct this error. You should, however, indicate that you are aware of the error. Insert the Latin word *[sic]* underlined and in brackets immediately after the term in question. Notice that brackets aren't the same as parentheses. If you can't make them on your typewriter, you can draw them in.

If you take a note that is a quotation, be sure to put quotation marks around the quoted material and to check carefully for accuracy several times. Students have been known to include misspelled words and many strange and doubtful facts in quotations they thought they had copied accurately.

At first it might appear that you would save time if you just took all your notes as quotations. But you probably won't need to use many direct quotations in your finished paper. If you use too many direct quotations, your final product is not much more than a cut-and-paste job and reflects little of your own thinking. Therefore, if you take too many notes in this form you will find that you later have to change them to another form for use in your paper; and it is easier to take them in the preferred form the first time. There are really only two reasons for including quotations in reports or other writing. First, you will use a quotation if the person who makes the statement is so important that the fact that these are his or her exact words will give weight to the material. Second, you will use a quotation if the phrasing is so excellent that changing the words would weaken the statement.

Because long quotations must be set off by indentation and single spacing, many readers have a tendency to skip them. You should use your own words most of the time, limiting your use of direct quotations to only those instances that specifically require it.

How do you take notes if you want all of the material and you do not quote it?

If you find a paragraph or similarly sized section of an article or chapter that seems to serve your needs in its entirety, you should *paraphrase,* put the material into your own words. To paraphrase successfully, you must read the whole section, being sure that you understand it thoroughly. Then write it in your own words without looking at the text. Now compare what you have written to the original to see if you recaptured the author's intent and detail. Here again, you must not misrepresent what is said. Here is an example of a good paraphrase compared with the original material.

Original

You should, therefore, exercise the greatest care in preparing your application. Type neatly on a good grade of white bond paper, $8\frac{1}{2} \times 11$ inches. Never use company letterhead stationery, hotel stationery, lined paper of any kind, or colored, gilt-edged, or decorated personal stationery. Follow an accepted form for business letters even if the prospective employer is your father's former roommate or a figurehead in the employ of your Uncle Albert. Before you mail your letter, double-check your spelling, grammar, and punctuation and be prepared to retype your letter or even to rewrite it if it is somewhat less than perfect. Of course, you can also ask your roommate, cousin, or next-door neighbor to correct it for you; and you should certainly do so if you plan to take this person to work with you to catch the little errors you make after you go on the payroll.

Paraphrase

The application should be prepared carefully and neatly. Plain white bond paper $8\frac{1}{2} \times 11$ inches should be used. An accepted business letter form should be used in all cases. Before mailing, check spelling, grammar, and punctuation. Retype the letter if there are errors. You may even need to rewrite it. Don't depend upon anyone else to make your corrections because nobody else is going to help you hold this job.

This example of paraphrasing is shorter than the original. Sometimes the paraphrase is the same length, sometimes it is longer. In any case, it contains all the information that is in the original, but it doesn't use the words of the original.

How do you take notes if you only want a summary of the original?

Frequently as you read to gain information, you find that the paragraph contains more than you want to include in its entirety, even as a paraphrase. You want to give the essence of this information, but you want to give it much more briefly; in short, you want to *summarize.* Your procedure is similar to that which you used in preparing the paraphrase. You read carefully all of the portion you wish to summarize before you begin to write; but your emphasis is a bit different as you read. If you read to paraphrase, you have to notice detail. If you read to summarize, you pay particular attention to the whole idea. The individual facts, ideas, and illustrations are important only as they relate to the whole. Find the topic idea of each paragraph. You will see the relationship of the parts of the material if you also notice such transitional words and phrases as "on the other hand" "to illustrate," "nevertheless," "consequently," "as a result," and "however." After you understand the relationship of all the material in the paragraph, concentrate on just the sentences which are necessary to explain the topic idea and ignore the rest.

Now write the summary. Don't look at the original as you do so. Your summary should be in your own words and style, not in that of the original author. Don't string together phrases or words from the original. Doing so may distort the original meaning, and trying to blend the author's clauses and phrases with your own word choice in your own sentence construction will be more difficult and will produce a choppy style much poorer than the kind of writing that is more natural to you. It may even produce a passage that doesn't make sense. When you have finished summarizing the paragraph, reread the original and compare it with your summary. Are your individual facts accurate? Is your overall meaning the same as that of the original? Make any necessary revisions, and then move on to the next paragraph.

The following summary shows that the writer understood the meaning of the original and was able to record for his or her own use the major idea and the proper relationships of the minor ideas.

Original

The employer is not interested in your need for a job, so don't take up time with a discussion of your financial problems or other difficulties. You will be hired not because you need the job but because the employer needs a worker and you seem to be the best-qualified applicant. Starting a new employee in a job costs the employer money. Someone must take time away from other work to teach the new worker, who will work more slowly at first and make more mistakes than one who has been on the job awhile. Therefore, the employer will be taking a smaller risk in hiring you if you can provide assurance that you are willing to learn and that you are genuinely interested in the job.

Summary

Because training a new employee costs money, the employer will hire the best qualified worker, not the one who most needs the job.

Even summary notes should be made in complete sentences. Taking notes that are made up of fragments rather than of whole sentences may be quicker at the time, but the practice may lead you into inaccuracies when you finally come to use the notes. If you make summary notes that are complete sentences while you have the original material before you, you can easily check for accuracy. If you make fragmentary notes and try to develop them into full sentences at a later time, you might distort the writer's original meaning and you would certainly find the process more difficult than when the passage was fresh at hand. You might also find that your fragments fail so completely to convey the original meaning, or any meaning, that you have to return to the article itself. Jotting down words and phrases instead of writing whole summary sentences may also lead you to plagiarism.

What is plagiarism?

Plagiarism is the practice of borrowing the words of another and passing them off as your own. Words belong to the person who publishes them. Claiming them as your own is dishonest. If your report is published, duplicated, or called to the author's attention in any way, the author may sue you. If your teacher detects plagiarism in your finished writing—and teachers have an uncanny ability to detect such things—you may receive a failing grade for your lack of honesty.

Some plagiarism is just that—a lack of honesty. More often than not, however, student plagiarism results from an unclear understanding of just how close to an original source one may write without using quotation marks and giving just credit. Most student plagiarism comes from the practice of reading the original source, almost copying it, but omitting a word here and there and, perhaps, changing one adjective for another.

The problem is one of using what someone else has written without proper credit. If the idea is someone else's, give credit. If the word arrangement is someone else's, give credit. After all, you probably wouldn't have arranged those words in *exactly* that manner if you had not had the original material in front of you. One old guideline that usually works states that you should use quotation marks and give proper credit anytime you use three or more words in exactly the same order that they are in the original.

Here is an example of plagiarism that has resulted from working too close to the original source:

Original

Whether you telephone or write for such permission, the person can give a more helpful and favorable recommendation if you give him certain information. Tell him something about the job you are trying to get, why you want that job in particular, and why you think you will do well in it. This information will allow him to focus on those qualities of yours that will be especially important in this job. If you have not seen this person in some time, you may make it easier for him to write a recommendation if you bring him up to date on your vocational or educational activities. After you have been hired, you should write a letter of appreciation to anyone who helped you get the job.

Plagiarism

If you telephone or write for permission, the person can help you better if you tell him certain things. Tell him about the job you want, why you think you will do well. Then he can focus on your qualities that will be especially important on this job. If you haven't seen him lately, bring him up to date on your educational or vocational activities. After you get the job, write and thank him.

Do you need to make a note of where you got the material?

Ideas and facts as well as words are the possession of the individual who originally recorded them; so you will have to give credit to the source from which you took them. Moreover, you will want to remember what authority is responsible for this opinion or piece of information. If you are gathering the information for use in a report or paper that someone else will need, your reader will also want to know the authority so that he or she can evaluate your material more intelligently. The reader may even want to refer to the source personally. You should therefore record the name of the writer, the name of the book, the publisher, the place of publication, the date, and the number of the page on which the information was found. If the material came from an article, record the name of the periodical, the date, the volume number, and the page number. This information should be recorded on a *source card* (sometimes called a *bibliography card*), one source card for each source. You should also include the call number of library material in case you need to use the book again. If you use more than one library, make a note of where you got this particular source. Figure 14-1 is an example of a bibliography card for a book, and Figure 14-2 is an example of a bibliography card for a periodical article.

If you have some questions about how to handle books with two authors, pamphlets, newspapers, or anything else that seems to be an unusual source, consult the explanation on bibliography in Chapter 17.

figure 14-1   Source card for a book.

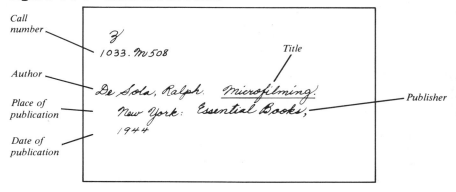

202

figure 14-2   Source card for a periodical article.

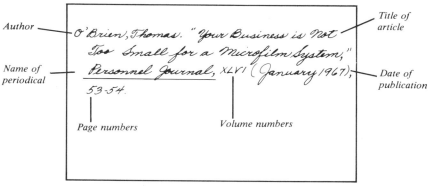

Author —

Name of
periodical

O'Brien, Thomas. "Your Business is Not Too Small for a Microfilm System," Personnel Journal, XLVI (January 1967); 53-54.

Title of
article

Date of
publication

Page numbers

Volume numbers

In what general form should you record the notes on what you read?

You might wish to summarize a whole article because you want the contents of the entire article for your files. If you want the whole article, you can often clip it from the periodical and file it. But many of the periodicals you will use will be from the files kept by your employer or from the library, and generally speaking, you wouldn't want to clip an article from a book, even if it's your own. In these cases you can reproduce the article on a copy machine in your office or at the local library for only a few cents. The time you save will be worth more than the cost involved.

Usually you take notes on your reading because you are gathering information to be used later in a paper or report. Perhaps only one portion of the article will pertain to your subject, or the material that you need may be scattered throughout the article. At any rate, you will want to use this material in your paper in a different order from that found in the original article or in combination with material obtained from other sources. You should try to take your notes with your final purpose in mind, but of course you won't know as you take them exactly what the order will be in your final paper. If you record your notes on sheets of paper, they won't be usable when you try to rearrange this information later. So you make each note on a separate 3 × 5 or 5 × 8-inch *note card.* Cards are handier than slips of paper because, being all the same size, they are more easily handled and they don't look like scrap paper. They are neat enough and of a proper size and shape to go into your file later, and they aren't large enough to tempt you into recording more than one idea or thought on each.

This last reason is extremely important. Later you will incorporate these summaries into your paper in an order and combination which isn't completely clear to you as you take your notes. If you have two separate facts or ideas on one card, you won't be able to sort them properly when you are ready to write your paper. You will have to rewrite the material on two cards so it will be in the order in which you will use it.

On each card you should make a note of the exact source for that piece of information. Write down the author's last name and the number of the page on which the information was found. If you have information from more than one article or book by the same author, you will also need to add the title. If the title is long, perhaps you can abbreviate it in some way or use only key words. Figure 14-3 is a sample note card:

Why is it necessary to use two different kinds of cards?

At first, you may think that using two kinds of cards will just increase the amount of writing you have to do, but this method really saves time. You might take ten notes from one source. Recording the full bibliographic information on one card will save you the trouble of rewriting the information nine times. When you multiply that nine times by perhaps a dozen sources, you can see how much time you will save. Moreover, having two kinds of cards makes several operations easier when you begin to prepare your final copy of your report. You will then be able to prepare your actual text material by using your note cards and to prepare your final bibliography by using your bibliographic cards. Having two separate sets of cards will reduce confusion.

ASSIGNMENTS

   I. Reread very carefully the first paragraph in Chapter 5 of this text ("The Job Application Letter"); then do the following activities:
      1. Paraphrase the paragraph in a manner that would permit you to use your paraphrase in a later formal report. Put your information on a note card.
      2. Summarize the paragraph so that you might use the information in a later report. Put your information on a note card.

figure 14-3

Verry, p. 103   *Reasons for Use*

   Microfilm provides the most organized method of storage. Facts are carefully stored and indexed until needed; they are never lost.

   3. Find one sentence in the paragraph that you might wish to use in a formal report in exactly the form that it appears here. Make a note card for this direct quotation.

 II. Select some subject or problem on which to prepare a formal report. Examine the sources in your school library that pertain to your subject. Preview the chapters or articles that you find until you locate at least five sources that will give you information that you need. Be certain the sources do not merely repeat each other. Make source cards for these five sources. You will then have completed a working bibliography. Later you will add other important sources as you discover them, but for now you will be reading and taking notes.

III. Following the instructions given in this chapter, prepare note cards from the sources you located for Assignment II. Include all of the three basic types of note cards—summary, direct quotation, and paraphrase. Take as many notes from each source as you feel necessary to cover the material properly.

15

Organizing

Why is an outline necessary?

An outline is nothing more than an organizational guide that you will use while preparing an oral or written report. Just as a football coach goes to the stadium with a detailed game plan worked out, so you as a speaker or writer need to have thought through your ideas to arrange them in their most impressive fashion.

Unfortunately, many students are frustrated by outlines because they have been drilled too hard on the techniques of the formal outline, which became, in many instances, more important than the speech or theme that it was supposed to be designed to help. From such experiences, students usually learned to write the theme or speech and then to develop the outline so that it matched! This procedure is obviously backwards and useless.

An outline is not useful unless it functions to help you while you do your writing. If you spend all your time getting the headings arranged correctly, spaced correctly, and capitalized correctly, you are spending time *building* a tool and not *using* a tool. An outline is a guide to your end product; it is not the end product itself.

Are formal outlines always necessary?

For some short speeches and themes you will not need to develop a formal outline before you begin to work. If your presentation is short and the ideas are readily before you, a brief listing of the order in which you will present them may be sufficient. Such a listing, most often arranged in order of decreasing or increasing importance, might look as informal as the example in Figure 15-1.

The speaker using this brief sketch of ideas would keep his or her main thoughts in the order that had been determined most effective earlier. If the speaker felt a need for more detail, he or she might, even without the use of elaborate subheadings, list them in a fashion similar to that shown in Figure 15-2.

What organizational principles work best?

An old but highly workable adage is that a writer (or speaker) should tell the audience what he or she is going to do, then do it, then tell the audience what has been done. Obviously this suggestion divides itself conveniently into the more typically labeled parts: introduction, body, conclusion.

A report, oral or written, should tell your audience (listener or reader) what you are going to do. That is, it should set the idea that you propose to investigate and should state the limits of your investigation. In conventional theme writing you have confronted this concept as the *thesis sentence.* A part of the introductory statement may also be used to get your audience's attention by use of a quotation, illustration, controversial statement, etc.

The body of your report is, of course, the most important. Here you must plan your strategy carefully: What facts do you present first? How much detail is necessary?

The two most frequently used systems for ordering facts are from the most important to the least important and from the least important to the most important. Experts themselves disagree over which is indeed the most effective, but a general suggestion will prove helpful: If your report is designed to present information, begin with your most important points while your audience is still most attentive (see Figure 15-3). If your report is designed to stimulate action (as the report urging a vote for more X-ray schools), then end with your most

figure 15-1

```
--quotation from Senator Fishburn

--need for more x-ray training schools

--cost for establishing such schools

--possible locations

--request for positive vote next week
```

figure 15-2

```
--quotation from Senator Fishburn

    "Unless we train highly skilled medical support teams,

    our population will be unable to receive adequate medical

    attention within the decade because of the increased

    workloads of the physicians themselves."

--need for more x-ray schools

    --only 2 in state now

    --train about 75 technicians a year

    --vacancies for skilled technicians exist in every clinic

        and hospital

--cost for establishing such schools

    --approximately $200,000 if built independently

    --approximately $75,000 if maintained as part of an

        on-going hospital program at established institution

--possible locations

    --4 schools in each of 4 major cities

    --3 schools in the largest cities and 2 schools to be

        built in yet-to-be-determined rural areas

--request for vote next week

    --Monday, April 10

    --will raise taxes only $0.50/year for average family
```

important point so that your conclusion can call for action immediately after your most impressive fact (see Figure 15-4).

Sometimes your points are of equal importance and are organized simply by enumeration: "There are four reasons why we should change the office duplication process," or "Three new proposals for redistricting of the sales staff must be reviewed."

The conclusion of your report should be brief but direct, and it should leave your audience with a feeling that you have finished. If your report is to give information, your conclusion might briefly rephrase the two, three, or four important points and tie them back

figure 15-3   **Most important to least important structure.**

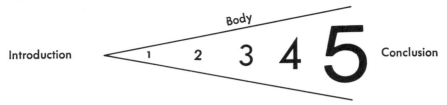

figure 15-4   Least important to most important structure.

Introduction   Body   1   2   3   4   5   Conclusion

with the thesis position you established in your introduction. If your report is to stimulate action, it might rephrase the points, but its emphasis will be upon the direct call to action. The conclusion is your final chance to speak or write about the given subject, and the words should be yours. Most rhetoricians agree that the use of a quotation at the very end of a report tends to weaken it.

When is a formal outline necessary?

A formal outline is necessary if your report is very long, because the brief informal jottings in Figures 15-1 and 15-2 are not detailed enough to hold together a 20-page report or a 30-minute speech. Sometimes, too, an outline is necessary in a formal written report because it precedes that report as a kind of table of contents.

What is a formal outline?

The formal outline is a structured listing of your ideas using various levels of importance and indicating these with indentations and the use of various Roman and Arabic figures and capital and lower-case letters. Again, structuring the outline should not take more time than producing the report because the outline is a tool to aid in that production. And the outline should never be produced after the report!

One important rule should be remembered: the parts that are marked equally (same level of Roman or Arabic figure, for example) must be of equal importance. The informal jotting of Figure 15-2 might be formally outlined to look like Figure 15-5.

Even Figure 15-5 is not a purely formal outline because the parts within a given unit (in II, A, for example) are not parallel with each other. Also, purists argue that the Introduction and Conclusion should not be listed the way they are here. However, this outline functions at three levels to organize the intended material, and it does this organizational task well. Remember the principle that the development of the

figure 15-5

```
    I.   Introduction:  Quotation from Senator Fishburn

   II.   Body

         A.  Need for more x-ray schools

             1.  Only 2 in state now

             2.  Train about 75 technicians a year

             3.  Vacancies now exist in almost every clinic and hospital

         B.  Cost for such schools

             1.  Approximately $200,000 if built independently

             2.  Approximately $75,000 if structured as part of a

                 program at an established institution

         C.  Possible locations for such schools

             1.  Locate 4 schools in 4 largest cities

             2.  Locate 3 schools in 3 largest cities and 2 smaller

                 schools in selected rural areas

  III.   Conclusion:  Request for vote

         A.  Monday, April 10

         B.  Will raise state taxes only $0.50/year for average taxpayer
```

outline should not be more involved than the subsequent development of the report itself.

What are the important principles of formal outlining?

You should keep the four following principles in mind when you need to develop a formal outline:

1. *The sum of the parts of the outline must equal the whole or total idea.* You will not have a valid outline if you omit any of the parts that are necessary to complete your defined topic. For example, Figure 15-6 is a valid one-level outline of the continents of the world. It would obviously have been incomplete if the writer had left out any one of the seven continents.

2. *An outline cannot contain parts that are not needed to make the whole.* The parts of your outline must not overlap, and they must not contain more divisions than are possible in the whole. For example, you would not develop an outline based on the three halves of a circle; a circle has only two halves. Figure 15-7 contains a part that overlaps one or more of the other three; "The problem phase" obviously has to come in either the initial, middle, or final phase.

3. *Only parts of the same thing or similar things can make the whole.* If you

figure 15-6

```
┌─────────────────────────────────────────┐
│                                           │
│      The Continents of the World          │
│                                           │
│                                           │
│           I.  Asia                         │
│          II.  Europe                       │
│         III.  Africa                       │
│          IV.  Australia                    │
│           V.  North America                │
│          VI.  South America                │
│         VII.  Antarctica                   │
│                                           │
└─────────────────────────────────────────┘
```

are not careful, you may have entries in your outline that are not actually parts of the whole. You would make this error if you were outlining your favorite movies and included an entry for *Kojak,* which is a television program. Figure 15-8 contains an entry, Atlantic, that is not a part of the continents of the world.

4. *The outline's label (title) must be specifically phrased to limit range of contents.* If you use an outline title that is too broad, you may not know whether you have included all necessary parts. For instance, it is impossible to tell from Figure 15-9 how complete the parts are because the title gives no direction. On the other hand, Figure 15-10 gives specific direction, and checking for completeness would not be difficult.

What are the principles for outlining the smaller parts?

The underlying principle behind all outlining, as you can see, is that the label of the outline is a whole that is divided into parts. The sum of the parts must be equal to the whole. Each part is itself a whole, although a smaller one, and it too may be divided. If it is, then the sum

figure 15-7

```
┌─────────────────────────────────────────┐
│                                           │
│    The Phases in Personal Development      │
│                                           │
│                                           │
│           I.  The initial phase            │
│          II.  The middle phase             │
│         III.  The final phase              │
│          IV.  The problem phase            │
│                                           │
│                                           │
└─────────────────────────────────────────┘
```

figure 15-8

```
The Continents of the World

      I. Africa
     II. Asia
    III. Europe
     IV. North America
      V. South America
     VI. Australia
    VII. Antarctica
   VIII. Atlantic
```

figure 15-9

```
My Senior Year in High School

      I. My classes
     II. My club activities
    III. My job
     IV. Baseball
```

figure 15-10

```
How I Spent My Time during My Senior Year in High School

      I. Attending class
     II. Participating in two social clubs
    III. Working afternoons
     IV. Practicing baseball
      V. Studying lessons
     VI. Going to parties
    VII. Dating
   VIII. Wasting time
```

of those parts must be equal to that whole. There must be no more parts than are needed to make a whole, and there must be no parts of something else or some different kind of part.

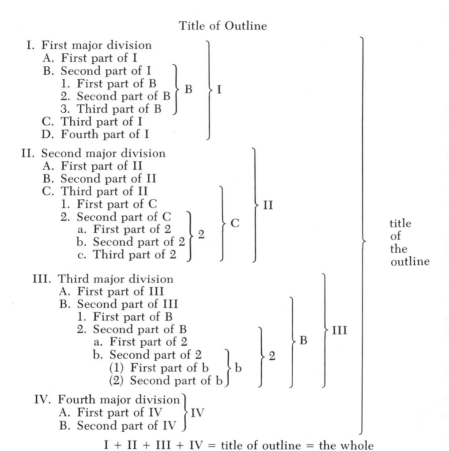

Title of Outline

I. First major division
   A. First part of I
   B. Second part of I
      1. First part of B
      2. Second part of B
      3. Third part of B
   C. Third part of I
   D. Fourth part of I

II. Second major division
   A. First part of II
   B. Second part of II
   C. Third part of II
      1. First part of C
      2. Second part of C
         a. First part of 2
         b. Second part of 2
         c. Third part of 2

III. Third major division
   A. First part of III
   B. Second part of III
      1. First part of B
      2. Second part of B
         a. First part of 2
         b. Second part of 2
            (1) First part of b
            (2) Second part of b

IV. Fourth major division
   A. First part of IV
   B. Second part of IV

I + II + III + IV = title of outline = the whole

How should you divide and subdivide the parts of an outline?

How many major parts there are in an outline and to what extent each part is divided depends upon the purpose of the writer and upon the amount of material. The writer may not want or need to divide some of the broader headings; other parts may need to be broken into very small units of thought. You might outline according to the simple scheme in Figure 15-11, or you might find that your purposes would be better served by the more detailed scheme in Figure 15-12.

figure 15-11

```
Money I Currently Have


    I. Bills
        A. Ten-dollar bill
        B. One-dollar bill
   II. Coins
```

figure 15-12

```
    Money I Currently Have
I. Bills
    A. Large bills
        1. Hundred-dollar bill
        2. Fifty-dollar bill
    B. Small bills
        1. Ten-dollar bill
        2. One-dollar bill
II. Coins
    A. A quater
    B. Four pennies
```

The outline in Figure 5-11 would be useful if you wanted to examine how much money you had and if you were not placing too much emphasis upon the value of your coins. The second outline is more detailed and would be helpful if you wanted organization into smaller units. It may be important to you, for instance, to separate large bills from small ones.

Order in arranging the headings and subheadings is also determined by purpose and material. The order in Figure 15-12 was determined by the importance (in this case the value) of the items being classified. In both I and II the movement was from the large to the small. Choose the ordering arrangement that best suits your needs and stick to it. If your arrangement is from large to small in I, then use that same arrangement in all related levels of your outline.

Are there any ways to be sure your outline follows the basic principles?

An arrangement of terms isn't an outline unless that arrangement has its basis in the principles of outlining discussed here, and there are several ways you can check your arrangement.

The first check is that afforded by the letters and numbers used to indicate parts. You would know immediately that you had made a mistake if you had written "I. Biology" and then under it "A. Science" because I is used to refer to larger groups than A and "Biology" refers to a smaller category than "Science." You could divide Science into Biology, Chemistry, Physics, etc., but you can't divide "Biology" into "Science" and some other similar parts of the whole represented by the label "Biology." Here is the usual order of letters and numbers used to represent the parts of an outline:

    I. Roman number
   II. Roman number
       A. Capital letter
       B. Capital letter
          1. Arabic number
          2. Arabic number
             a. Lower case letter
             b. Lower case letter
                (1) Number in parentheses
                (2) Number in parentheses
                   (a) Letter in parentheses
                   (b) Letter in parentheses
                      [1] Number in brackets
                      [2] Number in brackets
                         [a] Letter in brackets
                         [b] Letter in brackets

Notice that numbers precede letters; that the two alternate; and that although there may be no division under a number or letter, wherever there is one division there must be more than one.

The second check for your outline is found in the indentation system. The A and B under II have the same left-hand margin because they are part of the same thing and they are similar parts. They are indented under II because they are the parts into which II is divided. The 1 and 2 under the B have the same margin because they are part of the same thing and they are similar parts. The indentation continues to the right as the parts grow smaller.

The third check for your outline is found by applying the principle of outlining which applies to all the parts of the outline: make sure that all of the parts are there, that there are no extra parts, and that there are no different kinds of parts.

ASSIGNMENTS

    I. Make an informal jotting, similar to Figure 15-1, of the courses you are now taking and have taken in college. Then see if you can divide or group the courses in divisions and subdivisions so you have a two-level jotting similar to Figure 15-2.

   II. Prepare a two-level jotting of how you spend the hours of a typical day. Think first of the broad categories into which smaller things may be fitted. Perhaps you will want your final category to be "Miscellaneous" so it can serve as a catchall.

  III. Develop the material from Assignment II into a formal outline with appropriate numbers and letters and correct indentation.

  IV. The following outline is not arranged logically. Rework the outline into its logical form.

Animals I Have Had As Pets

  I. Members of the cat family
    A. Baby lion
      1. Three days old
      2. Mother died at local zoo
    B. House kittens
      1. Five of these

  II. Members of the dog family
    A. Two young dogs, mixed breeds
    B. A poodle
    C. German shepherd
    D. Other dogs

  III. Canaries
    A. Two males
    B. Three females
    C. Parakeet

  IV. Guppies

  V. Members of the reptile family
    A. Young grass snake
    B. Green lizard
    C. Two snails

  VI. Goldfish

After you have put the outline into correct order, go back through and see how you have arranged the material in the various divisions. Did you, for example, arrange it according to the size of pets? What other systems might have been used for arranging the material in each division?

V. Prepare two- or three-level outlines for each of the following topics. Be prepared to justify the groupings in each division.
1. Different types of employees in your vocational area.
2. Reasons why you are attracted to your profession.
3. Changes within your area in the last five years.
4. Different kinds of training programs for your area.
5. Kinds of equipment or tools that you will have to use in your particular work.

Oral Reporting

What situations require oral reports?

A large variety of situations require that you report your opinions or your researched ideas orally. Certainly you are asked to make oral reports in some of your college classes. Probably you will be asked to make oral reports on your job too; these reports at first may be so informal you might not even recognize the nature of what you are doing. As you continue to study and further your career objectives, the chances are that you will be asked to make more and more oral reports and that the nature of these reports will become increasingly formal.

If you're a member of a committee investigating a problem and you have been assigned to get some information, you will be expected to tell the committee what you have found. This report may contain only a few words that you can say from where you sit. It may, however, be longer and more formal. If your way has been paid to some workshop or convention, you may be asked to report on that meeting to the workers of your department or company. You may be asked to give an oral report on the success of some experiment or innovation made in your area. You may need to demonstrate the use of some machine or apparatus to a group of fellow workers. You may have many opportunities to stand up before a group of people and tell them what you know. If you're able to express yourself clearly and forcefully when you need to, you will undoubtedly have an advantage over your fellow workers.

What will happen to you if you have stage fright?

Some individuals are unnecessarily uncomfortable making oral reports; they prefer writing a report and submitting it instead. Some of these same persons are uncomfortable talking to someone on a one-to-one basis. Unfortunately, at some time in their lives they have been made too aware of their hands, arms, and legs. Now they don't know what to do with them. And they have grown to dislike watching their audience—be it one person or a large group—because they keep trying to "read" reaction from the audience while they are talking. Although speaking about an important matter to another individual, a committee, or a packed room may not be the easiest thing for someone to do, it need not be a frightening experience.

There is no great mystery surrounding the techniques of public speaking. Most of them are a matter of common sense. If you approach the matter with confidence, you can reason your way to the basic techniques. But the truth of the matter is that most of us become a bit panicky when we think about standing in front of a room full of people who are looking at us and listening to what we have to say. Everybody feels that way at first—ministers, school teachers, politicians, magicians, nurses, policemen—everybody.

But that tight feeling in your chest and that uncontrollable jiggle of your knees as you approach the speaker's platform are out of all proportion to the danger of the situation. You should depend upon the good manners of your audience for a quiet and attentive hearing. In fact you can depend upon more than that. For one thing, your audience is probably already interested in what you have to say. For another, the members of your audience are probably not professional speakers, and they don't expect you to be one. As they watch you take your place at the front, they will probably admire you for doing what they themselves find quite difficult. You may be acutely aware of your sweaty palms and the annoying lump in your throat, but they are not. Moreover, you know more about your subject than anyone present. Unless you call attention to yourself by a comment on your nervousness, your subject will be the first thing in the minds of your audience.

Are there any techniques that will help you handle your stage fright?

No doubt, these words have not removed completely your natural stage fright. But there are a few techniques that might help you. One of the things that will disturb you is the fact that your audience will be looking at you. You can relieve your mind considerably if you know you look your best. Give careful attention to your grooming. Be certain that your shoes are carefully polished, that your clothes are freshly pressed, and that your hair is neat and not too recently cut. Select an appropriate suit, shirt, and tie, or dress and accessories. You do not want your clothes to call attention to themselves and distract your audience from what you have to say. Do not wear anything that jingles and jangles or that feels uncomfortable. You do not want to be distracted by your clothes either. Give them your careful attention at home and then forget about them. Keep in mind that your audience will think about what *you* think about, so concentrate on your speech.

If you have to sit someplace on the platform before your turn comes to speak, sit at attention and look at the speakers preceding you, and listen to them, even though you might be having trouble concentrating enough to remember your telephone number. Naturally you will not drape yourself over the back or arm of your chair, cross your legs, or read or write while you wait. You can also take this opportunity to get used to the people in the audience.

If you make a habit of following these practices when you speak and you're still nervous, don't despair. A certain amount of stage fright is a good thing. Tension stimulates the release of adrenalin into your bloodstream. Adrenalin stimulates you to think and speak with greater energy than you do when you are calm and relaxed. You should try to channel that energy into productive activity rather than waste it on useless shaking and empty nervous gestures. You can channel this extra energy productively if you redirect your anxiety to a different subject. Instead of worrying about what your audience is going to think of you, concentrate on the subject matter of your speech. How do you want your audience to react to what you have to say? If their reaction is important to you, you should naturally feel some tension concerning that reaction. But use the extra energy stimulated by your tension to find and use the best method of getting the desired response. To get that response, you will need both a knowledge of the techniques of public speaking and thorough preparation of your material.

What are the techniques of public speaking?

When it's your turn to speak, rise and go to your place at the same pace you would go to any task that interests you. When you reach the speaker's desk, place your notes where you can see them; arrange them if necessary, but not too elaborately; then look at your audience. Really look at them; look right into their eyes. Good eye contact is one of the most important techniques in public speaking. Looking into the eyes of the members of your audience will also let you know how they feel about what you are saying. You may think you do not want to know, but how else are you going to tell when your explanation is a bit fuzzy and you should explain something more completely? Really looking at your audience will help to hold their attention in a way that looking at the tops of their heads or at a spot on the back wall will not. And not least in importance is the fact that somewhere along the way, if you really see your audience, you will discover that you are communicating with real people, that they are communicating with you, and that all of you are having a good time.

In that moment before you begin to speak, look pleasant if possible, unless the occasion is a very sad one. You also can find a comfortable posture. If your knees are shaking, flex them slightly. Relaxed knees are not so likely to shake. Take a deep breath. That breath is important: it enables you to gain control over your whole body.

Now you begin talking. You look at your audience as much as possible. You make whatever gestures are natural and easy for you. You say what you intended to say—probably a little better than you expected to. If you forget something, you look at your notes or you stand there and think of it. Do not be embarrassed if you forget; nobody expects you to be a memory expert. Don't panic if you have to think a minute. The time seems longer to you than to anybody else, and the vision of somebody really thinking hard is an admirable sight seen all too rarely.

The most important quality for effective public speaking is enthusiasm. If you are not enthusiastic, all the techniques in the world will not help you make a good speech. If you have enough enthusiasm, you can forget most of the techniques mentioned here and still be successful. Sometimes when you are first asked to present a certain subject to a group, you may feel it's not very interesting. But after you have done some research on the matter, thought about it, and become involved in it, you will probably be so excited about it that you are eager to communicate what you know to anyone who will sit and listen. If you can bring that kind of fervor to the speaker's stand, do not become too embarrassed to show all of your enthusiasm. If you are sold on the ideas you have to present and you sincerely wish your audience to be also, deliver your speech with all the energy and vitality you would bring to any talk that really mattered to you.

One word of caution: An audience can be turned off if you seem too pushy or too determined to persuade them to think or act the way you want them to. The key to showing an enthusiasm that is catching rather than repelling is having the desire to share what you have learned rather than to insist on its acceptance.

When you are finished, sit down. That last step is the hardest of all to take. Someone has said that the secret of public speaking is to get up, to speak up, and to shut up. How often have you listened to a speech and found several places for the speaker to stop before he did? Somehow it is quite difficult to believe you have communicated what you had hoped. But if you have reached your stopping place without selling your idea or explaining your process, you aren't going to do so in a dozen tacked-on sentences. Say the words you had planned as your closing ones, gather your notes, and sit down with a positive, decisive air.

How do you prepare the body of your speech?

All the public speaking techniques in the world will not help you give a good speech if you do not have something worthwhile to say, if you do not know your material, or if your speech is organized like a shopping list. Most of the public speeches you will give at first will probably be fixed as to content by somebody else. You will be asked to report on an investigation you have made, summarize the recommendations of a subcommittee, dedicate a drinking fountain, or introduce a speaker. But even if the subject is chosen by someone else, you will have to decide the purpose and scope of your talk yourself. Think about these things just as you do when you begin a written communication. Analyze your audience according to the knowledge and attitude they can be expected to bring to your subject. Note the place and occasion of your speech.

With all these things in mind, you should gather and organize the information and other material you will need for your speech. When you are ready to plan your speech in detail, read through what you have so that it is fresh in your mind. Then stand up and begin to talk about your subject. Remember, you will be standing when you deliver the speech. Don't write out a speech and read it. You don't write the way you talk. Also, unless you're quite unusual, you talk much better than you read aloud. You might be more comfortable reading than speaking, but you won't be communicating with your audience as well. Your purpose in speaking is to communicate; your comfort is much less important.

Don't memorize your speech either. A speech delivered from memory is only a little less indirect than a read speech. It is not flexible enough to allow you to answer the questions on the faces of your audience. It does not allow for the spontaneity of your own personality. Moreover, if you are relying on a memorized speech, you will be more nervous than if you plan to speak extemporaneously.

An extemporaneous speech is one that is carefully planned ahead of time and given from notes. Such a speech is appropriate for all but the most formal occasions. Radio and television speeches are normally read. But, other than these few exceptions, most speeches are given extemporaneously.

As you talk to yourself about your subject, you can try various methods of organization and presentation without spending the time that would be required if you wrote out your talk two or three different ways. Do not concern yourself with your beginning or your ending at this time.

When you're satisfied that you have found the organization and manner of presentation that you want to use for the body of your speech, sit down and make an outline of your speech. If you're still satisfied with it, transfer the outline to 3 × 5-inch cards. A large notebook or sheets of paper are distracting to an audience. The pages rattle when you turn them, and they may even blow or get out of order. Cards can be carried in your pocket or your purse; and if you discover that you will have to speak without the use of a desk or table, you can hold them in one hand.

On the cards you will probably want to put more than the bare outline, but you will not want to write out your whole speech. You will need the outline so that you will know what to talk about next. You may also need some names, figures, references, and quotations which you might forget. In general, put in your notes enough to remind you of what you had planned to say and to relieve you of the anxiety that arises from having to rely completely on your memory, but not enough to tempt you into reading exactly what you have written. Don't put so much on a card that you have to study the card closely. Either type double space or print in fairly large letters. The light on the platform may not be as good as it should be, or you may not be able to read as well as usual.

If there are any difficult parts in your speech—some highly technical explanation or some paragraph that, because of the emotions involved, is difficult to word—write those portions out and memorize them. You make take a card with the exact words written on it to jog your memory if you will be more comfortable doing so, but don't allow yourself to read it to the audience.

After you have completed your notes, get up and go through your speech, using your notes to see if they are understandable, usable, and complete.

What should you say in the conclusion of your speech?

When you are satisfied that the body of your speech as you have planned it is the most effective way to present your material, you are ready to plan your conclusion. A good conclusion is short, forceful, and conclusive. It serves a definite purpose which depends on the purpose of the speech. If your speech is to inform, your conclusion should summarize briefly the points which you have made. If you are reporting on a workshop or convention, you may want to close by dwelling on the general tone, the key thoughts, or the overall impression of the meetings. If your purpose is to convince your audience on certain points, you can summarize your arguments in the reverse order of their importance. If you seek to persuade your audience to action, you can summarize your arguments and then add an appeal to the desire for financial gain, long life, good health, family security, personal prestige, or public betterment.

Because your conclusion is your last opportunity to clinch your argument or sell your idea, you will want to plan it very carefully. Do not be satisfied with the first wording that occurs to you. Experiment. Try several ways for closing your speech until you have found the one best way to end with the proper emphasis. When you have found it, write it out word for word exactly as you plan to say it. It is a good idea at first to memorize this conclusion, because you may not be able to phrase your ideas as well in public as you can now.

What should you say in the introduction to your speech?

If you have noticed that you have not yet been advised to plan your opening remarks, maybe you have guessed why. The beginning of your speech should be designed to lead your listeners into the body of your speech, and you can't know the best way to lead them until you have made the trip yourself. A good introduction does two jobs: it catches the attention of the audience, and it leads the audience into the speaker's subject. It will defeat its purpose if it draws attention to itself or to the speaker rather than to his or her subject. Therefore, the best introductions often accomplish both of their purposes at once.

One of the most effective means of both catching attention and leading into the subject is the anecdote or illustrative narrative. Even if you have only a moderate ability as a storyteller, the ordinary listener will usually turn off his individual thoughts in order to listen to your story. If the problem to be solved in your story is concrete and close to the interests of your audience, you can build up some suspense as to the outcome. They will not only find your introduction irresistible, but they will continue to listen to you in case you should repeat the performance. A humorous anecdote can do much to get rid of tension and draw the audience to you and your subject. Because the humorous introduction is a very popular one, there are a few guides that you should observe in using humorous material:

Make the humor grow out of the situation or out of your subject.

Use a story, even a very funny one, only if it serves some definite purpose in your strategy.

Avoid using often-repeated jokes.

Keep your humor in good taste. Profanity, obscenity, and stories at the expense of minority groups or people with physical handicaps are not funny to everybody.

Be certain that you have the story straight, that the point is immediately apparent, and that you keep the story brief.

Do not label your humor either with your own laugher or with such an introduction as "That reminds me of a funny story."

If you cannot handle humor well, use something else.

Besides the anecdote, there are several other effective methods of opening a speech. You can ask a few provocative questions, make a startling but factual statement or two, or point to a paradox in the problem you will discuss. The striking first statement can be an epigram, a proverb, or a poetic quotation. It can be a thought-provoking prophecy. It can, by its references to local circumstances or to national, international, or historical happenings, be a bridge between the interests of the listeners and your topic. Tracing the background of your problem or subject may create a fascinating and useful introduction. If the occasion is associated with some special date or place, a well-chosen quotation or anecdote relevant both to the occasion and to your subject may perhaps be your best bet for an opening.

One type of introduction that you should avoid is the apology. Such a negative opening prepares the audience for a second-class performance. Moreover, the audience will think about what you tell them to think about. If you remind them to notice that your voice is shaky or that you have not given enough time to the preparation of what you are going to say, they will obediently do so.

Toward the end of your introduction you probably should make some easily recognizable and well-phrased statement of your thesis or aim. Occasionally you may find it wise to avoid a definite proposition early in your speech. If you make a bold statement that you are going to convince your audience that they should use peanut oil on the valves of their hydranagers, their immediate though silent response will probably be, "I'll bet you don't," or "Not if I can help it." Even if you don't want to make an explicit statement at the beginning, you still should make some statement to indicate what you are going to talk about so that your audience can put their minds in the proper gear. Never, however, begin with such an unsubtle remark as "I thought I would talk about. . . ."

How long should
the introduction be?

The length of your introduction will vary. In general, the length of your introduction should be proportionate to the length of the body of your speech. Some subjects, however, need longer introductions than others. A knowledge of a rather lengthy historical background may be essential to an understanding of your subject. This particular audience may need a longer introduction to arouse their interest in your subject. You may need to take time to break down prejudice or hostility toward your subject or yourself. If, on the other hand, the audience has the information they need to approach the subject, if they are already interested, and if they have no strong negative feelings, you can move into the body of your speech after only a brief introduction.

Your opening remarks will set the pace for your whole speech. If you lose your audience during the first few minutes, you may not recapture them. Apply imagination, resourcefulness, and even some research about your audience; arouse their interest in your subject, and set the tone for an interesting speech. Here again you should experiment until you have chosen the right words. Then write the opening paragraph down on a card and memorize it. After you have faced that audience and taken a deep breath, you can begin with the words you have memorized. By the time you have finished them, you will have your audience's attention, you will have gained some confidence and control, and you will be moving along into the body of your speech.

How should you practice your
speech?

Three or four short oral rehearsals at spaced intervals will give you a better preparation than one or two long ones. At your first rehearsal work on emphasis, and experiment with gestures that will help to underline your words. If you are the kind of person who stands at stiff attention, hands at your side, your face an inexpressive mask even when you argue with your roommate, then it probably will be natural for you to adapt the same posture for your public speaking. Natural, but certainly not effective. If, however, you are the kind of normal individual who scowls when you are insulted, beams when you are complimented, and doubles your fists when you are threatened, you will probably loosen up and make normal and appropriate gestures when you relax and become interested in your subject.

As you practice, you may pause as you try to think how to phrase a

228

thought, and you may fill your pauses with "and's" and "uh's." But don't worry about them now. Follow your outline and concentrate on your thought. At your next rehearsal you will have fewer such vocalized pauses. Your words and gestures will come more easily. Continue to experiment, however, as you strive for the clearest, most forceful means of communication. By the end of the second rehearsal you should have established the way you plan to deliver your speech.

At your third practice session, attempt to present your talk as you intend to before your audience. You may want to ask a colleague or friend to listen to you. If not, try to pretend that the chairs in your room are occupied and practice looking into imaginary faces as you speak. Do not practice in front of a mirror. Communication and not appearance is your first concern. You may record your speech so that you can listen critically to your phrasing. If you're not confident, if your speech is too long or too short, or if you're dissatisfied and decide to make some changes, you will need additional rehearsals. But don't rehearse so much that you have memorized your speech to the point that you can rattle it off like a robot. The emotion generated by the occasion and the friendly response of your audience may inspire you to more colorful and effective phrasing than you would now fix in your speech. Learn your speech completely enough to give yourself confidence but not so completely that your delivery is frozen and any chance of spontaneity is destroyed.

Should you use any mechanical devices in your speech?

In many public speech situations you may want to use some visual or auditory devices. Such devices can serve three purposes: they can help you make a clearer explanation, they can help you hold the attention of your audience, and they can help you fix certain facts in the audience's minds. Communication and teaching take place through the senses; and when more than one sense is used, their effectiveness is increased. Talking pictures are more popular than silent ones; television drama is more fascinating than radio drama. Some movie producers have even experimented with adding odor to their pictures.

Such devices include charts, maps, slides, moving pictures, phonograph records, sound tapes, manikins, puppets, and any kind of instrument, apparatus, or machine that can be demonstrated. Your choice of device should depend upon your topic and audience. No matter how fascinating you may find a given mechanical device, you should not use it unless it adds to your explanation, not distracts from it. It should not have such a complicated mechanism that either you or your audience becomes carried away with its operation. Don't twist your speech so you can use some clever gadget. Remember that the device is an *aid* to your speech. Don't depend upon it to clear the fog left by a muddled explanation or to demonstrate order in your reasoning where none exists.

How can you use your device most effectively?

You will get the best results with your device if you observe a few basic points. All of your audience must be able to see your device. Make your charts or maps large enough to be seen by everyone and place them where everyone can see them without strain. Make the letters large enough to be read and the lines of letters and drawings dark enough and wide enough to be seen. When you're planning your speech, consider the shape, arrangement, and lighting of the room where the speech will be given. It may be that these factors will make it impossible for your device to be seen no matter how large and clear it is.

After you have taken these precautions, don't spoil the effect by getting in the way yourself. Stand behind the device or well to one side; and, if possible, use a pointer to focus attention and to avoid obstructing the view.

Make your device easily understandable. Keep your labels short and simple and avoid unnecessary details in your drawing. Don't crowd the material in your layout. Spread it out well over the whole chart. If your chart or map is still too crowded, use more than one. Schematic drawings or charts that illustrate points progressively will emphasize the important features better than one complicated chart on which you try to show too much at once.

Because your device should direct attention to the points you are making, not distract from them, you should plan your device so that you can fit it into the talk at the moment when it supports a point. If you can, keep it hidden until you are ready for it and put it out of sight when you are through with it.

Don't devote more time to a device than it is worth. A very complicated device can take up too much time, delaying or interrupting your speech while you are getting something ready. Do any writing on the blackboard before the meeting and then hide it behind a screen until you need it. A machine should be set up, tested, and ready for operation before the meeting. If necessary, ask someone to help you so that you won't have to interrupt your talk to move furniture or adjust a screen.

When your topic involves an explanation of some complicated mechanism, you will find demonstration with the actual machine is not only helpful but absolutely essential. In making such a demonstration, explain the process first and then move into your demonstration without delay. Keep the demonstration short and as simple as possible, focusing on the specific points covered in your explanation. Practice ahead of time so that you can perform the demonstration with ease. If you are awkward, you will make the procedure seem more difficult than it really is. If you wish to show that a procedure is simple, perhaps you can take someone from your audience and teach him or her to do what you have just done. Such a demonstration probably will not be really effective if the audience is very large, very far away, or unable to move about and see the object from several angles.

Does the use of a device require any special rehearsing?

If possible, you should rehearse your speech using your aid in the room in which your speech will be given. Have someone move about the room as you talk to see if your device can be seen comfortably by all the members of your audience. Your slides may be excellent, but they will not do much good in the daytime in a room without dark curtains or shades. Your chart may show the relationship between your points in a memorable manner, but there is little chance it will be remembered if you are standing in front of it while you talk. Your drawings may be well laid out and reflect the orderliness of your thinking, but they will reflect only the late afternoon sun if you fail to take into consideration the placement of the windows and the time of the meeting. If you stage an early rehearsal with a friend to serve as a roving audience, you will have a chance to catch any problems that might later arise and to be certain that your device is really an aid and not a distraction or disappointment.

How did you do?

After you have given a speech, you probably would like to know how you did. Better yet, you would like to plan a superior performance. The following criteria will help you do both. Because you are used to measuring your performance with letter grades, they are used here.

How Well Are Your Notes Prepared?

    A. Your notes are brief, written or typed on 3 × 5-inch cards or small sheets which you can handle in one hand.

    B. Your speech is written out rather completely on cards.

    C. Your notes are on large sheets of paper that rattle.

    D. Your notes are in a notebook which you spread out in full view.

    F. Your notes are in your briefcase, and you have trouble with the lock.

How Well Do You Use Your Notes?

    A. You glance at your notes at brief intervals to guide you into the different divisions of your speech or to check figures or names.

    B. You interrupt your speech to consult your notes frequently.

    C. You rely heavily upon your notes.

    D. You read most of your speech.

    F. You read all of your speech.

Do You Have Eye Contact with Your Audience?

    A. You look into the faces of most of the people before you.

    B. You look at a few people that you think you can trust.

    C. You look at the tops of the heads of your audience.

    D. You look out the window or at a spot on the back wall.

    F. The audience looks at the top of your head.

Do You Keep Your Audience Interested?

    A. You have an enthusiastic interest in your subject that is contagious.

    B. Your audience listens attentively.

    C. Your audience is polite but bored.

    D. Some people are reading, writing, talking, or sleeping.

    F. Nobody is paying attention to you.

How Do You Use Your Voice?

    A. You can be heard and understood as you speak in a pleasant, expressive voice.

    B. You can be heard and understood.

    C. You drone in a monotone without expression or variety.

    D. You mumble.

    F. You are struck speechless.

Are Your Gestures Meaningful?

    A. You move your hands, arms, and face naturally and expressively.

    B. You make an unplanned, meaningful gesture.

    C. You stand relaxed but motionless.

D. You play with your notes, glasses, or pen, pace the floor, or fidget nervously.

F. You stand at rigid attention.

Is Your Word Choice Effective?

A. Your sentences are well constructed, your word choice is good, and you make no grammatical errors.

B. Your sentence construction and word choice need some improvement, but you make few errors.

C. You have given little thought to how you say what you say and you make a number of grammatical errors.

D. You make grammatical errors, and some of your words are inappropriate for the occasion.

F. Where did you learn language like that?

Do You Have Something Worthwhile to Say?

A. You have something to say that is important to you. You have done some reading and some original thinking about it, and you cause your audience to think a new thought or look at an old thought in a new way.

B. What you have to say is important to you, but you rely almost completely on what other people have written or said on the subject.

C. You had a good idea; and if you had started to plan your speech earlier, you might have been able to develop it well.

D. Your subject is large, abstract, and overworked. It is usually discussed in vague, abstract words, and clichés. Your discussion is no exception.

F. You have nothing to say, but it took you too long to say it.

Is Your Introduction Effective?

A. You catch the attention of your audience in an original way that leads easily into the body of your speech.

B. You catch the attention of your audience in an original way, but it has no apparent connection with the body of your speech.

C. Your beginning is quite ordinary, but it does introduce your speech.

D. You have no introduction at all; your audience figures out what you are talking about sometime after you begin.

F. You begin your speech by saying, "I'm going to talk about . . ."

Is the Body of Your Speech Well Organized?

A. Your organization of material is logical and clear; your subject is developed as completely as your purpose requires; and your emphasis is properly placed.

B. Your logic, clarity, completeness, or emphasis leave something to be desired but not a great deal.

C. The relationship between the parts of your speech is not completely clear.

D. You have trouble staying on the subject.

F. What on earth are you talking about?

Is Your Conclusion Effective?

A. You draw your speech to a close with a concise summary, an effective application or brief narrative, or an emphatic call for action.

B. You try to draw your speech to a close, but the results are less concise, effective, or emphatic than they could be.

C. You just quit talking and sit down.

D. The audience found several places for you to stop before you did.

F. Only the instructor, the bell, or exhaustion (yours or the audience's) could stop you.

ASSIGNMENTS

I. Prepare and deliver a three-minute speech on one of the topics below. Prepare your notes in such a way that they may be submitted to your instructor following delivery of your speech.

1. An appeal before your city council (or church group) requesting that there be more planned activities for the young people in the community. Offer some definite suggestions for what activities might be organized and show why they are needed. Keep your approach positive.

2. An appearance before your school's curriculum committee. Indicate to them one or two weaknesses that you as a student see in your present training program. Suggest what change(s) you think would be helpful. Don't argue; sell your ideas.

3. An explanation to your class of some important new concept in your own field of interest. This concept may be a revolutionary new idea, a new piece of equipment that has recently been discovered, etc. Assume that your audience is not as knowledgeable in the field as you; keep your presentation at a nontechnical level. Use whatever devices might be helpful to assist you in making your subject informative and interesting.

4. Brief comments to the local chapter of your vocational or professional group. Your purpose is to explain to them the positive points of the educational program that your school is currently offering in the area. These individuals are professionals, so you should speak professionally.

5. A brief speech before a group of graduating high school seniors. You have been sent as a representative from your technical area to sell them on the opportunities that your

profession can offer. Cite job openings in the area, expected job prospects within the next fifteen years, salaries, and fringe benefits. Make the job itself sound exciting by referring to some of the challenges it offers. They know a fraud when they see one, so be sincere.

II. After you have made your short speech in class, criticize yourself. What were your weak points? Were they matters of content or delivery? What were the good points? Write a short theme (about 500 words) in which you evaluate your own speech.

III. After you have carefully evaluated your speech, and after you have received comments on it from your instructor and other students, plan changes that will improve it. Perhaps you need more material. Probably you need to polish your delivery. Certainly you must look directly at your audience this time.

Using the same topic but adding to it and changing it where necessary, prepare and deliver a longer speech—a minimum of eight minutes. Include in this presentation at least one visual aid.

Good speaking opens the way for further communication with the audience, and communication is a two-way process. After you have finished speaking, take about two more minutes to answer questions from your audience. Keep calm. Remember that you are the authority on your subject.

Writing a Formal
Research Report

What is a formal research report?

Although much on-the-job writing involves short memos and informal reports, certain situations demand that your writing be more formal and that you document the sources of your information. For example, your committee at work may be asked to study several retirement programs and then to make a recommendation that your company select a specific program. This assignment is obviously of sufficient importance that you would not write a hasty paragraph or two in your own handwriting and submit this to your company president. Instead, you would study all available information carefully, organize your information into a tightly structured format, write your report in a dignified manner, and follow some system for showing exactly where you got your information. Finally, you would bind the entire report neatly and submit it to your president.

The formal research report is just that: a formally written report that presents the final results of an extensive fact-finding search. Although your report may end with your conclusions or recommendations, the bulk of your material is synthesized from the various sources that you have studied during the research phase.

What jobs do research reports do?

Both formal and informal reports can be classified by the job they do.

- Informational
- Analytical
- Special Purpose

Informational reports are reports that give information. In this type of report you will make no data analysis or recommendations.

> *Progress reports:* Reports of changes in conditions over a period of time. The progress report may cover a specific period—a week, thirty days, a year—or it may be a progress-to-date report which relates to events up to the time of presentation.
>
> *Status reports:* Description of conditions at a specific moment of time.
>
> *Narrative reports:* Description of an event. The narrative report can cover an event that happened at any time. It does not necessarily deal with changes in conditions or with changes at any given moment.

Analytical reports give analysis of data. In such a report you will always draw conclusions and make recommendations. Although there are three general types, in practice the three frequently overlap.

> Problem solving
> Proposal   Normal pattern: analyze,
> Research   conclude, recommend.

Special purpose reports are any reports not included in the above categories. Such reports may be informational, analytical, or both. They can present a summary, give progress and status information, draw conclusions, make recommendations, and predict future conditions. The following classifications refer to the stages, during the life of the assignment, at which a report is made.

> *Preliminary report:* made at the beginning of an assignment, a kind of preparation.
>
> *Interim report:* made at the halfway point or at a stated interval.
>
> *Final report.*

Where do you get the information you need?

The sources from which you will gather information are limited only by your subject and your resourcefulness. In the report involving the problem of the employee cafeteria, for instance, you might visit the kitchen when it is empty in order to analyze the layout, then again at various times of the day to observe the different phases of meal preparation, serving, and cleanup. You might also visit cafeterias in similar companies and commercially operated cafeterias. You can interview several individuals in the department to ask what they thought was the problem—the dietitian, the baker, the cooks, the servers, the dishwashers, the tray boys. The more people you talk to, the more suggestions you will hear and the less you will be influenced by a self-satisifed cook or server or an intolerant baker or dishwasher. Interviews with people involved in the training or directing of personnel in successfully operated cafeterias may yield ideas. You may need to call in several experts to advise you concerning the equipment and facilities of the kitchen. You may send for a relevant government bulletin. You might examine pamphlets put out by the utilities companies and brochures issued by appliance companies. Various professional periodicals published for business or industry managers or hotel and restaurant managers might contain helpful articles. Books at the local library may contribute general and background information. Your company may send you to a professional meeting or convention where you can attend workshops, listen to informative talks, and visit product exhibits.

How do you make notes on this information?

From all these sources you gather information on which you make careful notes. Whether you are recording information gathered from observation, interview, or reading, you will record it accurately only if you make your notes on the spot. Do not trust your memory for anything. Except for statistical information, specifications, or lists, use whole sentences. Clauses, phrases, and isolated words may seem meaningful to you while you are gathering information; but later, when your notes are cold, the bits and pieces that you have jotted down may not convey much information. Faced with such uncommunicating fragments, you will have several choices: you can go back and reread, reobserve, reinterview, and renote; you can forget the whole thing and change jobs; or you can string the clauses, phrases, and words together in what appear to be sentences and paragraphs, hoping your reader will know what was meant in the original sources although you do not. Your work will go more easily at each step and your finished report will be more usable if you take down your information in whole sentences you and your reader can understand.

You will find no need to quote excessively in report writing. When you do have such a need, check and recheck for accuracy. Nobody likes to be misquoted, and misquotations lead to misconceptions along the way and to errors in your conclusions.

Make your notes on 3 × 5 or 5 × 8 cards according to the form suggested in Chapter 14. You should be especially careful to take only one piece of information on a card. As you read and take notes, you will often find together in one paragraph or sentence several facts which the writer saw as closely related in a certain way. Later you may want to relate those facts to each other in a different way and to other facts in other ways. If you have blindly lumped several pieces of information together on one card, you may fail to see these new relationships. You will find it difficult to use your notes without violating the unity of your paragraphs, distorting the organization of your report, or tearing your notes into scraps of "subnotes." If for some reason you had to take some notes on a larger piece of paper or if you discover later that what you have on one note card is more than one piece of information, copy your notes over with one fact to a card.

You will handle your information more quickly and easily if you make two kinds of cards: a *source card* containing the complete information about the book, periodical article, interview, or meeting, and a *note card* containing the piece of information, the last name of the writer or speaker who reported the information, and the page number. If you put all the bibliographic data on each note card, you will just do a lot of unnecessary and repititious writing. Don't however, rely upon some code of symbols or letters which you plan to cross-match with some master list. Rely upon this simple method:

Long, p. 82
Abbott, pp. 69, 70.

Figure 17-1 illustrates how a source card might look. Notice that it contains the same parts as a formal bibliographic entry.
Figure 17-2 shows how a note card taken from Verry's book might look.

When you are satisfied that your outline provides the best organization of your material, finish arranging your notes. If you stack your

figure 17-1

figure 17-2

Page number — Page number

Label (to help fit material into section of report)

Author's name

Verly, p. 11   Types of Equipment

There are three general types of equipment : reduction, retrieval, and reproduction.

The note itself

cards exactly in the order in which you will use them, you can follow your outline, working each note into your report as you come to it. Writing your report will then be easy. You will just use the data you have gathered to put meat on the bare bones of your outline. Often by adding a transitional word or phrase or by shifting a clause, you can use many of the sentences you wrote on your note cards.

Where do you give credit to your sources?

When you write your formal research report, there are two important places where you give credit to your sources: footnotes and the final bibliography. Footnotes are used to indicate exactly where you got a specific bit of information. You will use footnotes throughout your paper, giving credit to your various sources as you use those sources. Your footnotes should be numbered consecutively throughout the report, and your numbers for footnotes are always to be placed just slightly above the normal writing line. In many contemporary specimens of research writing the footnotes now appear at the end of the report rather than at the bottom of the page. Although these are more accurately called end notes, they serve exactly the same purpose as footnotes. (In the sample paper at the end of this chapter the author has used end notes instead of footnotes.)

Although you give credit to your sources throughout your paper with footnotes, you need to present *all* of your sources again in a final, formal listing at the end of the report. This final bibliography is an alphabetized listing of all of the sources you have used in compiling your report. The form for the bibliography is not the same as the form for footnotes; study the following section of the text carefully to differentiate the two.

How should footnote and bibliography entries be made?

Examples of the type of reference material that you will most frequently use are given below. Any of several good research manuals can help you with forms not included here. Keep in mind that research forms vary from manual to manual and sometimes from teacher to teacher. The forms given here are quite standard and will be correct for this course, but another instructor may wish you to use a slightly modified form.

1. book with one author

F.N.
(footnote)
[1]Ralph DeSola, <u>Microfilming</u> (New York: Essential Books, 1944), p. 419.

The author's name is not reversed in the footnote, and commas separate the parts of the notation. Notice, though, that there is no comma between the title and the material in parentheses. Remember to put a period after p. and at the end of the footnote.

Bib.
(bibliography)
DeSola, Ralph. <u>Microfilming.</u> New York: Essential Books, 1944.

Notice that the book entry has three parts-author, title, and publishing information-each separated by a period. No page numbers are given. The entry ends with a period.

2. book with two authors

F.N.
[1]Henry Ewbank and J. Jeffery Auer, <u>Discussion and Debate</u> (New York: Appleton-Century, Crofts, Inc., 1951), p. 118.

Bib.
Ewbank, Henry Lee, and J. Jeffery Auer. <u>Discussion and Debate.</u> New York: Appleton-Century-Crofts, Inc., 1951.

When you have two or more authors, you reverse the name of only the first one in the bibliography.

3. book with three or more authors

F.N.
[1]J. N. Arnold <u>et al.</u>, <u>Introductory Graphics</u> (New York: McGraw-Hill, Inc., 1958), pp. 17-18.

Use the abbreviation pp. when you refer to more than one page of material.

Bib. Arnold, J. N., <u>et al</u>. <u>Introductory Graphics</u>. New
York: McGraw—Hill,Inc., 1958.

Et al. is a common bibliographic abbreviation meaning and
others. *It saves your having to list all of the authors for a work.
Notice that you write the name of the publisher exactly as it appears on the title page of the book, abbreviating only items that
are abbreviated there.*

4. book with author's name followed by a title

F.N. [1]Joseph L. Kish, Jr., and James Morris, <u>Micro—
film in Business</u> (New York: The Ronald Press, 1966),
p. 12.

*Observe that Jr. is a title and is set off from a person's name by
a comma.*

Bib. Kish, Joseph L., Jr., and James Morris. <u>Microfilm in
Business.</u> New York: The Ronald Press Company,
1966.

5. an anthology with one editor

F.N. [1]L. V. Ryan, ed., <u>A Science Reader</u> (New York:
Holt, Rinehart & Winston, Inc., 1959),
pp. 5—7, 9.

*List consecutive pages by connecting them with a hyphen; indi-
cate nonconsecutive pages by using a comma.*

Bib. Ryan, L. V., ed. <u>A Science Reader.</u> New York: Holt,
Rinehart & Winston, Inc., 1959.

6. an anthology with two editors

F.N. [1]F. R. Moulton and J. J. Schiffers, eds., <u>The
Autobiography of Science</u> (New York: Doubleday &
Company, Inc., 1950), p. 12.

Bib. Moulton, F. R., and J. J. Schiffers, eds. <u>The Autobi—
ography of Science.</u> Garden City, N. Y.:
Doubleday & Company, Inc., 1950.

7. an article in a magazine

F.N. [1]C. T. Graver, "Power Supply for Nuclear Research
Laboratory," <u>EE</u>, 72 (1953) 214.

*If the magazine is one generally known to the audience who will
read your paper, you may abbreviate its title in the footnote but*

not in the bibliography. Notice that no abbreviations come before the volume and page numbers. If the magazine can be identified by volume number, use that number only. If an exact date is needed (see example #9), you do not show volume number.

Bib.   Graver, C. T. "Power Supply for Nuclear Research
Laboratory." <u>Electrical Engineering</u>
72 (1953) 212–216.

Put the title of the article in quotation marks and underline the title of the magazine.

8. an essay in an anthology

F.N.   [1]Thomas Henry Huxley, "The Method of Scientific Investigation," in <u>Subject and Structure,</u> ed.
John M. Wasson (Boston: Little Brown and Company,
1963), p. 217.

Bib.   Huxley, Thomas Henry. "The Method of Scientific Investigation," in <u>Subject and Structure,</u> ed. John
M. Wasson. Boston: Little Brown and Company,
1963, pp. 214–219.

List the title of your essay. Indicate the editor of the collection immediately after the title by using the abbreviation ed. Note that no period separates the editor's name from the city of publication in the footnote.

9. an article without an author

F.N.   [1]"Coming Next: Push Button Banking," <u>U.S. News
and World Reports,</u> 14 Feb. 1966, p. 110.

Bib.   "Coming Next: Push Button Banking," <u>U.S. News and
World Reports,</u> 14 Feb. 1966, pp. 108–110.

Alphabetize your entry by the first major word in the title.

10. an article in a newspaper

F.N.   [1]"New Data Processing Procedures Employed by
Local Firms," <u>The Big City Register,</u> 8 July 1968,
p. 2., Sec. A.

Bib.   "New Data Processing Procedures Employed by Local
Firms," <u>The Big City Register,</u>
8 July 1968, p. 2., Sec. A.

If the name of the reporter is given, that name will go first in your entry.

11. pamphlet

F.N.   [1]"Communications Services Anytown," Promotional pamphlet published by Bell Telephone System, n.d.

Bib.   "Communications Services Anytown," Promotional pamphlet published by Bell Telephone System, n.d.

Alphabetize by title. If the pamphlet has page numbers, indicate page cited in footnote. Use the abbreviation n.d. (no date) when there is no publication date given.

12. interview

F.N.   [1]Personal interview with Fred Anderson, Austin, Texas, 10 January 1978.

Bib.   Alexander, Fred. Personal interview. 10 January 1978.

13. correspondence

F.N.   [1]Elizabeth Freeman, Letter to the author, 15 May 1977.

Bib.   Freeman, Elizabeth. Letter to the author, 15 May 1977.

14. encyclopedia

F.N.   [1]"Data Processing," The Modern Encyclopedia, 1966 ed.

Bib.   "Data Processing," The Modern Encyclopedia, 1966 ed.

Be certain to include the edition or the date of the encyclopedia. It is not necessary to give volume and page numbers in works with alphabetized entries.

How do you write subsequent footnotes?

Your subsequent references to the same work will differ from the first. You have the option of writing them in two ways. First, you may use the abbreviations *Ibid.,* for the Latin word *ibidem; Op. cit.,* for the Latin *opere citato;* and *Loc. cit,* for the Latin *loco citato.* Second, you may use the currently favored practice of merely citing the author's name, or name and short title if you use more than one work by the same author.

A. *Ibid.* means "in the same place." You use it to refer to the citation immediately preceding it. You may also use it in succession.

> ¹Ralph DeSola, <u>Microfilming</u> (New York, 1944),
>   p. 419.
> ²Ibid., p. 688.
> ³Ibid., p. 222.

B. *Op. cit.* means "in the work cited." You use it to refer to a work cited but not immediately preceding. Use it along with the author's name and page number.

> ¹Ralph DeSola, Microfilming (New York, 1944),
>   p. 419.
> ²J. N. Smith, <u>Graphics in Business</u> (Boston,
>   1977), p. 34.
> ³DeSola, <u>op. cit.</u> p. 82.

C. *Loc. cit.* means "in the place cited." You use it along with the author's name to refer to an exact passage cited but not immediately preceding.

> ¹Ralph DeSola, <u>Microfilming</u> (New York, 1944),
>   p. 608.
> ²J. N. Smith, <u>Graphics in Business</u> (Boston,
>   1977), p. 60.
> ³DeSola, <u>oc.cit.</u>

You should be aware of these methods of handling subsequent footnote form. However, while *Ibid.* is still widely used, most writers find the other Latin forms cumbersome and somewhat needless. The preferred current usage is as follows:

> ¹Ralph DeSola, <u>Microfilming</u> (New York, 1944),
>   p. 100.
> ²DeSola, p. 78.
> ³J. N. Smith, <u>Graphics in Business</u> (Boston,
>   1977), p. 20.
> ⁴DeSola, p. 83.

For usage with *Ibid.,* see the sample student paper at the end of this chapter.

How do you write
the introduction?

Some people write the introduction first and some write it last. If you thought through your report completely as you outlined it, you might have been able to write the introduction first. More than likely, however, you did not realize all the implications involved in your material until you actually shaped the sentences and paragraphs of your report. You can't write an introduction until you know what you are going to introduce; and the more completely you know what you are going to introduce, the better the introduction will be. Now that you have written the body, conclusions, and recommendations, you can decide what you need to include in your introduction.

Ask yourself what your reader will need to know before he or she can properly understand and evaluate your report. Go back and examine the kinds of information that are usually included in a report and decide what is the purpose of your introduction. You can write a paragraph or two telling why your study was made and explaining the problem you are trying to solve. You might also explain some aspect of the history or background of the problem. Then you may need to write one or more paragraphs defining some of the terms used in the report, describing the way you gathered your information, or explaining what your report will cover. Remember your reader as you plan your introduction, and be sure to mention the things he or she needs to know.

What belongs in
the conclusion?

Your conclusions are the crux of your whole report. They may be obvious to your reader after he or she has read your report or you may arrive at them only after you have carefully weighed bits of conflicting evidence. Your conclusion should not introduce any new evidence but should derive from the evidence presented in the body of your paper. The reader of your report should have been given all the information that leads to your conclusion, and should have been able to follow your logic as you weighed the information. Ideally he or she can now arrive at the same conclusions you do. If not, the reader should still be able to see how you got there. Present your conclusions clearly and support them with references to information in the body of your paper or in the appendix. You will not need to repeat this information, but you should refer to it specifically and indicate the page of your paper on which it is found.

The length of the conclusion will, of course, depend upon the length of your paper. If the body of your paper was four or five pages long, you may be able to present your conclusion in a paragraph or two. A shorter paper may require only a brief paragraph for its conclusion; a longer paper, a page or more. You should try to make your conclusion brief and to the point. A short conclusion, well phrased and definitely stated, will carry more weight than a longer one that has its complete meaning hidden under a blanket of vague and wordy sentences.

What do you do about recommendations?

Whether or not you will make recommendations will depend upon the type of report you are making. If your report is the type that should contain recommendations, these should derive clearly from your conclusion. If your report contains much conflicting evidence, bear in mind that conclusions can be interpreted differently by different people. Don't let such evidence keep you from making any recommendations, but be as objective as possible. If your facts lead logically to your conclusion and your conclusion logically to your recommendations, your reader will agree with you even if you state your recommendations cautiously.

What material belongs in the appendix?

If you have an appendix to your report, it will contain detailed data such as reference tables of statistics not immediately needed in the body of your report. The material included in your appendix should do one of two jobs:

> Give a picture. A photograph or artist's drawing can be used unless the report is to be reproduced by some inexpensive process such as mimeograph or letter duplicator. In that case, only line drawings (pictures containing no shading) can be used.
> Present data in an organized, easily understood form. Charts, maps, graphs, tables, or lists can be used.

Data that are too detailed to be presented easily in a paragraph should be summarized in the body of the report and reported completely in list, table, or chart form in the appendix. Preparing such a device may take extra time; but if it makes the material clearer and more usable to your reader, you should do so. If communicating your information to your reader were not important, you would not be writing a report in the first place. In some reports you may use vocabulary that is not immediately recognized by your reader or that is used in a different manner. If so, your appendix might well contain a vocabulary listing that gives key words and shows how you have used them in your report. The form you use to tabulate detailed information will be determined by your data. You can use a table to organize data into columns and rows; a table is useful if you want to present exact quantities. To make a chart or graph, you can use bars, lines, maps, circles, squares, stick figures, or any other kind of representation that will present your data clearly and forcefully. You can give the same information on both a table and a chart if your purpose requires doing so.

How do you bind your report?

Some companies have special binders for their reports. Others use a regular file folder. In either case the title of your report will appear on the cover. The title you give your report is very important. Most of the life of your report will be spent in a filing cabinet from which it can emerge to receive attention only if you have titled it so it can be recognized. Clever titles that catch the eye or ear, arouse curiosity, or provoke imagination may sell books and stories, draw long lines at the box office, or please a high school English teacher, but they are not appropriate or helpful on a report. You can choose a satisfactory title for your report by selecting and arranging the best words to give a preliminary description of your report. Here are some examples:

The Effect of Welding Thermal Cycles on the Microstructure of T-1 Steel

A Comparison of Three Intercommunication Systems for Installation in the Outpatient Department

A Proposal for Establishment of a New Department of Urban Ecology

An Analysis of Recent Job Openings in Accounting Careers

What does the written research report look like?

Following is a sample report for your examination. Notice how the various parts fit together.

THE PHENOMENON OF SUPERCONDUCTIVITY

Dan Blasdell

November 30, 1977

THE PHENOMENON OF SUPERCONDUCTIVITY

Superconductivity, a relatively new and not completely understood area of science, has been the subject of much new study and has over the past two decades undergone significant development. When this phenomenon was first discovered, it was not really considered a property of science that would be of any realistic use economically or technically speaking. But as knowledge and understanding of superconductivity grew, scientists found ways to put this phenomenon to work in our society.

As the name implies, superconductivity is a state in which certain conductors become extremely conductive and in essence have an infinite conductivity and/or an electrical resistance of zero. This superconductive state is reached by cooling the superconductor down to a very low temperature, near absolute zero.[1] When the critical temperature (Tc) is reached, the substance becomes a superconductor.

The discovery of superconductivity was made by H. Kamerlingh Onnes in 1911[3] when he was studying the relationship between temperature and resistance of a conductor near absolute zero. He discovered that mercury's resistivity suddenly dropped to an immeasurable amount at 4.2°K.

Little was done with superconductivity again until 1933, when W. Meissner and R. Ochsenfeld discovered that a substance in the superconducting state exhibits diamagnetism if the introduced magnetic field is not too strong,[4] i.e., a superconducting substance will expell a magnetic field from its interior if the field does not exceed a certain strength. This discovery showed that superconductivity involves more than its name implies.

If a normal conductor is placed in a magnetic field, the magnetic field lines of force are concentrated through the conductor. As mentioned, superconductors become diamagnetic, expelling the magnetic field. This was thought to be true of all superconductors until the metal Niobium (Nb_{41}) was tested for this property. Niobium was found to exhibit different magnetic properties than other superconductors and because of these differences, superconductors are now divided into two categories—type I and type II.

A type I superconductor is diamagnetic while below its T_c. If the temperature is raised above its T_c, the substance stops superconducting and any magnetic field is allowed to penetrate. Also, a superconductor can be

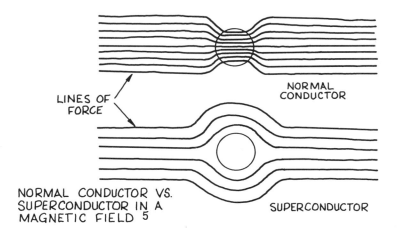

LINES OF
FORCE

NORMAL
CONDUCTOR

NORMAL CONDUCTOR VS.
SUPERCONDUCTOR IN A
MAGNETIC FIELD 5

SUPERCONDUCTOR

removed from the superconducting state by increasing the applied magnetic field beyond the H_c (critical field). At the point the magnetic field exceeds the H_c, the substance will stop superconducting.

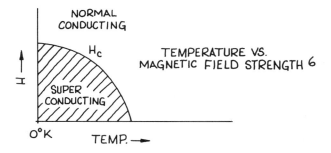

NORMAL
CONDUCTING

H_c

TEMPERATURE VS.
MAGNETIC FIELD STRENGTH 6

H

SUPER
CONDUCTING

0°K   TEMP. →

Type II superconductors have three states of conducting—super-conducting, mixed state, and normal conducting. Below T_c and as the applied magnetic field strength increases from zero, the substance will remain super-conducting until the magnetic field strength reaches a certain value (H_{c1}). At this value the type II superconductors will go into the mixed state of conducting. In this state the magnetic field penetrates the substance, but only in certain microscropic filament areas called fluxoids. In each fluxoid, normal conducting is observed, wheras outside the fluxoid the sub-stance is superconductive. As the magnetic field strength is increased

4

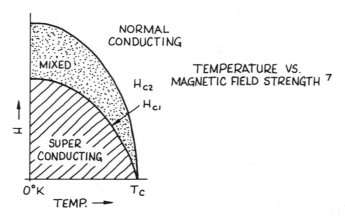

further, the substance remains in the mixed state until an H_{c3} is reached,
where the entire substance stops superconducting. Niobium is the only known
elemental type II superconductor[8] but there is a long and growing list of type
II (and type I) compound superconductors.

Uses for superconductivity are very specialized but in some cases
very economical in view of alternative methods of performing the task.

One such task that would be more economical to carry out using superconductivity than by conventional means would be the transmission of large
amounts of electrical power over long distances.[9] The boundary of where
superconductive lines would be more or less expensive than conventional means
would be transmitting over 100 gigawatts (100,000,000,000) of power over distances of 1,000 kilometers (ca. 600 miles). These parameters would make it
too expensive for the shipment of coal or similar sources and would also make
it too expensive for the building of high-voltage mormal conductor lines to
the source of consumption. The line loss due to resistance on a line like
this would be about $340 million a year.[10]

Quite obviously, the major problem of such a superconducting transmission line would be keeping the line cooled over the entire length. This
problem would be solved by using liquid helium as a coolant. Since helium
liquifies at 4°K, a superconductor was chosen with a T_c as high as possible

over the 4°K. Nb_3Sn ($T_c=18°K$) is the best choice economically and scientif-
ically. Since this line has to cover over 600 miles, it must be made as
thriftily as possible. The line would be insulated by vacuums and would be
embedded in the ground by concrete. Also liquid nitrogen (N_2) would help
cool the outside vacuum. The vacuums would be supplied by vacuum pumps every
500 meters and there would be refrigeration stations every 20 km. This
total system would be very expensive—about $806 million, not including the
on-site labor,[12] but would still be less expensive to build and run than other
alternatives.

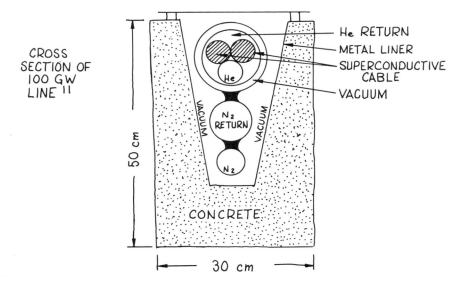

CROSS
SECTION OF
100 GW
LINE [11]

Another feasible use for superconductivity is superconducting
magnets. Normal conductor electro magnets are limited in their strength by
the high resistance of their coils, which develop large amounts of heat.
With the help of type II superconductors, large electro superconducting
magnets are possible. Type I: superconductors would be useless in such a
magnet because their H_c is too low. But type II superconductors remain
superconductive up to their H_{c2}, which is extremely high in some cases.
Today large superconducting magnets are very successful because of their

power savings and very high available magnetic field strengths.

Another possible use of superconductors is to employ them in computer memories. This is made possible by the phenomenon of superconductive
persistent currents. Since superconductors have no resistance, the current
flow in a superconducting circuit is continuous, even without a source of
potential difference. It has been estimated that the decay time for such a
curcuit is at least 100,000 years.[13]

Still other potential uses for superconductivity are gyroscopes,
bolometers, transformers, generators, motors, lenses for electron micro-
scopes, plasma containment magnets, linear accelerator resonant cavities,
and bubble and spark chamber magnets.[14]

The doors of this strange and fascinating area of science are just
beginning to open fully, and today's scientists are beginning to realize the
impact of this phenomenon. In the United States alone, at least 2,600
papers on superconductivity were published between 1961 and 1965.[15] The-
oretical conjectures have been made stating the existence of a possible
exotic compound that would become superconducting at room temperature.[16]
This possibility continues to be pursued. Superconductivity is beginning to
take on importance in many areas of science.[17] As today's world continues
to become more and more complex and problem-filled, superconductivity may
be turned to as a feasible and economical answer to tomorrow's problems.

7

FOOTNOTES

[1]Absolute zero is the temperature at which all molecular motion ceases, thus absolute zero is the lowest possible temperature, but has never been obtained. Values for absolute zero are $0°K$ (kelvin), $-273°$ C., and $-459.4°$ F. The size of one kelvin degree equals one celcius degree ($\triangle K° = \triangle C°$).

[2]D. N. Langenberg, "Superconductivity," McGraw-Hill Encyclopedia of Science and Technology, 1977 ed.

[3]Ibid.

[4]Ibid.

[5]B. T. Matthias, "Superconductivity," Scientific American. (Nov. 1957), p. 94.

[6]Langenberg, p. 311.

[7]Ibid.

[8]Ibid.

[9]Richard L. Garwin and J. Matisoo, "Superconducting Lines for the Transmission of Large Amounts of Electrical Power over Great Distances," in Superconductivity in Science and Technology, ed. Morrel H. Cohen (Chicago: University of Chicago Press, 1969), p. 79.
[10]Ibid.

[11]Ibid., p. 84.

[12]Ibid., p. 90.

[13]Langenberg, p. 310.

[14]Roland W. Schmitt and W. Adair Morrison, "Economic Aspects of Superconductivity," in Superconductivity in Science and Technology, ed. Morrel H. Cohen (Chicago: University of Chicago Press, 1969), pp. 147-149.

[15]Ibid., p. 151.

[16]Langenberg, p. 316A.

[17]For example, in astronomy, the interiors of neutron stars and possibly Jupiter may be superconducting. Taken from Langenberg, p. 316A.

8

BIBLIOGRAPHY

Garwin, Richard L., and J. Matisoo. "Superconducting Lines for the
Transmission of Large Amounts of Electrical Power over Great
Distances," in Superconductivity in Science and Technology, ed.
Morrel H. Cohen Chicago: University of Chicago Press, 1969,
pp. 77–101.

Langenberg, D. N. "Superconductivity," McGraw–Hill Encyclopedia of Science
and Technology, 1977 ed.

Matthias, B. T. "Superconductivity," Scientific American, (November 1957),
pp. 92–103.

Newhouse, Vernon L. "Superconducting Devices," McGraw–Hill Encyclopedia of
Science and Technology, 1977 ed.

Schmitt, Roland W., and W. Adair Morrison. "Economic Aspects of Superconductivity," in Superconductivity in Science and Technology, ed.
Morrel H. Cohen. Chicago: University of Chicago Press, 1969,
pp. 127–155.

ASSIGNMENTS

I. Working under the supervision of your instructor, select a suitable topic for a research project. Perhaps one of the following topics will work for you, or perhaps one of them will stimulate you to think of a good topic related directly to your area of interest.

  1. Changes in job demands within your vocational area during the last five years and changes that can be expected in the next five years.

  2. Changes in job training within your area during the last five years and changes that can be expected in the next five years.

  3. The importance of communication skills in your job.

  4. Specific qualifications that distinguish the two extremes (supervisors and subordinates) in your area of interest.

  5. Cost of preparing for your job, including education, equipment, supplies, etc.

  6. Specific needs in your geographic area for the skills which you will have.

  7. Salary structure within your job area, how it has changed during the last five years, and how it can be expected to change in the next five years.

  8. Different kinds of vocational training programs for the job you desire. How are they similar? How different?

  9. A review of a relatively new process that has changed or can be expected to change your field.

  10. A review of a relatively new piece of equipment that has changed or can be expected to change your field.

English Handbook

Introductory statement

Suggestions contained in the following pages are designed to assist you in your writing. Not every possible problem is confronted, obviously, but you will find presented in this *Handbook* the information you will need to avoid the major trouble spots as they have been defined by other students.

Language is fascinating, and though language study is interesting, it is not necessarily easy. You do not speak the way your parents or your grandparents do, and you definitely detect marked differences in the way you use the language and the way Shakespeare or Chaucer used it. But your grandparents, Shakespeare, and Chaucer all used English. The lesson is obvious: the English language is not fixed, but it changes constantly to meet the growing demands of its ever-changing audience. New words and methods of putting them together replace the old. Usage patterns acceptable fifty years ago may appear quite dated today.

From a purely technical point of view there are no *rules* for using the English language. Rather, there is a listing of the *conventions of usage* that have been found workable in given situations by a majority of people. For example, no English instructor sat up late at night figuring out that a comma was needed after an introductory adverb clause; it was simply observed that most writers whose work was clear and precise used commas in that position.

Although this *Handbook* will detail many conventions of usage, there are many times when you do not follow them and when you see them violated in newspapers and magazines of national repute. What are cataloged here for you are the conventions most acceptable to the business and professional communities; that is, most successful persons in these areas use these patterns when they communicate. Even though you may deviate from these conventions when you write a note to a friend or talk over a cup of coffee, you would do well to follow them in your more formal on-the-job communication tasks.

Sentences

what is a sentence?

Although definitions vary according to theory and situation, an English sentence generally meets the following two considerations:

- It is a two-member structure, having both a *subject member* and a *predicate member.*
- It expresses a feeling of completeness.

In its simplest form, then, such a standard sentence may be composed of only two words:

Secretaries   type.

Secretaries is the subject member, and *type* is the predicate member. The subject member is the part of the sentence which performs the action or is in a condition limited by the predicate member, and the predicate member defines the action or limits the condition of the subject member. In the example, *secretaries* names the performers, and *type* defines the action.

These two essential members form the *sentence kernel,* which may then be expanded to add further meaning:

The three new secretaries   type.
The three new secretaries in the office pool   type.
The three new secretaries in the office pool   type detailed reports.
The three new secretaries in the office pool   type detailed reports for the department supervisor.

You would obviously not have a sentence if you wrote the complete part of one member from the above examples but failed to include the other:

The three secretaries in the office pool

or

type detailed reports for the department supervisor.

what is a fragment?

A *fragment* is an incomplete sentence part. It may be incomplete because it is only one member of the construction, or it may be incomplete because it does not make complete sense. The following examples are fragments because they do not have both the subject and the predicate members:

Subject members only   The work on the corner of my desk

Predicate members only   The ringing telephone
             received the order yesterday morning
             set an appointment for Thursday afternoon

The above fragments could easily be corrected by supplying the missing member to the construction:

The work on the corner of my desk had been there for over a week.
The ringing telephone upset my train of thought.
Our order department received the order yesterday morning.
The receptionist set an appointment for Thursday afternoon.

The missing member is rather easily detected and the fragment completed, but often a more difficult task is spotting the fragment that results from a feeling of incompleteness. Read the following examples aloud:

After work, I always enjoy
The retyped report still looked
Because I got to work late today

If you stop to think as you read such statements, your mind immediately begins to ask questions: What do you enjoy? How did the retyped report look? What happened because you got to work late? The examples above contain subjects and predicates, but they are not complete because they leave you in need of additional information to complete the communication process.

Correcting such problems is much easier than spotting the problems might be. Simply supply an answer to the questions that come when you first read the fragments:

After work, I always enjoy a quick game of tennis.
The retyped report still looked too messy to submit.
I am not going to be able to take my afternoon coffee break because I got to work late today.

what is a clause?

A *clause* contains a subject member and a predicate member. If the clause makes complete sense, it is an *independent clause* and stands as a sentence. Many clauses, however, are used merely as modifiers and do not make complete sense by themselves. These *dependent clauses* should be recognized and their function understood so they will not lead you into writing fragments.

The greatest problem of dependent clauses' resulting in fragments comes from the use of adverb clauses at the beginning of sentences. Look carefully at these examples:

When I finish processing this set of X-rays
Although you are very tired
After she had completed her work
Until you get the replacement part

Each of the above examples has a subject member and a predicate member, but each also needs more information to avoid a feeling of incompleteness:

When I finish processing this set of X-rays, I must meet with the consulting physician.
Although you are very tired, I need your help with one more chore.
After she had completed her work, she left for the day.
Until you get the replacement part, you should work on another motor.

Some dependent clause structures are used as adjectives within the sentence, and these, too, can often lead to fragments. Observe these examples:

that you duplicated yesterday
who is usually conscientious
that I left on the counter

Again, each example has the two-member construction, but there is no communication because there is no feeling of completeness. The completed sentences might look something like these:

> Dr. Robertson needs to see the report that you duplicated yesterday.
> My assistant, who is usually conscientious, did not report for work today.
> Has anyone seen the wrench that I left on the counter?

what is a compound sentence?

A *compound sentence* is composed of two or more independent clauses, each of which might stand alone and be a complete sentence. Mature writers use compound sentences to put together closely related ideas and to avoid a series of short, choppy sentences.

and	shows simple addition of another idea
but	shows contrast with another idea
yet	shows contrast with another idea
nor	shows an alternative or gives a contrast
or	shows an alternative, gives a contrast, or indicates a condition
for	indicates a cause or result
so	adds an idea or shows a cause or result

To further separate the parts of the compound sentence, the coordinating conjunction is usually preceded by a comma:

> He sold his quota yesterday, *but* he is still eager for more.
> She asked for her vacation, *and* her request was granted.
> The supervisor does not want any more of those machines, *nor* do I.

Sometimes in very brief sentences where the subject of both parts is the same, the comma is not necessary, but it is never incorrect:

> I want to finish this work *and* I want to go home.

or

> I want to finish this work, *and* I want to go home.

When the subject of the second clause is not stated but is understood to be the same subject as that in the first clause, the comma is omitted:

> I want to finish this work and need to do so quickly.
> Larry talked for an hour on the telephone but claimed he did not neglect his customers.

The conjunctive adverbs used in compound sentences include *therefore, however, otherwise, furthermore, then, moreover, consequently, nevertheless, accordingly,* and *afterward.* A semicolon is necessary before the conjunctive adverb:

He did not meet the appointment; *however* he was charged the fee.
Ms. Alison will be in San Francisco in June; *therefore* she can personally check on the report.
You should complete the request form; *then* you should take it to the purchase counter.

The correlatives used in compounding sentences are *not only . . . but also, either . . . or,* and *neither . . . nor.* Correlatives are used in patterns similar to the following:

Not only was she the best salesperson of the year, *but* she *also* won the President's Award.
Either you must improve the quality of your work, *or* the supervisor will dismiss you.

For your convenience, the most used connectives are arranged in Figure EH-1 according to their usage.

what is a run-on sentence?

The label *run-on sentence* is often used interchangeably with the labels *comma splice* and *sentence fusion.* Although there are technical differences, the problem is the same in each instance: two or more main clauses have been joined without using proper coordination or punctuation.

The following sentences are run on because they do not have coordinating connectives between the two independent parts:

I hope that Ralph will finish the task you can learn from him.
You should report to the supervisor she can give you additional directions.

These sentences may be corrected by supplying connectives with appropriate punctuation:

I hope that Ralph will finish the task; *then* you can learn from him.
You should report to the supervisor; *afterward* she can give you additional directions.

A run-on sentence may also result when you use a comma instead of a semicolon before a conjunctive adverb:

figure EH-1   **Connectives.**

	To Add an Idea	To Show an Alternative	To Show Cause or Result
	and so furthermore then moreover not only . . . but also	nor or either . . . or neither . . . nor	for so therefore consequently accordingly
	To Show Contrast	**To Show Condition**	**To Show Time**
	but yet nor or however otherwise nevertheless not only . . . but also	or otherwise	then afterward

> Helen did an outstanding job, *therefore* she was rapidly promoted.
> Benjamin should finish the assignment, *otherwise* you must help him.

The correction is simple. Place a semicolon before the connector:

> Helen did an outstanding job; *therefore* she was rapidly promoted.
> Benjamin should finish the assignment; *otherwise* you must help him.

Subject and verb agreement

what is subject and verb agreement?

One of the basic conventions of good writing is that subjects and verbs agree in number. A singular subject always requires a singular verb, and a plural subject always requires a plural verb:

> The *mechanic is* ready to begin work on your car.
> The *mechanics are* ready to begin work on your car.
> The *secretary* always *answers* the telephone promptly.
> The *secretaries* always *answer* the telephones promptly.

The problem with such basic sentences as these is to locate the true subject and true verb and then to know the correct forms for singular and plural patterns. Although these forms are generally familiar to you, a good dictionary is a handy reference tool to verify your thinking.

what is the true subject?

You may sometimes have a problem with agreement if you fail to locate the true subject of the sentence. Do not become confused with intervening words, especially other nouns, that appear to be the subject. Look at these examples:

The *problem* with those reports *is* that they were filed too late.
Long forgotten in the corner of the desk drawer *were* the data *cards.*

The subject of the first sentence is *problem,* not *reports,* and the subject of the second sentence is *cards,* even though it appears at the end of the sentence.

Another problem with locating the true subject sometimes occurs when you have a singular subject followed by phrases such as these: *in addition to, as well as, with, together with, except,* and *no less than.* In these situations, the verb always agrees with the primary subject:

The *president,* as well as the board members, *was* excited by the report.
My retirement *income,* together with my social security, *provides* me sufficient money to live comfortably.
The *nurse,* together with the laboratory technician, *gives* the required medical attention.

what are some other problems with agreement?

A major portion of your agreement troubles will be solved when you correctly identify the true subject and make it agree in number with the verb. However, there are some instances that require special consideration:

- A compound subject (two or more parts) always requires a plural verb even if its parts are singular:

The *letter* and the *call do* impress me with your sincerity.
Dr. Haggar and her *nurse are* out of the office this afternoon.

- With subjects joined by *neither-nor, either-or,* and *not only–but also,* the verb agrees with the subject nearer to it:

Either the *supervisor* or his *employees were* at fault.
Either the *employees* or their *supervisor was* at fault.
Not only the architect's frontal *sketch* but also all other *plans* for the home
  were burned during the big fire.

- The pronoun *you* always requires a plural verb form:

You are the most capable person for the job.
You talk as though *you have* authority.

- These pronouns always require singular verbs: *anybody, anyone, anything, another, each, either, everybody, everyone, everything, nobody, no
  one, one, somebody, someone.*

Is anyone going to work overtime today?
Nobody wants to be the one to ask for a raise.
Either works just fine.

- A subject that is plural in form but suggests a singular unit always
  requires a singular verb:

Economics is a very difficult subject for him.
Seventeen *dollars was* not enough.
Two-thirds is a good majority.

- If the subject is *the number,* you should use a singular verb; but if the
  subject is *a number,* you need a plural verb:

The number of absences during the month *was* very high.
A number of workers *were* sick with some unknown infection.

- The relative pronouns *who, which,* and *that* require a verb that agrees in
  number with the antecedent of the pronoun (the word it modifies):

The students *who were* absent came to class today.
The student *who was* absent came to class today.

- The words *more, some, part, most,* and fractions and percents are
  sometimes followed by an *of* phrase. In such instances the verb must
  agree with the object of the *of* phrase:

Some of the money *is* missing.
Most of the students *were* present for the guest lecture.
One-fifth of the overtime *was* unnecessary.
One-fifth of the workers *were* absent from the meeting.

- A collective noun requires a singular verb if it is regarded as a unit and a plural verb if it is regarded individually:

The *crew was working* hard to prevent further flooding. (The crew is functioning as a single unit.)

The *crew were carrying* their tools with them. (Members of the crew are carrying individual tools.)

The *crew was carrying* its tools with it. (Members of the crew are carrying tools as a singular activity.)

Pronouns

what is a pronoun?

A *pronoun* is a word or word group that fills the same sentence position as a noun. Thus a pronoun may be used as a sentence subject, as a direct object, object of preposition, complement, or at any other sentence position where a noun might occur. Pronouns are most frequently discussed in terms of *case:* nominative, objective, and possessive.

what is the nominative case?

The *nominative case* pronoun is found as sentence subject, subjective complement, or appositive:

Sentence subject	*He* was late for the morning meeting.
Subjective complement	It was *he* who was late for the meeting.
Appositive	Two of us, *he* and *I,* were late for the meeting.

Here are the nominative case forms:

	Singular	Plural
First person	I	we
Second person	you	you
Third person	he, she, it, who, whoever	they, who, whoever

what is the objective case?

The *objective case* pronoun is used as a direct object, object of verbal, indirect object, object of preposition, object of infinitive, and subject of infinitive:

Direct object	The racing auto hit *her.*
Object of verbal	The telephone rang all day, making *him* very nervous.
Indirect object	The board gave *him* the raise.
Object of preposition	Give the finished report to *me.*
Object of infinitive	I want to give *her* the finished report.
Subject of infinitive	I want *her* to give you the finished report.

Here are the objective case forms:

	Singular	Plural
First person	me	us
Second person	you	you
Third person	her, him, it, whom, whomever	them, whom, whomever

what is the possessive case?

The *possessive case* pronouns are used to show posession and also to modify certain gerund structures:

Ownership	The board members left *their* reports on the table.
Gerund modifier	The board members were pleased by *your* reporting on the new developmental process.

Here are the possessive case forms:

	Singular	Plural
First person	my, mine	our, ours
Second person	your, yours	your, yours
Third person	his, her, hers, its, whose, whose ever	their, theirs, whose, whose ever

what are the indefinite pronouns?

The *indefinite pronouns* are so named because they refer to an indefinite person or thing. The list includes such words as *each, every, either, neither,* and the *-body,* and *-one* combinations: *somebody, anybody, someone, anyone, no one,* etc. The important things to remember about indefinite pronouns is that they are *always singular* and always require singular verbs:

Everyone is entitled to his/her sick pay.
Each wanted his/her just recognition for the task.

what are the demonstrative pronouns?

The *demonstrative pronouns* are those that demonstrate or point out. *This, that, these,* and those are demonstrative pronouns.

what are the relative pronouns?

The *relative pronouns* always introduce a relative (or related) clause that modifies the noun preceding the pronoun: Here is the book *that* you asked me to bring for your report. *Who, whom, whose, that,* and *which* are often used as relative pronouns.

Always use *who* or *that* to refer to people, and always use *that* or *which* to refer to animals and inanimate objects:

She is the employee *who* scored the highest on the exam.

or

She is the employee *that* scored the highest on the exam.
Here is the report *that* you requested.

or

Here is the report *which* you requested.

what are the three types of pronoun agreement?

Problems in pronoun usage occur when the pronoun fails to agree with its *antecedent* (the word it refers back to) in number, gender, and person.

1. Problems with *agreement in number* often occur when you do not carefully identify the noun to which your pronoun refers.

The causes of unrest are so intense that *they* must be studied. (Antecedent of *they* is *causes,* plural)

Two subjects joined by *and* always require a plural pronoun:

The supervisor and her assistant took *their* coffee break later than usual.

Two singular subjects joined by *or* or *nor* require a singular pronoun:

The supervisor or his assistant left *his* watch on the workbench.

Several specific problems with determining whether a pronoun is singular or plural are identical with determining whether a subject of a sentence is singular or plural. You might with to refer back to that section of the *Handbook* for review.

2. Problems with *agreement in gender* (masculine, feminine, or neuter sexual references) can be solved if you remember two basic guides:

Pronouns referring to masculine or feminine antecedents are always of similar genders:

Mr. Walker left *his* briefcase on the train.
Ms. Alison gave *her* comments to the board meeting.

Pronouns referring to neuter antecedents are always neuter:

Roger picked up the file but dropped *it* to the floor.
He brought the part *which* you ordered yesterday.

3. Problems with *agreement in person* can be avoided if you make certain your pronoun agrees with its antecedent in person and if you avoid shifting person when you make the same pronoun reference in a later sentence. Perhaps the most frequent problem with person occurs when you make an unnecessary shift from either the first or third person to the second:

Shift	A new worker in the department should be able to do some work on *your* first day.
Consistent	A new worker in the department should be able to do some work on *his* or *her* first day.
Shift	Even though we were new workers, the supervisor expected *you* to be familiar with the working area.
Consistent	Even though we were new workers, the supervisor expected *us* to be familiar with the working area.

how are the -self pronouns used?

Certain pronouns may be combined with *-self* and used in either a reflexive or intensive pattern:

Reflexive	The board chairman gave *himself* credit for the new profit showings.

Intensive   The doctor *himself* ordered the
                                      changed prescription.

You should never use *myself* instead of *I* or *me,* but you may use
myself to give emphasis:

Incorrect   *Myself* went to the library to research
                                      the report.
                                      John and *myself* went to the library to
                                      research the report.
Correct   I *myself* went to the library to re-
                                      search the report.
                                      (or)
                                      I went to the library to research the
                                      report *myself.*

Verbs

what is the function of a verb?

As you discovered in the first section of this *Handbook,* every
formal sentence must have a verb member that is composed of the
simple verb and its related modifiers. A *verb* may perform one of two
possible functions in the sentence: it may show an action or it may
describe a condition. The first example below describes an action, and
the second example indicates a condition of ownership:

The decorator *framed* the picture in a dark wood.
The decorator *has* a picture similar to that one in his own home.

what are the two major problems in using verbs?

You use verbs constantly in your talking and your writing, and
generally you use them without any difficulty. When you do encounter
problems, they are usually one of two types: failure to use the correct
tense, or failure to use the correct form for the tense even though you
may understand the tense correctly.

what are the principal parts of verb tenses?

Before you can familiarize yourself with the common tenses of
verbs, you need to recognize the principal parts from which those
tenses are derived. A good dictionary is an extremely valuable tool for
helping you determine the principal parts of any given verb: *infinitive,*

present, present participle, past, and *past participle.* Here are some sample verbs and their principal parts:

Infinitive	Present	Present Participle	Past	Past Participle
to type	type(s)	typing	typed	(have) typed
to listen	listen(s)	listening	listened	(have) listened
to have	have (has)	having	had	(have) had

what are the tenses most often used?

Although there are actually twelve tenses for most modern verbs, six of those are *progressive tenses* whose specialized use will be discussed separately. For practical purposes, you need to understand the tense ordering of only six tenses:

1. *Present tense* indicates action taking place *now:*
   I *listen* attentively to the conversation.
2. *Past tense* indicates action that took place before now:
   I *listened* attentively to the conversation yesterday.
3. *Future tense* indicates action that will take place in the future:
   I *will listen* to the conversation tomorrow.
4. *Present perfect tense* uses *have* or *has* plus the past participial form of the main verb to indicate action just completed or continuing into the present:
   I *have listened* to conversations all my life.
5. *Past perfect tense* uses *had* plus the past participial form of the main verb to indicate action that was completed at a definite past time:
   I *had listened* to the conversation until he began to bore me.
6. *Future perfect tense* uses *shall* or *will* along with *have* and the past participial form of the main verb to indicate an action that will be completed by a certain future time:
   I *will have listened* to his conversation for three hours by the time the plane gets to Atlanta.

what are the progressive tenses?

Each of the six tense forms discussed above has a progressive tense pattern also. This progressive pattern is used to show an action taking place (progressing) at the described time (past, present, future):

Present progressive	I *am listening* to the conversation.
Past progressive	I *was listening* to the conversation.
Future progressive	I *will be listening* to the conversation tomorrow.

Present perfect progressive   I *have been listening* to the conversation for an hour.

Past perfect progressive   I *had been listening* to the conversation for an hour.

Future perfect progressive   I *will have been listening* to the conversation for an hour by the time we get to Atlanta.

what are the correct tense forms?

Most modern English verbs form their tenses by adding -*d* or -*ed*. Other verbs, such as *swim, hang, lie, lay,* and many others are irregular and have their independent verb patterns. You have seen lists of such irregular verbs in the past. However, such lists are not helpful unless you memorize them entirely. Learn to use your dictionary to verify tense patterns for the irregular verbs. Also, do not fail in your writing to add the -*ed* or -*d* endings when they are needed by the regular verbs. Sometimes, as with such past forms as *talked* and *walked,* the ending does not receive emphasis in oral pronunciation patterns, and it becomes easy to omit it in written patterns.

what are some problems in consistency?

If you are not careful, you will sometimes shift verb tenses within the same sentence or in a sequence of sentences that all belong to the same tense structure. The following examples show tense shifts and then show how they should have been written to be correct:

Inconsistent   After she *went* to the office, she *answers* her letters.

When she *answered* the telephone and *took* the call, she *made* an immediate appointment with the doctor because the patient *is* obviously quite sick.

Consistent   After she *went* to the office, she *answered* her letters.

or

After she *goes* to the office, she *answers* her letters.

When she *answered* the telephone and *took* the call, she *made* an immediate appointment with the doctor because the patient *was* obviously quite sick.

Style

what is style and why is it important?

Style is the *how* of written communication, and *content* is the *what.* The same ideas may be communicated differently by two different persons, and the results may be quite different. When you are completing an order form or certain other types of formulaic writing, style may not be so important. But in your business letters and your detailed written reports, you may find the *how* to be almost as important as the *what.*

There are many aspects of style, and it is not the purpose of this *Handbook* to review all of them. Any of several excellent style manuals are available in libraries and bookstores. The following broad suggestions cover those areas of style most often abused in business and technical writing.

what is specific diction?

Specific diction is that word choice that explains exactly and to the fullest extent your intended meaning. Too often business writing is clouded by general catchall words and phrases. The more concrete your descriptions, the sounder your writing will be because your reader will know exactly what you intend to communicate.

Following is a listing of some general words and phrases along with a list of the same ideas as they have been specifically detailed.

General	Specific
window	third window from the left
desk drawer	second desk drawer from the top
tool	thin-nosed pliers
check	check for Invoice 23-78A
secretary	secretary for Mr. Rollins
walked into the room	strutted into the room

After you have finished a piece of writing, you should read it through to check the nouns and verbs. Will your reader know exactly what you mean by your nouns or do you need to add some details? Would more specific verbs add a dimension of meaning to your message?

what is connotative meaning?

Connotative meaning is the emotional meaning that a word carries with it. *Denotative meaning* is the dictionary meaning. If your goal in business and technical writing is clear, direct prose, then you should usually avoid heavily connotative words because they cloud your message with emotional overtones.

Some words have a connotative meaning only to certain audiences who identify the word with a particular experience or concept; other words have more universally identifiable connotative meanings. Each of the following words has a literal denotative (dictionary) meaning, but each also communicates either highly positive or highly negative emotional feelings:

left wing	honor	love
church	rightist	fat
bitch	muddy	home
security	religious	mongrel

are there some word clusters to avoid?

Some writers attempt to impress their readers by their ability to use long or impressive words or their ability to use a large number of words. Both attempts to impress merely result in weaker style for the entire message.

Sometimes writers put together word clusters that really say the same thing in two or more different ways. Here is only a partial listing of such phrases:

consensus of opinion	new innovation
final result	exactly identical
end result	free gratis
return again	completely finished
large in size	cooperate together
round in shape	quite unique
few in number	over again

Sometimes writers use pompous words or lengthy phrases that ultimately detract from their message:

Pompously Wordy	Straightforward
We *are cognizant* that you are *experiencing difficulty* during *this period of reorganization* of your central office.	We *know* that you are *having difficulty* during *the reorganization* of your central office.
Under ordinary circumstances we do not *in every instance find it necessary to make this request.*	*Ordinarily* we do not *need to ask this.*

how is brevity achieved?

No one likes to listen to a long-winded conversation, and no one has time to read unnecessary words to get at the meaning of a message. You can make your communication brief by cutting out unnecessary phrases that add nothing to the meaning.

Wordy

I have been wondering if it might be possible and convenient to make the necessary arrangements that might be in order for us to get together for a short conference to talk things over sometime near the beginning of next week, perhaps on Monday or Tuesday.

Brief

Could we have a short conference Monday or Tuesday?

Another way to make your writing brief is to pay close attention to sentence patterns. Often, attempting to pack too much meaning into one sentence results in a structure that is wordy or unnecessarily cumbersome.

Sentences That Try to Cover Too Much at One Time

Mr. Medwell tells me that several dealers in the area which you cover are disturbed because their orders are not always filled promptly and they are not notified when these items are out of stock and they don't know when new items are replacing older models which they wish to be notified of when such items will soon be released for sale.

Sentences That Cover One Item at a Time

Mr. Medwell reports that dealers in your area are dissatisfied for several reasons: (1) Their orders are not always filled promptly. (2) They are not notified when items are no longer in stock. (3) They do not know when new models can be expected to replace older ones. They would like notification of the date when new models will be released.

when is a sentence confused?

Confused sentences are usually the result of confused or unclear thinking. If you write ideas in the order in which they pop into your mind, you will probably leave your reader confused because there will be little connection between the various ideas. Always arrange your sentences so you omit the irrelevant material and put what is important in a clear and coherent order.

Here Is a Confused Explanation

We are writing to let you know that we have located the problem that was responsible for the shipment which you have not received. When the manager talked to Mr. Holdsome, the shipping clerk, he was certain that the merchandise could be obtained at once because

Here Is a Clear Explanation

We are writing to explain the delay in your shipment. There was a breakdown in one of the machines necessary to supply the product which you had ordered. The machine has now been repaired, and your order can be filled at once. We had not had such a machine failure in the he had inspected the factory's new machinery that has occupied the same premises for fifteen years and has never failed to produce the desired results which means it was natural to expect that it would now. The difficulty has been remedied and your order will be filled at once, but we thought you would appreciate understanding exactly what happened.

fifteen years that our plant has occupied these premises, and we trust that we shall not be so forced to disappoint you again. Thank you for your patience.

Study your sentence patterns carefully to be certain they show proper relationships between the facts that you wish communicated.

Sentences That Show No Relationship Between the Facts	Sentences That Show the Relationship Between the Facts
There is a strike at the steel mill. We have not received any parts from the factory for two weeks. We have been unable to make the repairs on your machine.	Because the steel mill strike has delayed our shipment of parts from the factory for two weeks, we have been unable to make the repairs on your machine.
We recommend the Type 182 amplifier. You can use it in your maintenance shop. It can be used for instrumentation and test purposes.	We recommend the Type 182 amplifier for instrumentation and test purposes in your maintenance shop.
The first large-scale computers were used during World War II. They were used for ballistic calculations. They were introduced in the early 1950's as commercial machines.	Although the first large-scale computers were used during World War II for ballistic calculations, they were not introduced as commercial machines until the early 1950's.

what words are often confused?

Some words are often confused with others that sound or look like them or that have similar meanings. Clear writing requires that you use the exact word to give your intended meaning. The list of possible problems in this area of diction is large, but here are some of the words that cause the greatest problems.

ability, capacity *ability* is the power to do; *capacity* is the power to receive.

accept, except *accept* is a verb meaning "to take"; *except* is most often a preposition meaning "but," and it is also used as a verb meaning "to exclude."

adapt, adopt *adapt* means to change in order to make suitable; *adopt* means to take charge of or to put into effect.

advice, advise *advice* is a noun; *advise* is the verb.

affect, effect *affect* is a verb meaning to change or modify; *effect* is usually a noun meaning the result of change and it is sometimes a verb meaning "to put to use."

among, between *among* refers to more than two possibilities; *between* is used when there are only two possibilities.

anxious, eager *anxious* means looking forward to something with fear or apprehension; *eager* suggests looking forward with desire.

can, may *can* signifies ability to do something; *may* suggests permission.

complement, compliment *complement* is a verb meaning "to complete" or is a noun naming that which completes; *compliment* is a verb meaning "to praise" or is a noun referring to the praise.

continual, continuous *continual* refers to an action that takes place at repeated intervals; *continuous* refers to an action that never stops.

decided, decisive *decided* suggests being free from uncertainty; *decisive* suggests having the power to decide.

desirable, desirous *desirable* refers to something that is worth wanting; *desirous* describes the person who wants something.

deteriorate, degenerate both mean to worsen, but *deteriorate* usually refers to things and *degenerate* to people or morals.

exceptional, exceptionable *exceptional* refers to something uncommon or rare; *exceptionable* refers to something likely to cause objections.

explicit, implicit *explicit* refers to something plainly stated or clear; *implicit* suggests something understood although not actually stated.

few, less *few* is used with units that can be counted; *less* is used with quantities not counted.

infer, imply *infer* means to draw an unstated opinion from something that is said; *imply* means to suggest something without actually stating it.

ingenious, ingenuous *ingenious* suggests something or someone clever or shrewd; *ingenuous* suggests frankness or candidness.

kind of, sort of both are very colloquial expressions better replaced by *rather, somewhat, a little,* etc.

last, latest *last* suggests the final member of a series; *latest* suggests the most recent member and implies that there may be more.

percent, percentage *percent* is most often used with a number reference (30 percent of the people); *percentage* is most often used when there is no number reference (a small percentage of the people).

practical, practicable   *practical* refers to something that can be done without much effort or money and that is sensible; *practicable* means "capable of being put into practice."

principal, principle   *principal* is a noun meaning head of school, amount of money owed on a loan, or an adjective meaning "main" or "major"; *principle* is a law or rule.

universally, generally   *universally* means everywhere at all times; *generally* means most of the time or most everywhere.

what is parallel structure?

Ideas that are written in a structural series or that have closely related meanings are often best cast in parallel form. The parallelism may be in the form of words, phrases, clauses, or even sentences. By placing related ideas in such a structure, you not only improve style but you also show the relationship of the items that are paralleled.

In each of these examples notice how much more effective the parallel structure is to the mixed structure.

Mixed	Laverne worked in an office that was too crowded and smelled musty.
Parallel	Laverne worked in an office that was crowded and musty.
Mixed	Seeing what needs to be done, knowing how to do it, then to do it are the traits of a qualified worker.
Parallel	Seeing what needs to be done, knowing how to do it, then doing it are the traits of a qualified worker.
Mixed	This outdoor work will help you in building muscles and to make money at the same time.
Parallel	This outdoor work will help you to build muscles and to make money at the same time.

what is a dangling modifier?

A *dangling modifier* is a word, phrase, or clause that dangles or does not connect because the word to which it should be connected either is missing from the sentence or is hidden internally.

Here are two examples of dangling modifiers that have resulted because their connected words were omitted. Observe how simply they can be corrected:

Dangling	Filing the reports, the error was quickly discovered.
Corrected	Filing the reports, he quickly discovered the error.
Dangling	Seriously wanting a raise, her work improved.
Corrected	Seriously wanting a raise, she improved her work.

Sometimes a modifier dangles because the word or phrase that it should be connected to (should modify) is hidden in the sentence. Most often in such situations, the word that should be connected to the dangling modifier is used in a prepositional structure:

Dangling	Speaking very loudly, the telephone was answered by the receptionist.
Corrected	Speaking very loudly, the receptionist answered the telephone.

when is a modifier misplaced?

A *misplaced modifier* occurs when the modifying element is placed at a spot in the sentence where a reader cannot tell clearly what word or phrase it is intended to modify. The most common problem is with the *squinting modifier.* In this structure the writer places a modifying element in a position where it might possibly modify two different words or phrases; thus the reader has to "squint" at them both for meaning.

Squinting	The sales representatives were told *by noon* that they were over their quota.
Corrected	*By noon* the sales representatives were told that they were over their quota. *(or)* The sales representatives were told that they were over their quota *by noon.*

Not all problems with modifiers occur in squinting structures, but most of the other problems can readily be detected by slowly reading for the logical structure in sentences. Notice the illogical structure of these two sentences:

Misplaced	The new plant was for sale with all of its fixtures.
Corrected	The new plant with all of its fixtures was for sale.
Misplaced	The safe in our office with the digital combination was stolen.
Corrected	The safe with the digital combination in our office was stolen.

The words *only, almost,* and *nearly* require special consideration because they can completely change sentence meaning if not positioned carefully:

The accountant was nearly always correct in his report.
The accountant was always nearly correct in his report.

I only want you to handle my account.
I want only you to handle my account.

Abbreviations

what are the important guides
for technical abbreviations?

Writers have always made use of abbreviations to aid them in their task, and perhaps nowhere has the use of abbreviations been so great as in business and technical writing. Almost every profession has its own abbreviation code that covers the terminology within its own specialty. Following is a basic guide for general abbreviation practices in business and technical writing:

1. Unless it is extremely short, a term used for a unit of measurement is abbreviated when it follows a figure:

92 ft.   200 hp.   50 cc.

A unit of measure is not abbreviated when it does not follow a figure:

The amount is given in cubic centimeters.
The molasses is sold by the gallon.

2. Some extremely short terms of measurement are not abbreviated:

day   mile   acre

3. The abbreviation for a unit of measurement is always singular:

5 lb. (not 6 lbs.)   10 gal. (not 10 gals.)

4. Some professional terms used with extreme frequency are abbreviated when it is reasonable to suppose they will be readily understood:

F.   Fahrenheit   C.   Centigrade
a-c   alternating current (only when used as an adjective)

5. Whatever practice you adopt for abbreviations, you should be consistent.

6. Some signs and symbols are considered standard:

$ dollar sign   ° degrees   ¢ cent (use with descretion)

Do not use symbols when words or abbreviations are usually used:

8 in. (not 8″)   12 by 15 ft. (not 12′ × 15′)   percent (not %)

7. In some professions the period is omitted after many abbreviations. Follow the practice of books and periodicals from your own field. Always use a period if its omission would cause misreading, as with the abbreviation *in* for *inch.* Use periods with these abbreviations:

A.M.   P.M.   c.o.d.   B.C.   A.D.
Fig.   ibid.   op. cit.   vol.   p.   ff.

8. Capitalization is not affected by abbreviation. Abbreviations are not usually capitalized unless the terms they stand for are capatalized.

what are the official abbreviations approved by the United States Postal Service?

The United States Postal Service recognizes only one officially approved abbreviation for each of the states. The abbreviations in the following list should be used in all business correspondence:

AL	Alabama	CO	Colorado
AK	Alaska	CT	Connecticut
AZ	Arizona	DE	Delaware
AR	Arkansas	DC	District of Columbia
CA	California	FL	Florida

GA	Georgia	NM	New Mexico
HI	Hawaii	NY	New York
ID	Idaho	NC	North Carolina
IL	Illinois	ND	North Dakota
IN	Indiana	OH	Ohio
IA	Iowa	OK	Oklahoma
KS	Kansas	OR	Oregon
KY	Kentucky	PA	Pennsylvania
LA	Louisiana	RI	Rhode Island
ME	Maine	SC	South Carolina
MD	Maryland	SD	South Dakota
MA	Massachusetts	TN	Tennessee
MI	Michigan	TX	Texas
MN	Minnesota	UT	Utah
MS	Mississippi	VT	Vermont
MO	Missouri	VA	Virginia
MT	Montana	WA	Washington
NE	Nebraska	WV	West Virginia
NV	Nevada	WI	Wisconsin
NH	New Hampshire	WY	Wyoming
NJ	New Jersey		

For the answer to particular problems not covered here, consult the pages of abbreviations in any collegiate dictionary.

Figures

what are the general guides
for using figures in technical writing?

The various charts and statistics necessary to much business and technical writing often demand more use of figures or numbers than is required in other types of writing. Although specific requirements vary from one type of writing to another, the following style is most often used:

1. Use figures for 10 and all numbers above 10:

10 sales   122 sales   four sales

2. Use figures for numbers below 10 when they precede a measurement unit:

3 in.   5 ft.   6 days

3. Use figures to express sums of money:

$5.95 $10 (or 10 dollars) $0.75 (or 75 cents)

4. Use figures to express decimal fractions. Place a zero before the decimal if the value is less than a whole:

1.33   17.56   0.89

5. Use figures for any section of writing where numbers are very frequent:

> The 7 board members met for 35 minutes to discuss the 9 proposals submitted by the 2 standing committees.

6. When one number appears immediately after another as part of some phrase, one of the numbers, usually the shorter one, is spelled out:

8 six-inch boards   two 5-person teams

7. Use words and not figures to indicate common fractions:

one-third   two and three-eighths

8. Use figures to indicate definite percentages:

80 percent   3.2 percent   10 percent

9. Use figures to precede the words *million* and *billion* when stating a quantity:

3 billion dollars   2.7 million people

10. Use words for numbers that are approximations:

The company was started nearly fifty years ago.
The building should stand for another fifteen years.

11. Use figures to indicate latitude, longitude, and temperature:

45° South   98.6°F.

12. Use figures to indicate time of day when followed by *a.m.* or *p.m.* but not when followed by *o'clock:*

3:00 P.M.   3:00 A.M.   three o'clock

13. Use figures for references to dates:

July 13, 1973   13 July 1973

14. Never use figures to begin a sentence; spell out the quantity:

Three billion dollars will be spent in marketing this year.
Sixty-two percent is too low a figure to justify the increased cost.

Index

Subject-verb agreement, 268–71
Subsidiary motion, 129–30
Summary, 195, 199–200
Suspend a rule, move to, 131
Syllogism, 143
Synopsis, 195

Table, motion to, 130
Telephone, answering a, 15–16
Telephone call:
  ending a, 20
  placing a, 17
Telephone image, positive, 18–19
Telephone information, 19–20
Telephone manners, 14–20
Telephone message, taking a, 17–18
Tenses:
  progressive, 276–77
  verbs, 275–77
Testimonial fallacy, 159–60
Testimonials, evaluation of, 160–61
Thesis sentence, 208
Title card, 183

Tone, 38–40
Transfer fallacy, 159

Usage patterns, 262

Verb, principal parts of, 275–76
Verbal skills:
  how to learn, 6–7
  other, 6
Verbs:
  function of, 275
  tenses of, 275–77
Verb tenses, parts of, 275
Visual aids, use of, 229–31
Vita sheet, 72–75

Withdraw, motion to, 131
Words:
  choosing the right, 23–25
  often confused, 281–83
Work experience, 74
Writing instructions, 116

DATE DUE

MAR 8			
FEB 2 9 '88			
MAR 1 7 1988			